Using
MODELS
to Improve
the
SUPPLY
CHAIN

Using
MODELS
to Improve
the
SUPPLY
CHAIN

Charles C. Poirier

S^t_L

ST. LUCIE PRESS

A CRC Press Company
Boca Raton   London   New York   Washington, D.C.

Library of Congress Cataloging-in-Publication Data

Poirier, Charles C., 1936-
    Using models to improve the supply chain / Charles C. Poirier.
        p. cm.
    Includes bibliographical references and index.
    ISBN 1-57444-347-X (alk. paper)
    1.Business logistics—Management. I. Title.

    HD38.5.P643 2003
    658.7—dc21   2003046600

Visit the CRC Press Web site at www.crcpress.com

© 2004 by CRC Press, LLC.
St. Lucie Press is an imprint of CRC Press LLC

No claim to original U.S. Government works
International Standard Book Number 1-57444-347-X
Library of Congress Card Number 2003046600
Printed in the United States of America 1 2 3 4 5 6 7 8 9 0
Printed on acid-free paper

DEDICATION

For Eric, Wendy, Casey, Jesse, Rachel, Jordan, Anna, Libby, and Amelia—
the next generation

PREFACE

Around the world, virtually every company of any appreciable size is engaged in some effort intended to improve the processing that takes place across an end-to-end supply chain system. Some of those efforts focus narrowly on a system that starts with raw materials, proceeds through manufacturing or conversion, and ends with delivery to a business customer — the so-called business-to-business (B2B) cycle. Others go from earth-to-earth, starting with basic raw materials, proceeding through complex conversion processing, and transferring to business intermediaries and on to retail stores, consumer selection, and return, either for rework or recycling — the business-to-business-to-consumer (B2B2C) cycle.

Perhaps as an extension of previous business process reengineering, total quality management, or continuous improvement efforts, companies are frantically trying to move their organizations to the next level of performance, and supply chain, particularly when enhanced with collaboration and Internet technology, fits the requirement. As these efforts get started, progress, and mature, businesses find themselves in one of five levels of supply chain progress — from an initial focus on internal excellence to some form of external network, and on to a state where full network connectivity links the end-to-end constituents in an online value constellation. In the process, they move from a collection of fragmented, noncooperative internal functions and business units to a single extended-enterprise network that dominates a particular industry.

As results from research and interviews with hundreds of organizations are documented, there's a continuum where these supply chain efforts are concerned. Those industries that took an early lead in introducing and pursuing the concept — computers, high technology, electronics, and entertainment — are further along the continuum, and most advanced stories still come from this sector. Next, we find the fast closers, those industries that are setting the new pace in implementation — aerospace, automotive, chemicals, consumer products, defense, office products, petroleum, pharmaceuticals, and utilities. Members of these industries are above the middle of the chase and are producing some very interesting advanced case examples.

The second half of the continuum begins with the slower industries, where progress is definitely not measured by the industry, but more by individual firms. Here we place banking, distribution, financial services, food manufacturing, healthcare, packaging, printing, and retailing. Finally, there are those industries having difficulty breaking away from old models — construction, farm products, forestry, furniture, industrial equipment, industrial products, outdoor products, publishing, and paper products. Good examples are emerging, but from a limited number of players.

Another important factor is that global differences are converging as advanced techniques are introduced and industry breakthroughs occur. Even among the apparently laggard industries there are cases where one or two progressive firms have broken out of the standard mold and are forging impressive leads over others in the industry. Examples include: Wal-Mart, Carrefour (France), and Tesco (Great Britain) in retailing; John Deere in industrial products; Broken Hill Properties (Australia) in mining and steel; Hochtief (Germany) in construction; IKEA (Sweden) in furniture; Nestle (Switzerland) in food processing; and Weyerhaeuser and International Paper in forest products.

The pathfinder firms could be in any country as the same desire to use supply chain and Internet features to dominate an industry exists everywhere today. Where there used to be significant gaps between the United States, Europe, and Asia, the differences have blurred. Individual firms have moved out in front and eliminated the gaps, as many of the action studies in this text verify. Today there is little global sector advantage, as even the leading industries have firms in front and those trailing the pack. It has become a nearly level playing field as the final stages of the progression are conquered.

One factor of importance is, of course, the starting position of the industry. Another is how far a firm within an industry must proceed in the five-level progression. Within industries such as computing and electronics, there was virtually no old model that needed breaking. Firms simply designed their own supply chain models and set about to quickly optimize the linked process steps. Adaptec, Dell, Intel, Sun Microsystems, Hitachi, Toshiba, and Hewlett-Packard stand out as leaders in this area. These firms are followed closely by a host of others rapidly moving to the highest level of the supply chain progression. Close behind in the middle industries are firms such as Boeing, Colgate-Palmolive, Procter & Gamble, Toyota, Wal-Mart, Prada, Dow, Federal Express, United Parcel Service, W.W. Grainger, and General Dynamics, moving substantially ahead of others in their industries, creating performance gaps that can be measured in years.

At the same time, there are firms doing very well in lower levels of progress, as the starting point came later than the leading industries and the needs are not as great. The developing wisdom in supply chain has schooled practitioners in the idea that the movement should be inexorably toward the highest level of progression. During the maturation process, however, it has become clear that some firms do not need to make such a complete trip. For firms engaged in the supply of primary commodities, such as grain, chemicals, ores, gas, and water, achieving internal excellence could be a feasible and effective strategy. For distributors and wholesalers, the need for full network connectivity might not have the same value as selective network formation in niche markets. For those engaged in global manufacturing and trade that ends with consumer purchases, however, the need to distinguish the network and constituent members probably demands full connectivity spanning the extended supply chain.

Across industries, most of the leading business firms realize supply chain optimization, advanced supply chain management, virtual logistics, e-commerce, digital communication systems, and other modern tools are essential factors that can converge into new strategies and business models that lead to the next level of success. What is less certain is how far a firm must progress into network participation and technological collaboration. The thesis in this text is to calibrate oneself, based on what's happening within and without the industry, and then decide just how much progress can and must be made to take a leadership position. Then the firm can create the necessary new implementation models and build in the features mentioned, with the help of willing and trusted allies.

In this text, we consider what the leading firms have accomplished and how they plan further progress in supply chain evolution. Beginning in Level 1, the entry point for supply chain, we consider what strategy works for firms engaged in supplying basic commodities or operating in a particularly narrow focus niche business. The models presented illustrate how to bring savings in such areas as sourcing, transportation, order entry, and order processing. Moving into Level 2, we see how it makes sense for a firm that needs to be the lowest cost, easiest-to-work-with commodity supplier to have a model focused on efficiency across internal functions and processes. We consider forecasting, demand management, and capacity planning.

Progressing to Level 3, we evaluate firms that understand there must be a customer focus driving the effort and external resources are necessary to build a definitive network. We investigate interactive information sharing and models impacting supplier and customer relationship management.

Advance planning and scheduling models illustrate how some leaders are widening the gap against less able competitors.

As we enter Level 4, where the number of firms and stories declines rapidly, we study what's happening with the real pathfinders, companies hard at work building value-chain constellations. With partner collaboration and enabling information technology, these firms create situations where important processing is supported with online visibility. Now we're in the area of collaborative design and manufacture and collaborative planning, forecasting, and replenishment.

Finally, we see how a very few Level-5 firms have taken the time and expended the effort to create full network connectivity through design and implementation of e-business models that span a single inter-enterprise network. With these most advanced models, we look at the future state of supply chain modeling and what it holds for those needing to be in the frontmost position.

By describing the means of calibration and the advantages of moving to higher levels of progress, as well as illustrating advanced conditions, we provide the reader with an opportunity to establish the starting point and the necessary most-advanced position. Some companies will view these conditions and decide they don't need to reach the full potential of a focus on supply chain. They will appreciate, however, the value of collaboration and technology applications designed to enhance the supply chain effort in whatever level they seek. They'll learn how to work with willing supply chain constituents to find extra values that have eluded their relationships. Cycle time reduction, joint product development, joint asset utilization, and virtual logistics systems become part of such an effort.

We explain just what's required as each function is considered and outline what takes place from lower to higher levels of progress. The key is to establish the desired pathway to success, find the correct models to guide the effort, and implement with the right combination of technology and collaboration, which enhances the elements of supply chain that set one network apart from another in the eyes of customers and consumers. B2B2C commerce, enabled by cyber techniques, must be a central concept in any future business strategy. Make no mistake, supply chains of the future will be technology chains, linking companies from each end of the chain in a digital framework that makes the most sense to the intended buyers. What we provide is a series of models that will guide any firm toward that state.

Throughout this text, we provide generic and specific models, with examples from many industries and companies. More importantly, we present how to use the models to develop solutions — complete with actual case studies and action stories showing how collaboration and proper application of Internet-based technologies are typically the keys to success. The work reflects years of in-depth research, interviews with hundreds of key players across the supply chain spectrum, case study analysis, and actual hands-on experience spanning a wide range of industries and firms. This book is rich in model details — how they are constructed and how they can be implemented. We define a course of action that ensures better performance. Business examples are documented for each chapter. The reader is given a framework for understanding the models and how to use them to build an effective supply chain improvement plan.

This book will be of interest to anyone engaged in, or considering being engaged in, supply chain management, particularly those supply chain professionals seeking answers to implementation problems. It will have meaning for executives looking to get to the next level of performance improvement and managers charged with getting the intended solutions and returns. It should be of interest to software suppliers and users, as we show how to get the right implementation sequence and raise the probability of success. Academicians will find it valuable as a guide for how to overcome the many obstacles that stand between good intentions and superior achievements. There should also be global interest as supply chain continues to circle our world, bringing new efficiencies to those willing to make the special effort to build a dominant value chain network.

Much remains to be accomplished in supply chain management. There is still time to gain the high ground in an industry, as no firm has mastered all of the techniques and tools to claim the dominant position. There are leaders and followers, but opportunities exist to take the inherent concepts to a position of leadership. Selecting and applying the correct models can only enhance the odds of eventually being the ultimate leader in a particular industry.

ACKNOWLEDGMENTS

As we recognize those who helped bring this book to fruition, there are more names than can be listed. The research into all of the models presented has taken a path around the world and into every conceivable source of expertise. Crediting these sources has been done as carefully as possible throughout the text. If a particular individual or organization has been overlooked, it is purely unintentional.

Special thanks do go to the usual cast of players, including: Michael Bauer, Alex Black, George Borza, Russell Brackett, Brad Barton, Brad Bush, Simon Buesnel, Chet Chetzron, Steve Caulkins, Dean Chandler, John Decker, Roger Doty, Dave Durtsche, Lynette Ferrera, Drew Gant, Steve Goble, David Groener, Robert Guzak, Deb Hageman, Adam Hartung, Ken Hill, Pat Holmes, Michael Holzer, Bill Houser, Dave Howells, Larry Huhn, Peter Ilgenfritz, Marty Jacobsen, Gary Jones, Jim Kennedy, Larry Lapide, Chris Lennon, Kevin Lynch, Michael McClellan, Paul Molineux, Tom Muccio, Joel Polakoff, Frank Quinn, Steve Reiter, Jeffrey Sica, Steve Simco, Elsbeth Shepherd, Greg Suberlak, George Swartz, Paul Thompson, Bob Trauner, Chuck Troyer, Ian Walker, Chuck Wiza, and Rick Zuza.

THE AUTHOR

Charles Poirier has more than 40 years experience in business operations, with senior executive responsibility in a broad range of disciplines, including engineering, productivity, cost control, marketing, sales, quality, multiple plant and business management, safety, purchasing, mergers and acquisitions, organization, and administration. He has significant experience in developing leading-edge techniques to create process improvements with major manufacturing firms.

His recent work has focused on finding opportunities for value enhancement across integrated supply chain networks. He is highly skilled at presenting information on global best practices to senior-level corporate executives. Information from these and other experiences are contained in his books, *Supply Chain Optimization* and *Advanced Supply Chain Management*.

Prior to joining CSC, Poirier worked in many capacities for Packing Corporation of America, a division of Tenneco. As Senior Vice President, his responsibilities included developing corporate-wide quality, productivity, and cost improvement processes; acquisitions and management of a $400 million business; manufacturing assignments across all divisions; and the development of a corporate-wide marketing and selling process based on concepts in his book *Business Partnering for Continuous Improvement*.

Poirier received a B.S. in industrial management from Carnegie-Mellon University and an M.B.A. from the University of Pittsburgh.

CONTENTS

1

INTRODUCTION: A SUPPLY CHAIN FRAMEWORK WILL GUIDE EXECUTION

Throughout my business experience, I have never encountered a company that did not have some form of improvement process under way. Most of these efforts were intended to cut costs as close to the bone as possible, while others had a slightly more noble intention. For a while, quality became a serious matter as we heeded the calls of Deming, Juran, Crosby, and others to pursue total quality management. Most firms set out to do things right the first time and bring processing under acceptable control limits. Some firms qualified themselves under ISO 9000, the Baldrige Criteria, or other standards, providing proof they were serious about the effort. A few even moved to six sigma standards by improving systems to generate less than 3 bad parts per million. The smart ones used quality as a rallying point to reduce costs while they made things better.

Next came a nearly universal attempt to reengineer business processing. Process maps detailing what goes on in a business became common and were useful in finding and eliminating all of the nonvalue-adding steps. As-is conditions were analyzed so teams could develop improved to-be conditions. Companies employed this technique to dramatically downsize their operations. Enormous removal of labor will be a lasting legacy for this effort as the focus was mostly on becoming a low-cost producer in an industry. What companies learned, however, was how to challenge the status quo and look for innovative ways to do the right things better.

SUPPLY CHAIN BECAME AN UMBRELLA PROCESS
FOR OVERALL IMPROVEMENT

Then we discovered supply chain and realized there is an *umbrella* process under which the best features of the previous continuous improvement efforts could be merged with a focus on end-to-end processing that results in superior customer satisfaction. The early practitioners saw an opportunity to rethink and redesign linked process steps, all the way from initial raw materials to delivery of finished goods and services. While pursuing this opportunity, the idea of supply chain optimization developed — the chance to bring all process steps to a best-practice level and thereby optimize the total effort. Now the better right things would be at the right place at the right time.

Next came the discovery that knowledge was as crucial to success as innovative processing ideas. Those at the forefront of supply chain turned to the Internet and cyber-based technologies became feasible as a means of enhancing the improved processing. With appropriate digital-based equipment, software, middleware, and business process applications designed to enhance knowledge across extended enterprises technology blossomed as the tool for success. Those at the front of this phase also discovered that collaborative use of cyber technology could play an enormously beneficial role in bringing the linked processing to the highest level of effectiveness. Online visibility of total processing became an important feature so firms could see the right things going to the right places on time and communicate quickly if changes were necessary.

A few parameters became necessary ingredients for combining all of these emerging capabilities into a sensible strategy. The first supply chain improvement need is to establish what *end-to-end* means for a particular firm in order to set limits on the span of these efforts. The next step is to determine who will participate in the digital knowledge sharing and what information they should receive. Another need is to establish the scope of the ensuing advanced improvement efforts so skilled (and scarce) resources can be appropriately applied to building the new network systems while assuring returns are matched with the effort.

In this chapter, we look at the current state of the supply chain effort and use a basic framework that has proven to be very useful for understanding the dynamism of such efforts and to help calibrate a firm on its pathway to the desired level of improvement. This framework is used throughout the text to guide readers in selecting the most appropriate models and then executing properly. The author is greatly indebted to Ian Walker, senior partner for CSC Consulting, and Dr. Larry Lapide, VP of Research Operations and Business Applications at AMR Research, for their assistance in the supporting analyses presented in this chapter. The foundation for building sound and appropriate models was created with their help.

SUPPLY CHAIN DIMENSIONS SET THE STAGE FOR IMPROVEMENT

When defining the scope for a supply chain effort, it is always advisable to adopt as broad a definition as possible. That way the most process steps are included and, therefore, the greatest opportunity for improvement is considered. The only caveat is to exercise caution and not make the scope so great that insufficient resources are available to reach effective conclusions. When enthusiasm builds for such efforts, it is not unusual to see long lists of improvement initiatives generated. Too often, due to talented resource constraints, these efforts get bogged down in completing the list, rather than bringing the right initiatives toward an aligned and logical strategic intention. With that in mind, the firm gets started by deciding where its supply chain begins and ends — the dimensions for the effort. The traditional view of supply chain starts with an illustration as simple as that displayed in Figure 1.1.

The front end, or upstream dimension, begins at the point at which the firm acquires the wherewithal to start its processing. That requires a look at incoming materials and services so an immediate effort to reduce the total number of suppliers can take place. Further work in this area generally results in identifying the core group of important sources on which the firm depends. Supply chain improvement always progresses with the help of these *key suppliers* — never with the total array of sources. How the materials and services arrive is also documented as inbound logistics come under study. There are simply too many modes of transportation being underutilized for a serious supply chain advocate to overlook this important area. Here we consider the timing and cost of getting the materials and services to the appropriate destination.

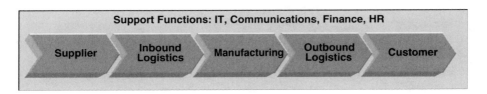

Figure 1.1   The Traditional Supply Chain

Since some improvement effort will already be under way, the next step is to draw a process map linking these incoming supplies and services with the important internal process steps. This map need not be elaborate, but it must show the flow of products and information that results in the firm delivering products and services. The map continues through the manufacturing or production processes and on to delivery to the next link in the supply chain. Steps used for outbound logistics of what has been made must be recorded. Here we take note of the shipments leaving manufacturing or production and going to places where the goods are stored — generally called warehousing. This sector could include an intermediate distributor, but results in shipments of goods to a business customer. For some firms, the map ends at this point and the improvement process can commence. Most firms have begun their supply chain effort with a business-to-business (B2B) map.

In the modern sense, the chain continues and is complete at the downstream side when the consumer is satisfied with the delivery. When that does not happen and something is returned, the chain continues in reverse. Figure 1.2 illustrates this more extended business-to-business-to-consumer (B2B2C) view. Regardless of which format is chosen to optimize any supply chain effort, a company must define the breadth of its end-to-end processing so people seeking improvement know where to begin and where to stop. That means the map must include the intermediate steps that define what happens to the products and services after the immediate business customer has been satisfied. For goods that go on to retail outlets and into consumer purchasing, the map gets extended all the way to the consumer and shows a channel for any possible returns.

The map gets more complex as this analysis progresses and multiple supply sources and channels to market can be depicted. Figure 1.3 shows a complex supply chain system more closely depicting a modern, large-scale network. In this flow chart, the supply side is far more complex, involving multiple incoming sources of materials, as well as subassemblies, work from subcontractors and contract manufacturers. The intermediate processing could involve other network partners with better core competencies handling part of the process steps. The channels to market could include distributors and several types of business customers, including

Figure 1.2 The Extended Supply Chain

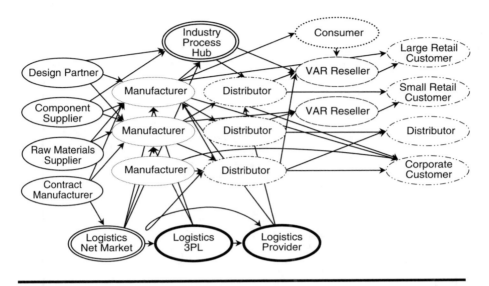

Figure 1.3   A Complex Supply Chain Network

multiple retail customers. To complete the map, it should then extend to the designated consumer markets targeted for selling by the network partners.

With the end-to-end dimensions determined, the Level 1 firm returns to the starting point where the attention is going to be on internal processing. Once a rough supply chain map is completed, the firm focuses on what happens within its four walls. Here the map takes on more detail as the firm decides the definition and scope of what is going to be improved. Figure 1.4 shows a detailed map of the internal processing that takes place within a particular factory making desert boots. On this map, the time frames and estimates of current costs have been included to make the map more of a depiction of what's transpiring, so it becomes a detailed value chain.

The internal supply chain map should cover all of the physical processing — from supply through manufacture, transport, and storage to eventual sale. As each connection is made along the chain, group together the products that share mutual resources and segregate products that operate separately. The result will be a series of self-contained product flows where sharing of resources is minimal (warehousing and storage) and where competition for resources becomes a problem needing management (shipping and customer service).

Clarks Shoes made the map in Figure 1.4, one of twenty produced for each major product family. This map for desert boots immediately revealed several problem areas:

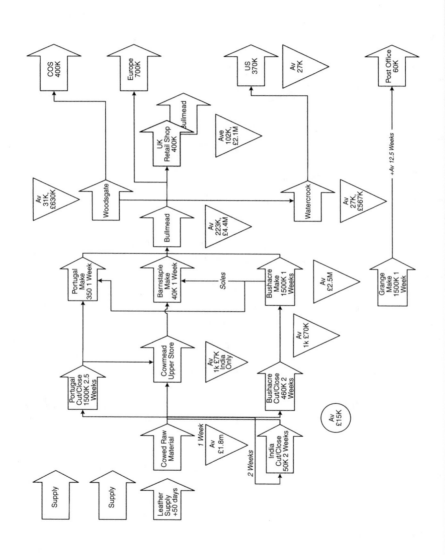

Figure 1.4 A Detailed Internal Supply Chain

- This one product flow was mapped by several functions in the organization, each having its own local performance measures.
- Production resources were often fully loaded but the result was a lot of inventory in the supply chain.
- The customer service goals were often not defined precisely, so no one knew how much it cost to provide a given level of service (Walker, 2001, p. 40).

Clarks took the segmented flows shown by the mapping exercise and created horizontal structures, what they called supply chain tubes, across the organization. Teams responsible for each tube took control over the products to be made and sold and the assets used to make the products. Each tube, or product line, is largely self-contained in this approach. As a firm pursues its mapping, groupings could be based on an identified set of assets, or a market-facing product group. When correctly depicted, there's little trouble beginning a process improvement effort that starts with suppliers and moves through the channels to market.

With this information, teams can begin working to bring this map to a new and improved state. Such an effort always starts with a focus on internal functions and processes — to clean up existing problems, mistakes, and errors, and optimize internal efficiency. Then the focus can move outside to look at how every hand-off in the end-to-end processing can be improved and made as effective as possible for customer needs. Eventually, the effort spans a full network — an extended enterprise — and applies the appropriate cyber-based technologies to establish the most effective value chain in the eyes of the desired customers and consumers. This most advanced level will contain the greatest span of supply chain dimensions and, of course, the most work to reach completion.

Figure 1.5 illustrates a supply chain process map that spans a high-technology network. In this advanced stage, all the players are collaborating on improving the linked processing so the network gains a market advantage. Firms won't get to this stage for a while. They need to evolve to such a stage and will have to struggle along the way with the possibilities offered by applying the new cyber technologies. These features must be built into the models used to progress across the five supply chain levels.

WITH SUPPLY CHAIN COMES AN EVOLUTIONARY PROCEDURE

Along this evolutionary pathway, firms will pass through one level at a time and must determine whether further progress is warranted. The levels

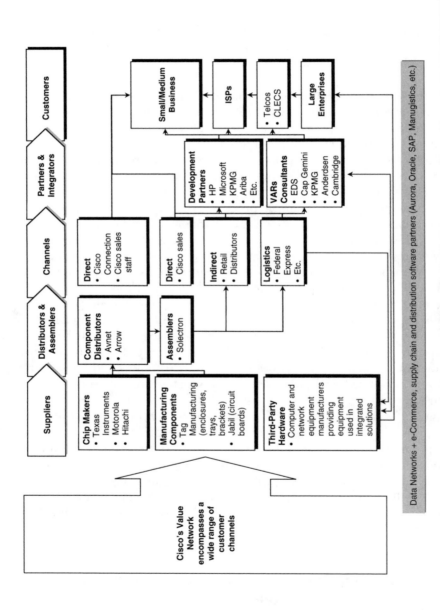

Figure 1.5   A Detailed Internal Supply Chain (From Cisco Systems, San Jose, CA)

in this evolution start with an introduction of the umbrella supply chain effort and move methodically to the optimal business model that makes sense for the firm and its circumstances.

Level 1: Internal/Functional

Level 1, internal/functional, focuses on sourcing and logistics, concentrating on internal needs and business unit efficiency, while neglecting organizational synergies.

In the first level of supply chain evolution, the firm invariably works on an internal basis, seeking to expand its cost improvement effort, while focusing on total supply chain processing. The methodology is to look at functional improvement (getting better at buying, planning, warehousing, and shipping) and operational efficiency (lowest cost to manufacture), typically within a specific business unit. Departmental silos and independent operating units cover the landscape. Little cross-organizational cooperation exists in this early level and is rarely encouraged. Real savings are possible, particularly from improvements to sourcing and logistics within a business unit. The supplier base is reduced, volumes are leveraged, and costs decline. So long as quality is not impaired, savings can be significant and funding is created to continue the effort into the other levels.

In the area of logistics, transportation costs are reduced, warehouse space is matched with need, and inventories are scrutinized for possible reduction. Transportation management systems (TMS) and warehouse management systems (WMS) are features of this part of the evolution. Most firms finish Level 1 with an improved order entry and order management system that eliminates errors that confound such systems and speeds the cycle time from receipt of order to receipt of cash payment.

Some Level 1 firms try to apply these improvements across business units to establish a basis for intra-enterprise interaction and cooperation, but are generally driven back because the units and functions refuse to share resources and information or accept help outside their limited boundaries. I have never encountered a firm that wants to remain in Level 1, but I could name several that will never leave that part of the progression. The potential to add profits to a firm's profit and loss (P&L) probably peaks around 1 to 1.5% in this Level. That means a company's profit margin before taxes can increase from 5% to 6 or 6.5%.

Level 2: Internal/Cross-Functional

Level 2, internal/cross-functional, focuses on internal excellence, breaking down the internal walls and beginning intra-enterprise integration.

In the second level of progress, the company remains internally focused, starts to move away from functional organizational structures and begins building a foundation for an optimized internal supply chain. The walls that typically separate parts of the organization and inhibit leveraging the full scale of operations are broken down. Now the company starts cooperating within itself and a cross-functional effort begins. Separate business units come together to see what they buy in common, what they process and ship, and to determine where the opportunities exist to collaborate without harming market capabilities or functional excellence.

Some form of shared services based on aggregated demand is created within the firm to take advantage of the full size of the organization. Transportation needs across the firm are studied to see where synergies can be applied. Sharing of best practices starts to move across functions and units. The seeds of advanced technology are planted as a communication intranet is established and software introduced to enhance planning and scheduling. Features will include advanced planning and scheduling (APS) and sales and operations planning (S&OP). It is a time for getting the organization primed with respect to supply chain process steps that are vital to market success.

Level 2 companies sort out their customers by segmenting them into classes that define their importance to the firm and the needs important to each class. Performance metrics that relate to customer satisfaction begin to appear as the idea is to match service with value rendered and received. Technology, as an enabler, also begins on an internal basis as the *intranet* is used for sharing information across the firm. Enterprise-wide resource planning (ERP) systems come into the picture as the transaction engine for the firm. Some form of advanced supply chain planning solution, from such firms as i2 Technologies or Manugistics, will be in place to identify system constraints and smooth planning and manufacturing flows. Leaders will reach the point where they have an available-to-promise capability to show the best customers what is in the supply pipeline and to make delivery date commitments that are kept.

Somewhere close to 70 to 80% of all companies studied fall into this level, although many of those firms have footsteps in multiple levels. Because some business units will progress with or without the rest of the company, firms can find themselves with parts of the organization spread across the entire evolutionary progression. Not every firm, or all parts of a firm, must leave this level. In a later section of this chapter, we will consider which firms ought to stay and which should progress. Another 1 to 1.5% can flow to the bottom line in this level.

Level 3: External Network Formation

Level 3, external network formation, focuses on the customer through collaboration with selected partners.

A strong cultural wall stands between Levels 2 and 3 — a wall that schools all effort should be focused on internal excellence. Customers are an important by-product of the effort, but compensation, bonuses, and payoffs are still strongly related to what gets pushed through the improved internal supply chain. Only with an external view can the firm move forward with the help of partner collaboration. Now the company begins to link its processes with selected customers via the previous market segmentation, while eliciting the help of a few key suppliers to make sure promises made can be promises kept. An *extranet,* designed to link these partners, comes into being.

The company seeks out willing constituents of the supply chain that can assist in finding the next level of improvement. An extended enterprise perspective is brought to the discussions as the firm realizes it is only one part of the network of companies focused on a particular customer or consumer group. Together, these allies focus on customer satisfaction and align supply chain efforts so a distinctive advantage is gained in the eyes of those customers. ERP-to-ERP connections and alignment occur in this level, as those typically large investments begin to pay off from an external perspective through the valuable integration of knowledge that helps all network partners. Vendor managed inventory (VMI) and customer replenishment planning (CRP) systems mature in this level. The firm finds it can now offer available-to-promise (ATP) and capable-to-promise (CTP) features as well.

Only about 10 to 15% of my sample of supply chain firms has made it over the cultural wall and is firmly planted in Level 3. Here we find the companies that determined it was necessary to take an external viewpoint to process improvement and to elicit the help of willing and trusted partners. It is here that companies really work for the benefit of their customers and do all they can to optimize the end-to-end processing that results in satisfaction for those customers.

A caution must be mentioned here. There are as many stories of failure in this transition from Level 2 to 3 as there are success stories. The failures typically involve firms trying to move too much of the company to a higher position too fast before the internal house is in order. Most firms successfully reach this level, not because of a corporate-wide effort, but because one or two visionary business leaders take the initiative and moved their units into the necessary external environment. With proof of success, others then follow the example. A full two points of profit can be added to the P&L when this level is completed.

Level 4: External Value Chain

Level 4, external value chain, focuses on the consumer with partners and establishes inter-enterprise synchronization.

As collaboration succeeds and technology is used as a key improvement tool, the linked firms move into an industry leadership position where a value chain constellation begins to form. This entity is a set of firms cooperating as an extended enterprise to dominate a particular market or industry by virtue of having the delivery system of choice in the eyes of the desired business customer. Now the firm is part of a constellation of companies that represent the end-to-end value chain, with all of its complexities understood and under an overall improvement effort. Firms in this level look seriously at supply chain outsourcing to find the most capable constituent for process steps. E-procurement systems are in place and supporting Internet communication systems link the partners.

A new dimension is added. Realizing that any supply chain ends with consumption, the focus moves to a targeted end-consumer group. Now network resources move from attention to the bottom line (cost reduction) to the top line (new revenues in the desired market sectors). The supply chain becomes a value chain effort in this level, as enough information is shared to pinpoint all the costs and values from end to end of the network, and partners focus on how they can optimize all the process steps. Working together, members of the value chain begin to synchronize efforts across the inter-enterprise network. That means firms align the supply chain process steps into a single, logical, extended enterprise, operating as a fully linked and optimized end-to-end B2B2C network from suppliers to consumers.

The number of firms in this level is very small and rates only 1 or 2% of the total sample. Here we find the firms that have worked collaboratively with suppliers, distributors, and customers to build new business models focused on end consumption. These models are enhanced front to back with e-commerce features and the best cyber-based technologies. Another one to two points can flow to the bottom line in this level.

Level 5: Full Network Connectivity

Level 5, full network connectivity, focuses on cyber technology as the value chain enabler to achieve network optimization.

The final level of progress is more theoretical than factual because of the limited number of firms that occupy this space. It is an area where full network connectivity has been achieved in which all of the important transactions are visible online. Partners share vital information electronically and bring an unprecedented low cycle time to the processing that takes place across the full network.

Supply chain visibility is achieved, inventories are viewed on a real-time basis, and forecasting error is reduced to workable levels or banished ? in favor of direct linkage to consumption. Manufacturing, distribution, and transportation are virtual efforts taking advantage of all the modes in a system. New products come out in a fraction of typical time frames with a higher possibility of success. The opportunity to create savings while generating new revenue is possible for all parties in the value chain.

There are so few Level 5 organizations, we cannot give it a percentage. This is the land of opportunity where the final points are added to profits, bringing a total improvement of 5 to 8% to the bottom line of the P&L. That means a firm starting with a before-taxes profit margin of 5% can increase that figure to 10 to 13%.

THE FIRM MUST DECIDE ON ITS REQUIRED POSITION

As already explained, a firm moving into and progressing through a supply chain management effort must decide on the dimensions of its end-to-end processing, and then determine its position on the described evolutionary progression. With the help of material supplied by Dr. Larry Lapide from AMR Research, we now take a look at how that part of the process goes forward.

Figure 1.6 shows a simple way to get under way by creating a graphical questionnaire to help define the path forward. On a chart depicting a time frame across the horizontal axis and strategic impact of the supply chain effort on the business on the vertical axis, the firm establishes where it is at the current time, the starting dimension. There does not need to be much precision in this early exercise, only a relative rating. Next, some rough estimate, based on general or industry study, is made of where the firm should be headed — the final dimension. A simple estimate that states the firm should double its earnings per share within three years will suffice.

Since no pathway is a straight line in supply chain, a roadway must be constructed from Position 1 to Position 2, moving through the levels described. This pathway will be far from clear in the beginning and will take time and patience to outline as the firm goes forward. For the preliminary exercise, some general ideas regarding where to get started, what type of first initiatives make sense, where models will help, and where some measure of significant improvement could be gained, starts the roadmap.

The general ideas now get specific as we question: What are the practical next steps? No firm is going to get the necessary support for its effort unless there are early savings or significant improvements. For this reason, smart leaders always select some early initiatives that yield some

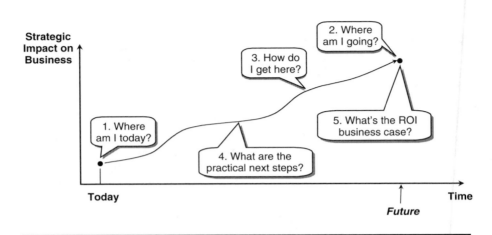

Figure 1.6 Supply Chain Strategy Development

low-hanging fruit or quick-hit gains. The corollary question then becomes how to measure the return on our efforts. Metrics should be quickly established for measuring progress and what we term the return on investment for the business case that will be made for the overall effort.

With an idea of where we are beginning, where we want to go, and how we might get there, attention turns to more detail on establishing the ranges of improvement that might be achieved and the strategic thinking needed to get to the higher levels of progress. Figure 1.7 helps with making such determinations. In this illustration, Levels 1 and 2 have been combined as the first part of the progression, which we now term *getting the house in order*. These two levels are for those firms intent on getting internal excellence as close to optimized conditions as possible.

Here we see the kind of application models that get accomplished in the first two levels of the evolution, including TMS and WMS, focusing on moving transportation and warehousing systems to state-of-the-art conditions so the costs of staging, storing, and shipping products is as good as or better than industry standards. The beginnings of some type of inventory management system, APS, and S&OP are targeted accomplishments.

When a firm decides it must move into Level 3, termed *enhancing partner relationships*, the focus moves to such matters as supplier synchronization to make sure planning systems involve the key suppliers mentioned. The idea is to make certain these suppliers are bringing the right materials forward to meet actual production needs. The current use of demonstrated best supply chain practices is considered, regardless of the industry from which these practices derived. Suppliers manage inventories through VMI systems and replenishment is based on information

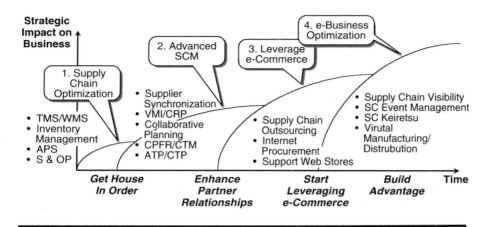

Figure 1.7   Where Is the Firm Today?

supplied through CRP systems. Other features include collaborative planning, Collaborative Planning, Forecasting, and Replenishment (CPFR), Capable-to-Manufacture (CTM), ATP, and CTP.

As we approach the rarefied air of supply chain, Level 4 is now termed *start leveraging e-commerce*. Here we see the firm using e-procurement features with its key suppliers to find catalog suppliers of indirect materials and services. Private buying portals or aggregated consortium systems are present. Outsourcing becomes a viable option to find the best partners across all process steps. Supporting Web-based systems are in place to aid in knowledge transfer and virtual e-business models are coming into view. Firms must assess their e-commerce capability in this area and that of their supporting partners, so partnering is accomplished at each point of the linkage. There can be no tolerance of weak partners that might slow or interfere with the system.

In the most advanced area, Level 5 is termed *build advantage*. It is at this level that firms and their key partners use their models and implementations to dominate an industry. Here we see full supply chain visibility from end to end in the processing. Event management for promotions and special applications is cyber-based and controlled from the stores to key suppliers. Virtual manufacturing and distribution uses the online extranet systems to track, divert, and move the right amount of goods to the right point of need. A form of supply chain keiretsu becomes a reality as the members of the existing value chain network work in a trusting atmosphere, sharing knowledge vital to each partner's ability to enhance profits. Joint investments in assets are a special feature at this level.

In Figure 1.8, the firm draws another pictorial representation of the supply chain under consideration. Taking note of both the flow of goods and information, the firm begins to position itself and lists those constituents important to the end-to-end processing. For firms content with a Level 2 position, this picture will be fairly compact. For a firm seeking Level 5 status, the chart will be far more complex. In any event, exchanges that could help the network are considered next. Such exchanges as exist or could be created for suppliers, logistics providers, or customers are listed, along with what value will be added by participating with such entities.

Finally, the firm considers exactly how far it wishes to progress in the evolution. To assist that determination, Figure 1.9 repeats the progression shown in Figure 1.7 and lists some of the companies in each level. If getting the house in order, Level 2, is sufficient for at least the early supply chain effort, the firm sets that as its target. Small companies and Tier 2 suppliers (suppliers two steps removed from an OEM or final manufacturer) fit this part of the evolution. Consumer products firms are advised to adopt this level as minimum progress. Firms well upstream in a supply chain, supplying minerals, power, water, chemicals, or farm products, also fall into this area of concentration.

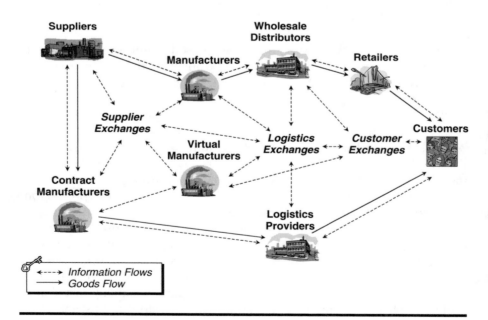

Figure 1.8   Where Does the Firm Fit?

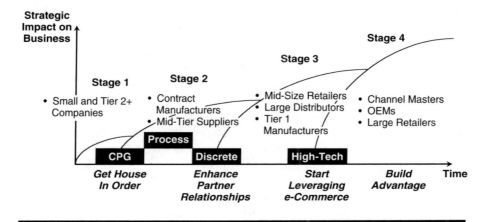

Figure 1.9 Where Should the Firm Go?

As the firm moves to Level 3, enhancing partner relationships, we find mid-tier processing firms (office products, manufactured sub-assemblies, plastic products), manufacturing automobile assemblies, airplane parts and sections, and defense equipment. Financial service organizations typically fall in here with banks and lending organizations. Discrete manufacturers making products for retail sales also span this and the next level as they need to link their output with what is being demanded in the stores. Examples include sports gear, clothing, cosmetics, furniture, and accessories.

As the firm moves into Level 4, start leveraging e-commerce, the need for connectivity with partners begins to increase dramatically. Now we find medium-size retailers, large distributors, and Tier 1 manufacturers. High-technology firms must have a footstep in this and the next level of the evolution, as that entire industry is on the forefront of moving to Level 5. Firms engaged in electronic equipment and entertainment also have little choice but to move to this level. Appliance manufacturers are well advised to follow suit.

When the determination is Level 5, build advantage, the need to have full network connectivity is essential. Now we see the nucleus firms or channel masters that will dominate their industries. Original equipment manufacturers (OEMs) and the very large retailers fill this space. Names like Ford, General Motors, Kraft Foods, Boeing, Procter & Gamble, Siemens, General Dynamics, Nestlé, Sainsbury, Kroger, Carrefour, Sears, and Wal-Mart fit in this level.

RESULTS CAN BE SIGNIFICANTLY BETTER FOR THE EFFORT

The different positions offer decidedly different returns on the effort. For Level 2 organizations, returns may be sufficient as they avoid the cost of building the e-commerce connectivity, but the maximum benefit to the bottom line will be in the range of 2 to 3%. The differences for those firms that take the lead and move to the highest levels can be dramatic, reaching seven to eight points of new profit. How well the job is done in the chosen level of progress also affects the results. Research from Computer Sciences Corporation (CSC), based on responses to an annual survey of organizations engaged in supply chain, indicates a significant difference in results achieved between those firms in good supply chains and those in poor supply chains. See Figure 1.10.

Before proceeding to the specific models and solutions that are recommended, it is critical that we establish some points of importance. First, supply chain optimization is a concept that can only be approached. So much progress has been made and so many new innovations introduced that the end line becomes a moving target. Only a few firms come close to best practices across an entire extended enterprise. Nevertheless, the

Benefits	% of Companies in Good Supply Chains Experiencing	% of Companies in Poor Supply Chains Experiencing	All Companies Surveyed
Increased Sales	41%	14%	26%
Cost Savings	62%	22%	40%
Increased Market Share	32%	12%	20%
Inventory Reductions	51%	18%	35%
Improved Quality	60%	28%	39%
Accelerated Delivery Times	54%	27%	40%
Improved Logistics Management	43%	15%	27%
Improved Customer Service	66%	22%	44%

Figure 1.10   Effectiveness of Overall Supply Chain Effort Does Make a Difference (From Computer Sciences Corporation, El Segundo, CA)

effort is extremely valuable, as the magnitude of improvement to performance is potentially the difference between survival and failure.

Second, each level of progression requires time and patience to accomplish. The necessary understanding and requisite behavioral change (business transformation) is not easy and requires sustained executive endorsement. Experience schools that getting to Level 3 takes at least three years, and then only a few business units will move into that level. For some firms and industries, achievement of the most advanced levels could require a decade of effort.

Third, the rewards for the effort can truly be the difference between leading an industry in performance or perpetually following. Research underpinning this text shows those companies (leaders) implementing Levels 3 and 4 are experiencing significant advantage over other firms in their industries and are benefiting from profitable revenue growth that wouldn't otherwise have been achieved.

Fourth, companies in earlier stages (followers) will continue to see margin erosion while trying to catch the leaders, unless that is an acceptable level of progress for their business. The gap between leaders and followers shows a one- to two-year advantage. At the same time, very few firms have reached Level 5, although many are in pursuit of this position. Therefore, the opportunity exists to make supply chain progress and thereby close the gap and attain dominance.

What is required is a solid understanding of what end-to-end means for a particular organization, what the dimensions of the improvement effort encompass, and how to merge technology with sound business practices to become the chosen network of supply by a particular business customer or end consumer group. The following chapters provide specific models for getting through each level of the supply chain management progression.

SUMMARY

Supply chain is the latest business performance improvement effort for good reason as the results are proving. It is the umbrella process under which a firm can merge the best of its previous continuous improvement efforts to gain the next level of better performance and customer satisfaction. Taking best advantage of supply chain management requires defining the end-to-end process steps involved, the scope of what must be achieved, and then progressing through evolutionary levels to the level necessary for the firm to achieve a market advantage. Moving through each of the intermediate levels is important to bring the organization to optimum conditions, as the house must be in order before working on alliances with external partners. As firms move to the external environment required for the higher level of progression, they find getting to the most advanced levels requires collaboration with a select group of supply chain partners working as a network focused on specific customer or consumer groups.

As this collaboration proceeds, the network of partners will get to the highest level by working through models that guide progress and show where appropriate technology and Internet-based applications will enhance the effort. We will expand on this thinking as we now begin to consider the many supply chain models that can result in a firm and its partners dominating a chosen market or industry.

2

A CALIBRATION MODEL ESTABLISHES POSITION AND PERFORMANCE GAP

With the five-level framework as a guide to movement through the supply chain evolution, it is possible to point out where progress has been made by firms across many industries, and to establish a format for calibration. By considering where others have advanced, a firm can determine if similar progress is advantageous. It can also create an order of magnitude gap describing the difference between current best practices and the firm's performance. Analyzing this gap provides a guide for choosing the areas that need improvement and the models that could help close the gap.

In this chapter, we consider a calibration model, descriptive practices across the supply chain evolution, and a self-administered exercise to assist with the suggested analysis. Michael Bauer, partner at Computer Sciences Corporation, made substantial contributions to this chapter.

COMPANIES ACCOMPLISH PROGRESSIVE IMPROVEMENTS WITH SUPPLY CHAIN

As mentioned in the previous chapter, supply chain efforts progress through five levels in a sequence. As a firm or business unit moves through these levels, the various functions make progress or they restrict the overall effort. Considering each of the major functions in a typical firm and the levels of evolution provides an opportunity to begin the calibration exercise. Figure 2.1 presents an overview of the major business applications matched with the five levels of supply chain evolution.

Progression Business Applications	Levels 1 & 2 Internal Supply Chain Optimization Supply Chain Optimization	Level 3 External Network Formation Advanced Supply Chain Management	Level 4 Value Chain Constellation e-Commerce	Level 5 Full Network Connectivity e-Business
Design, Development Product/Service Introduction	Internal Only	Selected External Assistance	Collaborative Design – Enterprise Integration and PIM-Linked CAD/CAM	Business Functional View – Joint Design and Development
Purchase, Procurement, Sourcing	Leverage Business Unit Volume	Leverage Full Network Through Aggregation	Key Supplier Assistance, Web- Based Sourcing	Network Sourcing Through Best Constituent
Marketing, Sales, Customer Service	Internally Developed Programs, Promotions	Customer-Focused, Data-Based Initiatives	Collaborative Development for Focused Consumer Base	Consumer Response System Across the Value Chain
Engineering, Planning, Scheduling, Manufacturing	MRP MRPII DRP	ERP – Internal Connectivity	Collaborative Network Planning – Best Asset Utilization	Full Network Business System Optimization Shared Processes and Systems
Logistics	Manufacturing Push – Inventory- Intensive	Pull System Through Internal/External Providers	Best Constituent Provider	Total Network, Virtual Logistics Optimization
Customer Care	Customer Service Reaction	Focused Service – Call Centers	Segmented Response System, Customer Relationship Management	Matched Care – Customer Care Automation and Remediation
Human Resources	Regulatory Issues/Hiring, Recruiting, Training	New Work Models, Training	Inter-Enterprise Resource Utilization, Training	Full Network Alignment and Capability Provision
Information Technology	Point Solutions Internal Silos	Linked Intranets Corp Strategy/Architecture	Internet-Based Extranet Shared Capabilities	Full Network Comm. System Shared Architecture Planning

Figure 2.1　Levels of Supply Chain Maturity

Levels 1 and 2 have been combined in this matrix to represent the starting position. The majority of companies occupy these two levels, focused strictly on internal supply chain optimization within the four walls of the organization. The degree of internal cooperation will determine a higher or lower position. Level 3 is where aspiring firms begin to use external resources to reach advanced benefits. It is here that the external network formation begins, as the focus is on advanced supply chain management. The value chain constellation appears in Level 4, as current leaders display features of e-commerce, collaborate with allies in the digital economy, and apply cyber-based technologies in their relationships. In Level 5, full network connectivity is established and e-business models begin driving the linked firms. These models will define the roadway into the new economy and the direction in which superior business relationships are headed.

On the vertical axis, the business functions and corresponding applications are listed and the changes in roles and activities that take place are matched to the various levels of progress. The calibration starts by comparing current conditions to what can be achieved. The chart in Figure 2.1 begins with design and development, as this function affects new product and service introduction. In Levels 1 and 2, this effort generally revolves around internally oriented activities. There is a sense that no sharing should be done externally, as that could jeopardize the secrecy normally attached to these efforts, and practitioners fear a competitive advantage would be lost. For firms engaged in patented processes and products, this fear is probably justified. For others, it might be a bit overcautious.

The design and development effort for new products is usually engineering driven, with pressure on creating best product features, designing breakthrough innovations, and finding applications of current technologies. For industrial products, quality is often worked into the designs after products are manufactured and tested. For consumer products, there's a long list of developments in the queue and a considerable amount of marketing input, with only a slight guarantee that any new introduction will become successful after reaching the market. Only about five percent of Level 1 and 2 developments achieve commercial acceptance.

In Level 3, this function seeks external advice as the firm forms a network. Selected suppliers are invited to participate in the design process and some external ideas are accepted. Suppliers of important subassemblies begin experimenting with how to move away from paper blueprints and apply some form of electronic data interchange. A serious effort is made to facilitate engineering and design changes without the normal delays in seeking access to prints and specifications, getting approvals, and making engineering changes. Industry seminars are accessed, functional workshops attended, and some consumer clinics aimed at discussing actual customer needs are conducted. Contract design firms may also be used.

Hewlett-Packard has a network of internal and external designers working around the world and around the clock to sustain a lead with products that seem to have an ever-shorter life cycle. Their extranet, linking valuable players in the design effort, is online on a 24/7 format and keeps new designs going on a perpetual basis.

In Level 4, there are elements of collaborative design, even if on a pilot basis, as teams that include selected suppliers begin to develop products. Enterprise integration of planning systems, including computer-aided design and computer-aided manufacturing, are linked to take advantage of multiple constituent skills, shorten cycle times, and increase the probability of commercial success. Product information management systems are a feature of this interaction as firms collectively make use of the engineering and design information in their databases to improve the design phase and create new products that are manufacturing friendly. Consumer products firms work very selectively with a cadre of suppliers and key customers to increase the likelihood of success with new product introductions.

In Level 5, a business functional view appears and the constituents are involved in joint design and development, focused on what their collective database information shows as the trends, preferences, current popular innovations, and actual customer and consumer needs. Often the relationship leads to a truly collaborative endeavor where all constituents do what they do best and all participants bring their views of the market needs into play. The best concepts are used to create new prototypes or product offerings. Joint development of new equipment is likely to occur. Consumers are a key part of the design team and participation extends across the network. This phase of the effort could include joint investment in new capital assets.

This is the area where Boeing is found working as a nucleus firm, with very selected suppliers, to create the new 777 airplanes in industry-record times. This airplane was designed in cyberspace. Electronic sharing of design tools and processing techniques occurred with engineers, customers, maintenance personnel, project managers, and key suppliers of components and subassemblies. There were no paper blueprints. The work was done interactively over the Web using Boeing's extranet for communication. The normal three-year delivery for a new airplane of this size was cut to twelve months or less with this Level 5 application. Boeing found it could also increase its capacity to build twice as many airplanes in a year.

There are other examples of Level 5 design efforts, but we will have to wait until they come out of the pilot stage. The big four automakers, for example, are working diligently with their network partners to deliver a new automobile from dealer order through manufacturing to home delivery in something under 14 days. Toyota is working on a six-day cycle. The U.S. Department of Defense has made great strides with its military network to deliver bombs on target in 72 hours. The Defense Logistics Agency is becoming a model for how to use e-commerce and collaboration to have the correct supplies in the hands of their end consumers — the battle-ready warriors — in unprecedented short cycle times. In another automotive example, Ford was able to bring its European model — Monde — to market in 16 months through the same type of collaboration between designers, suppliers, and manufacturers.

PURCHASING AND SOURCING MOVE FROM TACTICS TO STRATEGY

The purchasing, procurement, and sourcing functions demonstrate another progression. In Levels 1 and 2, the emphasis is typically on leveraging volume and supplier share for the lowest unit cost. That's generally done at the individual business unit level first, but could progress across the firm, especially in nondirect categories of buy. It is difficult for any firm concentrating on internal excellence to do much more than hammer its supply base for continual cost reduction. A few strategic relationships will be found as the number of suppliers is reduced, but true collaboration comes later in the progression.

In Level 3, purchasing is better understood as a strategic tool and leveraged at the full intra-enterprise level. Then comes a move to expand the leverage through aggregation across the network. Initially, key suppliers and customers are invited to take advantage of the buying power of the nucleus firm. This is also the time when some meaningful diagnostics are conducted with a few very important and strategic suppliers to begin discussion on enhancements that do not involve price concessions. The seeds of supplier relationship management (SRM) are sown in this level, as the closest and most strategic suppliers are used to develop a future state template.

In Level 4, the role of purchasing expands dramatically in the eyes of senior management, and this function begins to play a central role in the network formation effort by bringing in key suppliers to make an impact on design, planning, and manufacturing. Supplier expertise is sought and used to enhance the production processes. As the emphasis also shifts to core competencies, this function plays a critical role in identifying the suppliers that can provide larger assemblies or take responsibility for entire parts of the production process. The function also finds new sources, often in nondomestic locations, where superior parts, delivery, and pricing can be found. This is definitely an area where the typical engineering and manufacturing push back has been subdued. E-procurement begins to be a factor as transaction costs are reduced by virtue of having a buying robot do a lot of the tedious work involved in catalog search, bidding processes, and vendor selection.

The key elements of this automation include a Web browser user interface, use of standard Internet communication and security protocols, and software supporting the requisitioning process. These elements and others require a new orientation for the sourcing group, a move directly toward strategy and away from tactics. Network-wide purchasing becomes a real opportunity as the collaborating partners start turning over their indirect categories of buy to the constituent having the best expertise for contract negotiation. Procurement portals become an option to consider to further streamline the processing. A variety of online auctions are used to find the best possible arrangement on specific commodities, usually turning up some very interesting new scenarios. It's a time when all of the fresh ideas for improving this function become operating techniques as the linked companies spend less time on negotiation and more on building network strength.

When the nucleus firm reaches Level 5, the role of sourcing is firmly entrenched in business strategy as the value chain constellation is driving for best overall performance and the most capable constituent is responsible for each process step. That means letting the most capable member of your value chain constellation purchase goods and services for the entire network. Full electronic catalogs are made available to all constituents.

MARKETING, SALES, AND CUSTOMER SERVICE MOVE THROUGH ROLE CHANGES

The marketing, sales, and customer service functions collectively take on new roles as well. In Levels 1 and 2, the emphasis is on internally developed programs and promotions, as the firm is convinced the route to success is through providing what they think is best for the customer and the need to push production toward the customer. It is in these levels that we hear a lot of talk about the importance of the customer but very little real meaning. Compensation systems are an inhibitor here as they generally favor the push system and rewards for volume outweigh any customer satisfaction measures. Account ownership is a central issue and is viewed as a sales strategy.

In Level 3, the emphasis shifts toward the business customer as firms begin to share what is in their databases and use it effectively to generate new revenues. The role of selling changes dramatically here, from that of information provider, order seeker, and negotiator to becoming the voice of the key customers. The new salesperson functions as an advocate for these strategic customers, often with the best salespeople representing only one or two of the highest-valued customers. These representatives now bring back information on what needs should be resolved, what can be improved in the relationship, and how the firms can work more closely by applying their mutual knowledge of the marketplace.

Marketing moves from doing research and building planning systems that create new demand, to collaboratively analyzing data on customer buying patterns and habits to develop new revenues with the aid of network partners. Customer service moves from being the repository of complaints and customer anguish to being a proactive partner in planning, as they possess the vital information about what irritates and pleases the customers.

In Level 4, the transformation continues. The strategic account sales representative is an integral part of the network, actively processing collaboratively developed new solution sets for customers. The sales representative becomes the initiator of critical responses that cut cycle time, provide the necessary information to solve problems, and offer consultative advice on potential supply chain improvements. This representative also becomes instrumental in providing the resources for the inevitable team processing that comes from pilot projects designed to enhance the relationship and build new revenues.

Marketing works proactively with these strategic account representatives and key suppliers to maximize the insights on promotional, advertising, and other support mechanisms. They develop working sessions with strategic customers identified by the sales group and design the necessary multi-channel response systems. Customer service uses its front-line connections with customers to not only eliminate the root causes of problems but build a realistic interface with customers. The idea is to match the level of service with actual need through the appropriate response channel — from a special telephone number for direct conversation with a dedicated representative to Internet response and self-help features.

In Level 5, marketing and sales plans are developed collaboratively across the value chain with the emphasis for most networks shifting to the end consumer. Now the firms use all their collective knowledge and expertise to design fresh business models to secure new revenues for all partners. The purpose of the value chain is to know before any other network what these consumers want and will buy. The sales representatives become the mechanism for translating these needs into the appropriate cycle times, to advise what inventories should be in the system and where, and to provide even more e-commerce recommendations for streamlining the relationship. These representatives, moreover, will benefit from customer relationship management (CRM) systems, providing the kind of data that pertains to the here and now problems of their customers so they can be a real factor in designing new and successful sales efforts. In short, the salesperson will be someone intimately involved with the key customers, a crucial communication link, who adds value at numerous points in the supply chain, often using an extranet he or she helped create.

As success is achieved, the nucleus firm can extend what has become a very special system for the most important customers to a larger segment of its customer base and build even more revenues. U.S. Steel is an example. This firm has typically sold direct to its largest customers with a built-in supply chain and order management system. They went further and introduced an e-business venture named Straightline. This is a new middle-tier of e-business systems designed to aggregate demand from smaller buyers and deliver steel direct to the point of need. The virtual service center that has been created eliminates the need for traditional service centers and wholesale distributors. Over Straightline, USX will manage customer relationships, providing instant quotes and 24/7 services — via the telephone or Internet — from orders to fulfillment to post-sales support. The pilot for this advanced-level effort began in North Carolina, South Carolina, and Tennessee.

ENGINEERING, PLANNING, SCHEDULING, AND MANUFACTURING BECOME LINKED PROCESSES

Next we look at the engineering, planning, scheduling, and manufacturing portion of supply chain. In Levels 1 and 2, these functions are discrete, without any formal linkages and collaboration, a truly silo type of environment where the emphasis is on MRP, MRP II and distribution resource planning. This is an area where the poor planning function struggles with weak forecast accuracy, trying to satisfy customer needs and falling back on schedule interruptions and expediting to meet many of those needs. Multiple processes and functions can and often do originate change requests.

In Level 3, a sharing of manufacturing schedules begins so there is less confusion and expediting. Engineering specifications are shared and standardized, and external resources used to make them stronger. First-tier suppliers are made aware sooner of manufacturing plans for new products and often make valuable contributions to the design. Some suppliers are used to assemble tools. Here we see serious progress with the network partners making an effort to integrate their planning systems. This sharing does not come easily, particularly as most members of the network will be using different systems.

As the firms progress to ERP systems, integration of planning becomes a very serious effort. The nucleus firm must play the central role, working with the partners to integrate the disparate systems so crucial information sharing can begin. Now interactive planning and scheduling makes sense, as the partners work together to determine the actual demand and match it with the actual capability to manufacture.

Level 4 sees the introduction of collaborative network planning, with a team-focused approach to engineering, and production planning appears. The partners seriously evaluate which has the core competency and how best to utilize network assets. Suppliers have access to CAD/CAM and PDM tools and information. An example shows what an early pioneer accomplished. The U.S. unit of Taiwan Semiconductor lets customers such as Intel, Motorola, and Adaptec access its order-management system through their ERP systems to help them monitor the manufacture of integrated circuits at Taiwan semi-conductor manufacturing's (TSCM) factories. The company selected software from CrossRoute at its San Jose, California, operation, an application integration suite from CrossRoute Software, Inc., to connect TSCM's order management system directly to their key client's ERP systems. It took nine months to link its system to Adaptec's SAP R/3 system, but the result was faster data transmission and shorter production cycle times.

In Level 5, which very few organizations have mastered, the constituents work hard at full-network business-system optimization. Collaboration takes place across the entire value chain. Market insight and analysis are shared. All firms have full visibility of the entire supply chain with the ability to see how changes will impact performance. They view the value chain constellation as one operating system and they're looking to make the best use of shared processes and systems. A company knocking on the door to this position is Miller SQA, a Holland, Michigan, business that builds made-to-order furniture. Part of its business strategy is to compress information and manufacturing cycles as much as possible. As part of this strategy, Miller SQA linked its planning systems with key suppliers and business customers so they work as part of a fully integrated supply chain. What resulted was a supplier extranet. As soon as an order is accepted, the material requirements are immediately made visible to key suppliers.

The firm has created real-time integration between its sales configurator and its scheduling system. The firm also developed an application to attract customer orders that get published on the site. This integration, combined with improved supply chain planning, has enabled Miller SQA to reduce order fulfillment time from 21 days to fewer than 5 days. The most advanced networks are now hard at work on collaborative planning, forecasting, and replenishment (CPFR).

LOGISTICS MOVE INEXORABLY TOWARD VIRTUAL SYSTEMS

In the logistics function, the Level 1 and 2 firms work with a manufacturing push system. That means the function is primarily in house and oriented around maximizing internal efficiency, and is less focused on customer satisfaction, so the emphasis is on moving products to market in the most efficient manner. These firms tend to be very heavy in inventories as the drive is to push product toward consumption. Incentives are based on high utilization of manufacturing capacity, which rewards a full truck, even at the expense of delayed shipments to customers. Many firms maintain their own assets to make sure they have strong control over this function. When they do turn externally for shipment, carriers are worked to find the best shipping lanes and the lowest cost per mile.

In Level 3, the focus still may be on manufacturing capacity, but begins to shift toward a pull system and customer satisfaction. Existing linkages connect orders to shipments, but there is still a lot of expediting to meet actual demand. Then the same people start looking at having the right product at the right place just in time to meet need without all of the commotion. They begin looking at metrics that calculate on-time delivery and fill rates. Often, where the customer has strong leverage, the firm is required to meet time slots when their equipment can be unloaded — true collaboration hasn't blossomed. Logistics lag the supply chain process in that respect. Now third-party logistics providers (3PLs) enter the picture and discussions begin on why the firm is in the transportation business and not working on core competencies. At that point, many firms give up ownership of the logistics assets to one of these 3PLs as this entity accepts responsibility for equipment, drivers, and delivery.

In Level 4, the network view causes those in logistics to consider who is the best constituent for providing transportation for the pieces that go into the final product. The best constituent provider means a part of the transportation function could be outsourced to let a supplier deliver and pick up finished product. Now a global view of warehousing, transportation, and delivery comes into play, as the nucleus firm drives an effort to seek lowest-landed cost with the right products being at the point of need. With inbound and outbound freight on either side of each constituent, the question becomes how to make the best use of all available equipment and resources. Truck utilization on a nationwide basis, for example, is estimated to be no better than 60 to 70%, because of all the less-than-full outbound loads and empty backhauls. That becomes an opportunity to better utilize assets.

In Level 5, the idea of virtual logistics is part of the collaboration that takes place as the network members want to find the best costs and satisfaction, whether the orders go through traditional channels or are processed through an Internet channel. With residential package delivery, for example, expected to top 2.1 billion per year by 2003, this latter situation is of great interest to business to consumer (B2C) channel providers. Here lead logistics providers (llp) can enter the equation — firms with little to no physical assets, but the wherewithal to find the best answer to logistics needs, inbound and outbound.

Consider the description in Figure 2.2. A number of firms as diverse as Agilent Technologies, Fort James Paper, General Mills, and Nabisco got together and decided there had to be a better way to get raw materials into their manufacturing plants, finished goods into warehousing, and final shipments to retailers. Working with software created by Nistevo, the result was an alliance through which the members of the consortium can post a load between two points and, via the established extranet, check the

- Logistics consortium
    - Agilent Technologies
    - Coca-Cola Enterprises
    - Con Agra
    - Envera
    - Fort James Paper
    - General Mills
    - Graphics Packing
    - Hormel Foods
    - International Multifoods
    - Ivex Packaging
    - Kellogg
    - Land O'Lakes
    - McCormick
    - Monsanto
    - Nabisco
    - Niagra
    - Nestle USA
    - Pillsbury
- Optimized transportation routing is online, carriage by Dart and others, software by Nistevo, from manual routing to e-tool
- Alliance is working on 15 routes in North America
- Goal is transportation optimization – deadhead mileage under 5%
- Last company to use the truck picks up responsibility

Figure 2.2   A New Logistics Model

responses of hundreds of carriers. They can then select a carrier with equipment having the capability to carry the load and with open space to accommodate the load. Working through a pilot on 15 routes in North America, the members found they could reduce the deadhead mileage to less than 5%. Inbound and outbound usage of equipment reached better than 95%.

CUSTOMER SERVICE PROCEEDS FROM COMPLAINTS TO PRO-ACTIVE MATCHED CARE

Moving into the area of customer care, we find a function that is still being defined. In Levels 1 and 2, the firm concentrates on a vanilla version of customer service. Representatives are given the responsibility for responding to customers and helping them with their needs. Much of this work involves dealing with problems, changes, and expediting situations. It's basically a complaint-reaction system. Statistical information is kept on these complaints and Pareto charts are created to get to root causes. Rebates and incentives are often used to promote sales.

In Level 3, most firms move to a more focused customer service effort, with call centers to handle the wide variety of inputs received. Call centers are a mechanism to provide some level of consistent service to customers seeking information or redress. These centers are primarily cost centers inside the firm. Some efforts are made to generate new sales by having reps suggest extra values for adding to orders or entering new orders, and thus offsetting expenses. The familiar 1–800 locations have people handling phone calls and trying to satisfy customers, but now an effort is also made to shift customers to the most experienced personnel at the call center and away from the salesforce.

In Level 4, with the help of segmentation analysis and network partners, the care gets more specific as the intent is to build a segmented system that works with the customer relationship management system. Help is also available through the company's Web site and references to constituent partners. Caterpillar will route a customer's need for hydraulic parts to the actual supplier of those parts. Tremendous advances have also been made in automatic-response e-mail systems to answer questions. The crucial shift must be away from using the service to cut costs and more toward finding out what services customers need and giving them the responses they seek.

In Level 5, the care is matched with need and, in many cases, automated. Customer care becomes a serious effort and will transition into a profit center as it leads to new revenues. Activities work across the value chain, at times with a single contact responsible for the entire network. Customers have full access to a customized experience delivered via individuals or systems. Key customer records and transactions are available to all constituents.

Figure 2.3 shows an advanced system provided by Cisco. This firm has taken the time to study what their customers really want when they contact customer service. Since Cisco is a Level 5 company, most contacts are made via the Internet. Because many customers indicated they would be just as happy with a self-service feature as having a person assist them, the site was set up to let the customer move through a menu to find the help wanted. Many discover they can get to a solution without needing direct human contact. The troubleshooting engine even has a scoring system to allow you to determine if the solution meets your need.

HUMAN RESOURCES REMAIN A FUNCTION IN TRANSITION

The Human Resources function is another area going through a transition to keep pace with the changes brought on by the digital age. In Levels 1 and 2, the efforts tend to focus on regulatory, hiring, recruiting, and training issues. Screening applicants is done with internal views for staffing and resources. Little involvement occurs in business planning and strategy.

Level 3 of Human Resources involves new working models and using the intranet for creating better communications with employees. Access to training that many might overlook, for example, becomes a feature. Seeding academic programs and career enhancement with business requirements appears. One big U.S. issue was telecommuting as employee lifestyles changed. It is a time when larger firms move a serious amount of data onto the intranet for employee access.

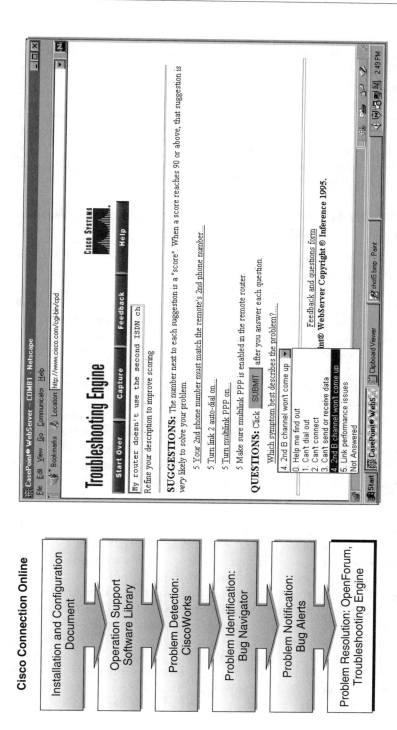

Figure 2.3 Cisco Customer Care

Level 4 of Human Resources is something of an untested area where a few firms are experimenting with inter-enterprise resource utilization. Work streams begin to extend across the enterprise and some supply chain training develops, using the help of external constituents. And Level 5 of Human Resources is really untested, as the external environment still needs greater clarification. The idea is to establish full network alignment and provide for the capabilities demanded of the various network members. All resource loading and acquisition will be done across the value chain. Cross-enterprise training should also be available. Much testing and validation will be needed before this area contributes in the way it can.

INFORMATION TECHNOLOGY MUST BECOME THE ENGINE DRIVING THE EFFORT

Levels 1 and 2 of Information Technology are characterized by point solutions, generally intended to improve some facet of performance for an internal function and, as we note, a silo mentality exists within the company. No consistent use of technology resources occurs as most work is devoted to getting the basic systems in place, particularly accounting. Companies often outsource a portion of the effort with little or no strategic benefit. Few corporate standards are in place as divisions and business units set their own directions. The architecture is usually product based. If there is a corporate architecture, it is from a centralized team and is often an academic exercise that is little used.

In Level 3 of IT, the intranet appears and flourishes, linking the various internal groups. A corporate architecture begins to appear, which connects to the corporate strategy. It is a voluntary system but used fairly often. Migration from silos is under way and intra-company communications are improved dramatically. Some published standards are in place to assist in communication with key suppliers.

E-commerce appears in Level 4 of IT and brings the Internet-based extranet into play as the firm begins to partner with other firms to build a network. The corporate architecture is in place and adherence is mandatory. Capabilities are shared to find the best systems solutions for what becomes an effort focused on satisfying customers. Initiatives are made in establishing inter-company technology standards. Focus groups are working on integrating systems with the most important customers so a template can be created for full inter-enterprise communications.

Level 5 of IT introduces a full network communication system with a shared architecture that integrates planning across the value chain. Extended enterprise architecture is in place. Strategy and implementation resources are extended across the value chain. Internet tools are the dominant technology infrastructure. Processes and standards extend across the network.

A CALIBRATION EXERCISE ESTABLISHES POSITION

With the information contained in Figure 2.1 and the preceding discussion, it is possible to calibrate a function or business organization in the five levels of supply chain evolution. Figure 2.4 is a useful tool for that purpose. This matrix should be completed with the help of some friendly advisors with or without a deep analysis. We find it is best simply to make a reasonable estimate of the firm's or business unit's position for each of the eight major functions listed. A check mark can be placed in the appropriate block for each function to signify the best estimate of current position.

Figure 2.5 provides a diagnostic scoring system to connect some numbers with the check marks. By placing an X in one cell per row on the calibration grid, a pattern quickly appears showing the organization's supply chain readiness. As noted, if there is doubt about a particular entry, favor the left-most column. The scoring is as indicated in the figure and brings a dimension to the final analysis. The rule-of-thumb scoring provides a means to determine a relative measure of supply chain readiness.

	Levels 1 & 2	Level 3	Level 4	Level 5
Business Application	**Internal Optimization/ Supply Chain Optimization**	**Advanced Supply Chain Planning**	**e-Commerce**	**e-Business**
1. Design/ Development of Products and/or Services				
2. Purchasing, Procurement and Sourcing				
3. Marketing, Sales and Customer Service				
4. Engineering, Planning, Scheduling and Manufacturing				
5. Logistics				
6. Customer Care				
7. Human Resources				
8. Information Technology				
Column Totals				
			Totals	

Figure 2.4   The Calibration Grid

• Based on the results of the internal, supplier and customer interview(s)/work session(s), calculate a "supply chain readiness" score	**"Rule-of-Thumb Scoring"**	
	7 – 16	**Internally Focused.** You are lagging in the market; look into advanced supply chain management tools
• The company's position is charted in each of the categories by placing an 'X' in one cell per row of the calibration grid	17 – 32	**Some External Focus.** You are with the majority of firms. You are likely well positioned to move quickly ahead. As an example, examine the possibility of providing vendor-managed inventory/ scheduling via a secure extranet.

- If in doubt, choose the left-most column
- Scoring: for each 'X'
  • In Column 1, 1 point
  • In Column 2, 3 points
  • In Column 3, 5 points
  • In Column 4, 7 points
	33 – 45	**Good External Focus.** You are well positioned as a potential market leader. Examine the possibility of taking the next step of forming a value chain with key customers and suppliers in order to focus on and fulfill the needs of a particular segment

	46 – 56	**Congratulations!** You are a market leader! Look into your one or two areas for improvement.

Figure 2.5   Diagnostic Scoring

A view of the position of the X marks indicates the level for the firm in any particular function.

Now the viewers take a step back and decide which functions need the most attention, how far the firm needs to progress overall, where major competitors might be if they had filled out the same diagnostic, and what the value is for closing any gaps or taking a leadership position. In general terms, we have found that the Level 3 firm has added about three points of new profit to the bottom line. Level 4 firms add another two points and the Level 5 firms another two points.

The calibration exercise can be done in greater detail, if desired. Experience has schooled, however, that it makes little difference how rigorous the effort. A firm and its members typically come to quick conclusions as to where the organization is positioned and what areas need attention. What becomes important is determining what further efforts are needed to transform the business processes to gain greater value. Figure 2.6 is useful in making that decision. There are processes that can be selected, which will have more impact than others depending on the previous calibration. In the figure, such processes as customer relationship management (CRM), collaborative design, procurement services, advanced supply chain management, and information technology are the areas most often selected for immediate attention. Others can be added if significant to a particular firm.

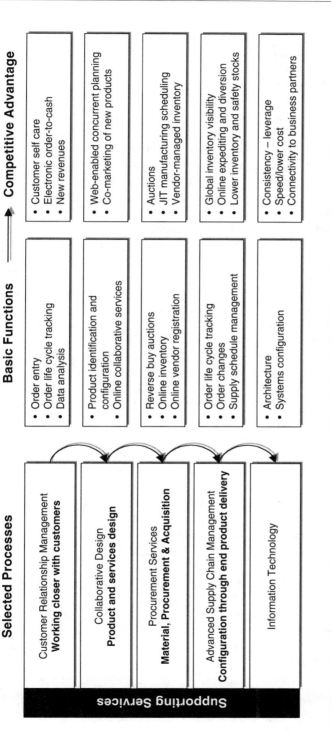

Figure 2.6 Transforming Business Process Is the Key

The figure goes further to list the basic functions impacted by a focus on these processes and the kinds of improvements that lead to a competitive advantage. CRM, which will be discussed in greater detail in Chapter 10, is concerned with, among other things, order entry, order lifecycle tracking, and data analysis. Additional functions important to the firm can be appended to this short list. The competitive advantages come from moving to a position of customer self care, an electronic order-to-cash system, and using the shared data to generate new revenues.

Collaborative design includes product identification and configuration, as well as establishing some form of online collaborative services to get suppliers and other enablers into the system, to help the firm shorten the new product introduction cycle and raise the possibility of success in the marketplace. Advantages come from the Web-enabled concurrent planning that results, as well as the co-marketing of new products with the highest success rate.

The list can be enlarged by adding other selected processes and by including other items under the basic functions. The purpose is to establish where the focus must be concentrated to take advantage of any advanced supply chain management effort. Figure 2.7 is a list of ten process issues developed by one company after such an analysis. The firm took the time to chart the key process steps in its supply chain, did the calibration exercise, and then listed the top issues that needed attention. Note the movement was from a high-level evaluation to the specific functions and issues needing attention to close the gaps the firm determined were inhibiting the company's processing.

This firm went further with its diagnostic efforts and listed the top ten systems issues, as illustrated in Figure 2.8. The firm took the time to determine where systems enabling was missing and where such capability would improve the current situation. The result was a clear road map for how this firm would move from its present Level 2+ position to one of an electronic nature, which would differentiate it in the marketplace. This company went on to become a supply chain channel master, or what we term a nucleus firm, driving the network changes it determined were required.

Similar stories point out that significant improvements can be the result of a focused advanced supply chain management effort. According to William Copacino, managing partner of Accenture's Global Supply Chain practice, "Companies that have successfully mastered their supply chains have realized documented gains measuring up to 35% in market share" (Copacino, 2001, p. 25).

The beneficial results don't just come from large firms, either. Small- and medium-size firms can reap improvements as well. Consider these examples of Level 4-type efforts. "Sport Obermeyer worked to tightly

Process

| Order Entry | Planning | Manufacturing | Ship Product | Invoice | Accounts Receivable |

Engineering · Returns 1,2 · Credits 1,2

It takes a long time for orders to be entered — Product development is cumbersome — Can't give order status once in the plant — Can't make on-time delivery — A/R is high

Gaps crossing all processes:
- Communication between departments, Corporate, and customers is difficult, at least (regardless of communication tools)
- No marketing/sales input to forecast
- Inter-company delivery service is poor
- High freight costs
- Customers are invoiced late and/or incorrectly
- Customer shipping requirements are not computerized or well documented

Engineering systems lack connectivity — Lack of understanding of business and application processes — 2-way match in purchasing -A/P is causing problems

European systems not Euro compliant — Some plants don't have cycle count programs — Forecast customer data not available to planners

Application support is not customer oriented — No engineering 'where-used' functionality — Call mgmt, service and tracking metrics are missing

NOTE: Shaded process is out of scope for this project

Top Ten Process Issues

- Little proactive tracking of shipments
- Poor communication of late or partial shipments to customers
  - Delays response to customer
- All carrier package tracking systems are separate
  - Require separate access
  - Difficult to get a status overview
- Sending most customers' ASNs is not automated
  - There are 4 ways of generating ASNs today
  - Time consuming
  - Trend is for more ASNs
- Bar coding is done manually and is only available to customers
  - Trend is for more bar coding
  - Manual process increases errors and makes it difficult to expedite orders
- Bill of lading and packing list are generated automatically through the system, but documentation required for proof of delivery exists only in hard copy
- Difficult and time consuming to access and forward to customers
- Limited technology enablers to meet emerging customization requirements of OEMs and distributors
  - Co-location
  - JIT
  - Kitting
  - Building sub-assemblies (including parts other than xxxs)
  - Postponement
  - Vendor-owned or vendor-managed inventory
- The current order fulfillment process does not facilitate the handling of national accounts
- Return process is costly and time consuming (e.g., shipments are often returned without referencing RMA numbers)
- Inconsistent quality information on material returned
  - Various formats for information
  - Various states of use of materials

Figure 2.7   An Example of Process Issues

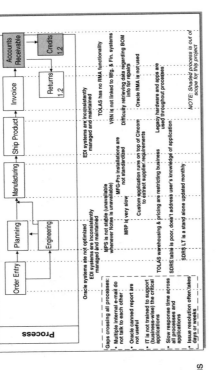

Top Ten Systems Issues

- No customer online access to shipping status of an order

- No online system for monitoring order shipping status to automatically identify problems

- Need a tracking system that integrates the separate systems to provide easy online access to status information

- No single integrated system to automatically, electronically send appropriate ASNs

- Bar coding is a stand-alone system, not integrated with the manufacturing or shipping systems

- No connection/integration of XXX systems with the shipper's systems
  - Cannot electronically access all proof of delivery documentation

- Systems not flexible to meet various customization requirements from OEMs and distributors

- Systems are not flexible to handle multi-tiered national accounts

- No automated systems to facilitate returns (i.e., automated screening to validate RMAs)

- Need an online system available to customers to support material returns, providing consistency and clean data

Figure 2.8 Key Application and Technology Gaps That Inhibit the Processing

integrate its overseas manufacturing bases with its customers and retailers. This effort resulted in a 60% increase in profits and a top ranking in customer satisfaction surveys. National Bicycle, a Japanese manufacturer, applied innovative supply chain strategies to create a new product and penetrate market segments that no one else in the industry was able to do. The result was a doubling of market share in a matter of years" (Lee, 2000, p. 31).

SUMMARY

Before applying models to better enable a firm to take advantage of supply chain management, it is advisable to take the time to make an assessment of the current position against what has been accomplished elsewhere. Using a simple technique, which matches various functional progress with what can be achieved across the five levels of the supply chain progression, can show a firm the gaps between where it currently is and where it wants to be in order to gain a market and financial advantage.

A simple calibration exercise has been provided with ideas on where leading practices have progressed. The firm is well advised to use a similar exercise, with detail pertinent to industry and market conditions, to establish its present position and where it should be to gain advantage. Then an effort can be made to attach customer satisfaction and financial metrics to the value of closing any gaps in a particular area or segment of the calibration matrix and moving to an advantageous position. This advantage can be the difference between dominating a market and industry and perpetually following the leaders.

3

MODELS FOR PURCHASING, PROCUREMENT, AND STRATEGIC SOURCING

As a factor in supply chain management, the combined entity of purchasing, procurement, and sourcing is one of the most important. Indeed, supply management is the first area of focus for virtually every firm embarking on a supply chain effort. It continues to have major importance throughout any advanced effort, moving from tactical initiatives to a position of strategic importance. The degree of emphasis may shift during the firm's supply chain evolution, but there is never a time when the buying function is not under pressure to reduce costs and find extra value-added features from supply management. The nature of the role for those professionals pursuing procurement as a career is to respond to that pressure.

In terms of the five supply chain levels being considered, the first two are a time during which those in procurement seeking improvement leverage volume for price concessions. The supply base is reduced and volumes are awarded to fewer suppliers for better prices. Attention is also given to better order management procedures and the means to reduce transportation costs.

Level 3 is a time to build network relationships with the most trusted and important suppliers willing to collaborate to find further mutual benefits. The top 5 to 10% of suppliers become strategic sources and offer values beyond those directly associated with pricing. At the same time, experiments are conducted, using techniques such as online auctions to determine the feasibility of making further gains through technology.

Level 4 is a time to work these key suppliers into the nucleus firm's extranet, again using technology to enhance the processing by providing online visibility across the full value chain. The advanced extranets also involve suppliers providing information that is beneficial in gaining a market advantage. Intel has such a supplier network, helping that firm develop new products worldwide on a full-time basis.

Level 5 is a time to build network connectivity with those select suppliers willing to work with the firm to build revenues in targeted end consumer markets. Few firms occupy this space, where the suppliers sit next to the nucleus firm's strategists, working on plans designed to pull new sales through the networked enterprise. Boeing and Toyota stand out as two industrial products firms moving consciously in this direction. The former has been successful in establishing an extranet by which suppliers play an important role in designing new airplanes without the usual complications surrounding handling paper blueprints, dealing with engineering delays, gaining approvals, and making changes.

In this chapter, we review all five levels of the evolution and describe models that enhance the buying effort. The theme being carried forward is that, in spite of the unrelenting executive pressure placed on the procurement function for ever-decreasing costs, there must be a shift in focus from such tactical initiatives to a realization that the most advanced firms use strategic sourcing as a key business tool. By elevating the importance of the buying function and establishing procurement positions reporting to the most senior office, such firms identify this importance. These procurement executives, moreover, make direct contributions to strategy formation and revenue generation for the firm.

To set the stage, it is important to understand that, for purposes of this discussion, the three concepts of purchasing, procurement, and sourcing will be combined into one entity, which can be improved through the use of the suggested models and techniques. In the broadest sense, procurement is the sum total of all activities involved with the acquisition of materials and services used by the firm. Purchasing is one part of that effort, which results in the placement and processing of orders. Sourcing is a further subset of activities, including identifying viable sources, making evaluations, implementing contracts, and monitoring supplier performance. The combined activities are what will be considered as we go forward and use the terms interchangeably while describing models to enhance the effort. This chapter has benefited greatly from contributions made by Chet Chetzron, Partner, and Steven Goble, Managing Partner, at CSC Consulting.

THE NUMBERS FORCE THE ATTENTION

To appreciate why procurement is of such importance to supply chain, one only has to look at the firm's P&L statement, and determine what percent of sales revenue comes from purchased goods and services. In Figure 3.1, PeopleSoft has supplied a listing of 18 major industries and calculated purchases as a percent of sales. We can see the range is from 18.5 to 64.6%. Based on this data, a company spends, on average, $.45 on external purchases for every dollar it earns in revenue. There should be little wonder then that, when asked what their five highest priorities for success might be, CEOs inevitably list reduced costs through better procurement as one of the top factors. Improvements in this area are the most immediate and tangible means of garnering cost savings and achieving higher profits. Benefits accrue directly and flow undiluted to the bottom line.

Experience has schooled, however, that the amount of savings is a function of time and the intensity of the focus given to the effort by senior management. Figure 3.2 describes the phenomenon being considered. When a single sourcing project is initiated, the typical results are a bell-shaped curve. There is a ramp up to improvements, with a tailing off as the project is completed and suppliers recoup the concessions made. The savings are real, but are not sustained — a typical Level 1 and 2 phenomenon. When the effort is reinforced, but without elements of strategic supply management, the curve can be extended, but again reaches the point of diminishing returns, usually in Level 3. Only when there is continuing executive support, collaboration with the key suppliers, and recognition of the strategic importance of the ongoing effort does it extend indefinitely into Levels 4 and 5.

Regardless of the amount of return or the time frame in which savings derive, the potential is significant and virtually every business organization that embarks on a supply chain effort begins in the procurement sector. They go in search of savings, which can be used to fund further efforts, and to make an immediate positive impact on profits. The reasoning is simplistic — there are too many dollars involved not to leverage for savings. But regardless of the amount of savings generated by a procurement effort, there remains an unrelenting senior management insistence that further savings be found.

THE SAVINGS ARE REAL

Studies that show just how much can be saved validate the effort. In terms of the supply chain evolution considered, many firms have done a very good job of improving the procurement function and have recorded

Industry	1999 *Fortune* 500 Sales ($ Billion)	Profit Average (% of Shares)	Purchase $ (% of Sales)
Metals	$114	0.3%	64.6%
Chemical	$257	5.4%	61.6%
Engineering/ Construction	$154	-0.5%	58.6%
Beverages	$86	9.8%	51.7%
Computers/Office Equipment	$282	3.6%	50.8%
Motor Vehicles & Parts	$1,110	4.0%	47.2%
Electronics, Electrical Equipment	$779	3.6%	45.6%
Railroad	$102	1.3%	42.4%
Aerospace	$184	4.2%	42.1%
Airlines	$120	4.2%	40.0%
Scientific, Photo, Control Equipment	$40	7.9%	40.0%
Forest & Paper Products	$86	3.5%	36.2%
Telecommunications	$521	9.6%	35.6%
Mining, Crude Oil Production	$54	-3.6%	34.3%
Pharmaceuticals	$204	17.3%	34.0%
Food	$218	3.6%	25.5%
Petroleum Refining	$748	3.6%	25.5%
Utilities, Gas & Electric	$338	3.6%	18.5%

On average, a company spends $.45 on external purchases for every dollar it earns in revenue!

Figure 3.1 Why Does Sourcing Matter? (From PeopleSoft, Supplier Relationship Management: Why Does It Matter? Pleasanton, CA, May 2001 With Permission)

tangible benefits. A Level 2 firm will have reduced the supply base by a significant amount, often more than 50%. Bills of materials will be standardized, SKUs rationalized, parts reduced, selective outsourcing arranged, and a holistic approach to evaluating costs and benefits will have led to closer relationships with a few strategic suppliers. Firms generally achieve a 5- to 8-percent reduction in buying costs, most of which will be found on the bottom line.

As the transition to Level 3 and higher is made, the difficulty of leveraging volume for price concession increases, and purchasing managers turn to auctions, aggregation, use of marketplaces, e-procurement, and other techniques to reach a higher plateau. Savings are derived from lower transaction costs, access to new sources (often global in nature),

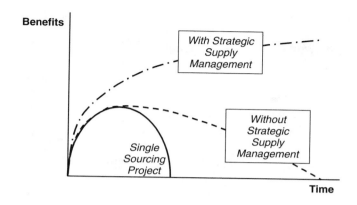

Figure 3.2   Sourcing Improvements Are a Function of Time and Focus

lower transportation and logistics costs, use of contract suppliers for sub-assemblies, and reduced inventory and carrying costs. Another point or two will be added to profits.

By the time they reach Level 4, most firms have faced the point of diminishing returns and are seeking the next level of performance enhancement with the help of their most important and trusted suppliers. It is a time for partnering with some key suppliers as the search is extended to finding other elements bringing further benefits, but not through the pricing route. Virtual logistics, or the use of pooled resources for transportation and storage, a further reduction in total inventories, reductions in selling and administrative costs, and better use of joint assets are techniques that work in this area. Another two to three percentage points of savings will be found.

The higher-level savings are often not as important as the extra value a closer networking relationship with these strategic sources can bring, particularly if they are instrumental in helping the buying firm better satisfy customers, find new markets, and build new revenues. In the search for the next big benefit area, technology, and especially the ability to communicate seamlessly between enterprises, provides new options. In the business-to-business (B2B) channel especially, the opportunity to work with strategic suppliers has worked well for a few leaders, resulting in online visibility of all inventory and orders, better correlation between demand signals and supplier capability, and collaborative efforts on design, development, and event management. Moen, the Ohio-based manufacturer of plumbing fixtures, stands out as an organization that parlayed two definitive supplier network efforts into a system that dramatically reduced the cycle time for new product introduction with better market acceptance.

One result has been a movement to a virtual tie for first place in market share in a very competitive industry.

Logistics savings loom prominently on this advanced horizon, as attempts to use suppliers to consider total assets and rationalize the use of space (warehouses and distribution centers) and equipment (tractors and trailers) is another plateau to conquer. Use of third-party or best-able supply chain partners to negotiate purchasing contracts in specific categories across multiple enterprises is just one example of what occurs in this rarefied area and the final benefits are achieved. General Mills has been particularly active in this area, working with other firms to aggregate shipment needs and build a network view of transportation options so buyers and sellers can access the most favorable alternatives. Shipment costs between pick-up and drop-off locations are minimized as the number of third-party alternatives considered increases dramatically through an online system. Utilization of available assets is the key to creating a win-win situation for the carriers, as well as the firms using the Web site solution.

A MATRIX MODEL HELPS ESTABLISH THE SOURCING STRATEGY

With so much occurring and so many different options from which to choose as the evolution proceeds, a special need arises for those in procurement. Effective procurement and supply management demands a range of strategies that are appropriate for current market conditions and matched with the realities of the business environment in which the firm operates. In the early levels of the supply chain progression, this requirement is easily met; as the supply chain effort matures, it becomes more critical and more difficult. One helpful technique is to apply a matrix model to establish what strategy is most applicable, depending on the circumstances affecting the firm and its procurement needs.

In a noteworthy *Harvard Business Review* article, Kraljic introduced a simple matrix intended to help purchasing managers decide on strategy by applying a portfolio type of analysis (Kraljic, 1983, p. 112). Figure 3.3 illustrates Kraljic's 2 × 2 matrix based on portfolio management concepts. The vertical axis is arranged to differentiate purchases by profit impact to the firm from low to high; the horizontal axis is arranged by supply risk to the firm, also from low to high. Kraljic theorized that, if the firm could classify categories of purchased materials in terms of profit impact and supply risk, the buyers could then analyze the supply market for these materials and determine the overall strategic supply position to implement. With a defined strategy, they could then develop actions for each sector of the matrix.

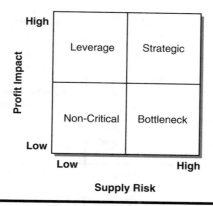

Figure 3.3 The Kraljic Matrix (From Kraljic, P., *Harvard Business Review*, 61, 1983 With Permission)

In a manner similar to that used for evaluating investment opportunities as part of the firm's portfolio of assets, those in procurement evaluate opportunities by segment and determine the appropriate action. Where the impact of a category is low from both considerations, the sector is labeled *noncritical* and calls for such tactics as efficient processing, product standardization, and inventory control. Where the risk is high and the profit impact low, the sector is called *bottleneck* and supply control is in order, along with volume assurance by the suppliers and contingency plans for emergencies. If the profit impact is high but the supply risk low, the area is dubbed *leverage* and the buyer would seek to exploit purchasing power. It is in the sector where the combined factors are the highest that special *strategic* approaches are taken to the buying-selling relationship, as the success of the firm could be tied directly with supplier performance.

The Kraljic matrix found wide use in Europe and eventually was imported to the U.S. with many variations appearing. C.J. Gelderman, for example, enhanced the model by introducing a variation that gave consideration to insights from a mutual buyer-supplier dependence theory (Gelderman, 2000). The elements of power and dependence are two very important concepts for further understanding relationships and deciding strategy in his advanced version of Kraljic's matrix.

Figure 3.4 is another expanded model drawn from the sources cited and personal applications that have proven helpful as firms progressed through their supply chain evolution. It requires very serious consideration by representatives beyond those from procurement before it is completed, and becomes an important tool in deciding on higher-level relationships and supply arrangements. When representatives from operations, sales, finance, materials management, and information technology are involved,

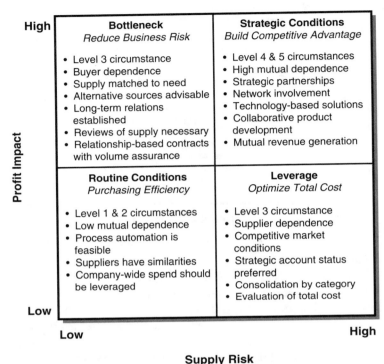

Figure 3.4 An Expanded Sourcing Strategy Matrix

the matrix eventually reflects the collective thinking of an organization regarding sourcing strategy as a function of the supply market risk and the impact on performance from the purchases. Its use and application increase in value as a firm moves from lower to higher levels of supply chain management.

Beginning in the quadrant where the business impact and the supply risk are low, *routine conditions* are found, and the emphasis should be on purchasing efficiency. This is a sector where much of the early Level 1 and 2 emphasis will be placed and the strategies are basic to finding the best suppliers and the least difficult means of securing supply. As firms attempt to generate savings by leveraging buying power in this area of low importance, a general problem is encountered.

Most large firms have great difficulty pooling the total purchases across all business units and functions that wish to retain autonomous control over any buying that occurs. Silos of separation continue to be an obstacle to optimized results until a cultural barrier is crossed and movement into Level 3 is achieved. By focusing first on those purchases that do not affect market advantage (i.e., indirect materials and services, office supplies, travel, telecommunications, and so forth), a sourcing group can generally rally agreement to centralize some of the buying and find savings. Nevertheless, most often, this segment moves forward on a business unit strategy basis.

As the effort progresses, a deeper look at more direct categories can be added to this sector, but organizational indifference will still be a limiting factor. Purchasing efficiency demands that such a pitfall is eventually overcome before proceeding to the next level. Consider the case of the *29 brands of vanilla*. Nestlé USA, a major division of the world's largest food company, encountered this problem as it progressed through its supply chain evolution. In 1997, a team examining conditions within the firm found that the business unit was paying 29 different prices for vanilla, all to the same supplier.

According to Jeri Dunn, Vice President and Chief Information Officer (CIO), "Every plant would buy vanilla from the vendor and the vendor would just get whatever it thought it could get." This is not an unusual situation for those embarking on supply chain. Business units are autonomous and the supplier is not being proactive in suggesting a uniform pricing scheme. Because no one takes the time to seek a better solution, the problem proliferates. "Every division and every factory got to name vanilla whatever they wanted," Dunn reported. "So you could call it 1234, and it might have a whole specification behind it, and I might call it 7778. We had no way of comparing" (Worthen, 2002, p. 64). The problem was eventually solved and savings realized, but not until such commodities were forced through a rigorous standardization process and the category given to a central buyer for purchasing.

Consistent strategies are basic in this area of the matrix. There is low mutual dependence between buyer and seller, and most suppliers have similar capabilities, so long-term relationships are not an absolute requirement. Once agreement is reached on the strategy, process automation is feasible through the application of buying software provided by a number of firms, including Ariba, Commerce One, Harbinger, Oracle, and Right Works. As success is achieved and savings documented, the company-wide spending usually finds its way into this sector and the total buy can be leveraged.

The sector involving high supply risk and low impact on performance is again labeled *bottleneck* to reflect the need to make certain a lack of supply does not disrupt efficient production and delivery. This is a typical Level 3 circumstance where there is high buyer dependence on the suppliers, but the procurement function has worked the supply base down to those companies where a degree of reliability exists. Alternative sources are advisable because even the best of sources can encounter trouble. A major-minor (75/25 split) type of arrangement is not uncommon, with long-term commitments being made through a relationship-based contract. Reviews of supply performance are necessary to make certain smooth flows are present and agreements kept.

This area also offers an opportunity for more synergies to be applied across the firm. Working with key suppliers and software specialists can bring focus to eliminating potential bottlenecks, and the procurement group can play a key role in selecting another partner to help operations. Manugistics and i2 Technologies, for example, provide very comprehensive application suites, which can trace supply back to tier-one or tier-two suppliers and alert an organization to impending shortages, while providing the means to match needed supplies with manufacturing schedules. Selection of such software proceeds best when multiple functions are brought into the evaluation and the strategy includes finding systems that provide better manufacturing efficiency and greater customer satisfaction.

GREATER IMPACT ON PERFORMANCE CREATES GREATER NEED FOR COLLABORATION

When the impact on business performance is high and the supply market risk is low, there is a definite opportunity to *leverage* the buy position. In this typical Level 3 area, the supplier dependence is high, particularly where large volumes are involved under competitive market conditions. The buyer will typically have a specific list of preferred sources in this area and will be receiving strategic account attention. The strategy is to consolidate the firm's total buy by category and aggregate the buy with selected external partners, such as other suppliers needing the same materials or noncompeting firms using the materials for other purposes. It is essential to determine the total cost of usage in this area, especially where inventories are kept at the supplier's point of distribution until needed or payment is made only upon use. This need requires greater attention by the supplier's account representative. Where volumes are large enough, such a representative may have office space within the buyer's headquarters.

Pfizer Inc. provides a specific example of accomplishment in this sector. Following that firm's merger with Warner-Lambert Company to create a $32 billion global pharmaceutical company, a special procurement strategy effort was instituted as part of the goal to integrate the two firms and take advantage of the scale of operations. According to Lisa Martin, Vice President of Global Sourcing for Pfizer, the objective had two key areas of focus: to "develop a strategic sourcing plan with a holistic approach to procurement and to incorporate new procurement process and technology solutions in cases where they add clear value" (Martin, 2002, p. 20). The firm was clearly looking for ways to leverage its new position, while building on past accomplishments and taking advantage of collaboration and technology as enabling tools.

Three initiatives were incorporated into this effort. To help unite the various internal constituencies, an e-procurement system was implemented providing internal buyers with an Internet-based means of procuring indirect goods and services. The potential to use e-marketplaces, buying portals, and exchanges was considered as a means of finding potentially viable new sources while leveraging a larger buy. And a test of reverse auctions helped evaluate the use of that technique as one application for specific commodity categories.

Since Pfizer worked in a decentralized culture and believed strongly in maintaining good supplier relations, two constituents played important roles in the evaluation that went forward. Representatives from a number of the divisions were invited to participate in a cross-organizational collaborative analysis of alternatives. The firm also invited several key suppliers to participate and help determine how the new systems could deliver improved return on investment for both parties. Pfizer expected it could automate time-consuming and costly manual processing, increase purchasing efficiency, eliminate off-contract purchases, and achieve global economies of scale. These benefits would accrue to any division taking advantage of the enhanced processing. The firm also believed suppliers "would benefit from reduced costs per transaction and increased revenue per customer, as well as from gaining new customers" (Martin, 2002, p. 21).

After considerable evaluation, in November 2000, the firm elected to implement the Ariba Buyer e-Procurement System in conjunction with its existing American Express Purchasing Card program to automate its indirect buy. On the back end, they integrated the Ariba system with the Pfizer financial system to optimize payment processing and eliminate steps that added no value. The firm did evaluate electronic marketplace options only to conclude that their scale was so large that such an alternative offered little added value.

Reverse auctions bore more fruit. In January 2001, Pfizer created a reverse auction project team to review and evaluate the process as an online tool. Working through the cross-divisional team to identify the *appropriate categories* to test, Pfizer planned and conducted seven pilot auctions by June 2001, allowing the company to evaluate at least one auction within each procurement organization (manufacturing and research, for example). The auctions proved to be a good fit with the existing sourcing process and the company achieved an average savings of 11% across the seven pilots. Of note, Pfizer discovered some extra benefits making reverse auctions an attractive approach for the correct categories. It shortened the price review cycle and provided an opportunity for new suppliers to participate while establishing a look at the true market pricing for commodities. The challenge was to convince their suppliers of the value, which they did by discussing the increased efficiency and the advantage of gaining familiarity with a process they expected more buyers to be using in the future.

The final sector of the matrix is the most important and requires the greatest degree of skill to make the best arrangements. Here we find a high degree of market supply risk and a high impact on business performance. This sector is typically where Level 4 and 5 firms are found working together to build long-term relationships benefiting buyer and seller. The mutual dependence is high and strategic partnering is a viable option for both parties.

Network involvement becomes a reality in this area as mutual resources are applied to find solutions to long-standing problems affecting both firms. These solutions are often technology based, as the participants are working together over a communication extranet that flows vital information from end to end in what has become a value chain of connectivity. Firms can be found working on collaborative design and development and building plans to create new revenues benefiting both companies. Planning is linked and active as the firms discover the means to link their ERP systems together.

In this area, it is extremely important that other members of the firm are involved. As network arrangements develop, it is not only cost improvement that is analyzed, but also asset utilization and how the partners can work together to build new revenues. That requires sharing information that has previously been kept under close control, and the involvement of multiple parts of both organizations. The best technique is to pilot such arrangements with one or two of the closest and most-valued suppliers, working from a jointly created plan that clearly defines the end objectives, what data can and will be shared, and how mutual resources can be applied to specific actions designed to help both organizations.

The modified Kraljic matrix is a model that can help any firm determine how to evaluate, refine, and enhance its buying strategies and build the kind of longer-term relationships necessary to optimize supply chain management conditions. It can be modified to meet the actual needs and circumstances of any firm or market environment. When developed, it must include the participation of other functions and certainly should be worked out across business units to create the kind of consistent features that characterize leading procurement efforts. Soliciting the advice of a few friendly and trusted suppliers only improves the effectiveness of whatever matrix is implemented.

TACTICS MUST BE MATCHED WITH STRATEGY

With the matrix as a guide to strategy, tactics must be applied to implement the purposes of the matrix. Figure 3.5 provides a model that matches the five levels of the supply chain progression with the type of tactics that are typical as a sourcing strategy matures. The tactics placed in each sector of the progression are what typically takes place, but a firm is advised to construct its own list of tactics pertinent to local conditions.

In Level 1, the focus is placed on reducing *prices* to generate quick improvements to the cost of purchases. The spending remains fragmented by business unit and function, but can be leveraged in a decentralized manner to achieve better pricing, particularly as the supply base is reduced. Lack of knowledge regarding total spending and no separation by specific categories will inhibit progress, as there is minimal authority exercised by any central procurement organization.

Despite the lack of total leverage, the number of suppliers is consolidated and whatever volume is available redistributed among the smaller number of sources. Transportation costs are reduced as buyers work with fewer suppliers to cut shipment costs, and some effort is made to standardize specifications to further enlarge the potential purchases by category. Order entry and management are discussed and some effort made

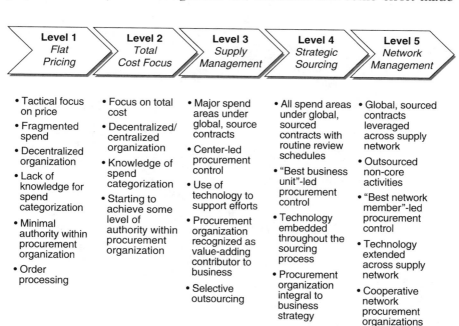

Level 1 *Flat Pricing*	Level 2 *Total Cost Focus*	Level 3 *Supply Management*	Level 4 *Strategic Sourcing*	Level 5 *Network Management*
• Tactical focus on price • Fragmented spend • Decentralized organization • Lack of knowledge for spend categorization • Minimal authority within procurement organization • Order processing	• Focus on total cost • Decentralized/centralized organization • Knowledge of spend categorization • Starting to achieve some level of authority within procurement organization	• Major spend areas under global, source contracts • Center-led procurement control • Use of technology to support efforts • Procurement organization recognized as value-adding contributor to business • Selective outsourcing	• All spend areas under global, sourced contracts with routine review schedules • "Best business unit"-led procurement control • Technology embedded throughout the sourcing process • Procurement organization integral to business strategy	• Global, sourced contracts leveraged across supply network • Outsourced non-core activities • "Best network member"-led procurement control • Technology extended across supply network • Cooperative network procurement organizations

Figure 3.5   Levels of Sourcing Progression

to automate order processing. The payback in this latter area comes from error elimination and the need for less reconciliation.

Most of the early savings are generated in Level 2, as the focus moves to *total cost* with the reduced supply base. Now some form of centralized buying or shared services organization appears, and there is knowledge of total organizational spending, usually gathered through cooperation with the business units and the CIO function. This total buy is then separated by prioritized categories. Following evaluation of business needs across the firm, those most capable of developing the best suppliers and contracts are given control of specific categories and a measure of procurement authority is established, typically through the direction and support of the CEO. Features of order automation are found and the most important sources are identified as strategic suppliers so they can work more closely with the firm to find savings beyond direct price concessions.

Evaluation of the total cost of supply advances in this part of the progression. Joint efforts result in finding the best solutions for operational needs. Other members of the organization join the discussions as the search includes cross-divisional benefits. Key suppliers are enjoined in the processing to determine how the total cost can be reduced, rather than concentrating on specific commodity pricing. Make-versus-buy decision making is enhanced through sharing cost information. Logistics are approached as a joint interest and warehousing space better utilized. Third-party transportation providers are used to reduce inbound and outbound freight costs. Substitute materials will be considered, as well as the possible outsourcing of some noncore capabilities.

SUPPLY MANAGEMENT EMERGES AS A STRATEGIC TOOL

In Level 3, interest moves to *supply management* and work begins in earnest with the most trusted and strategic suppliers to find the hidden values that have so far eluded the relationship. Major spending categories are under some form of contract, often of a global nature for large, nucleus firms. A central authority is established for the most critical items of supply, as the effort moves from indirect categories to direct materials and assemblies. Technology, through a growing use of an extranet between buyers and sellers, becomes an important element in the relationships and selective outsourcing is arranged with more capable suppliers. Most importantly, the procurement function and organization are now recognized as a value-adding contributor to the business and increase in importance within the firm.

Product value analyses becomes a feature of the evolving relationships with the most important suppliers. Joint design efforts begin as the partners look at optimizing the total lifecycle costs. Key suppliers participate in product development through linking computer-aided design and manufacturing capabilities. Sourcing is conducted on a global basis, with suppliers encouraged to be proactive in suggesting process improvements.

Strategic Sourcing becomes the focus for a Level 4 organization, as all categories of the total spending, beyond the most trivial items, are under the direction of a procurement professional, backed by long-term contracts that are honored across the firm. With less time spent on mundane actions, such as searching for suppliers and reviewing catalogs, these professionals concentrate on eliminating bottlenecks, moving to advanced just-in-time supply arrangements, working through systems integration, and minimizing inventories necessary to fully meet market conditions and customer satisfaction. They work at finding technology solutions that further improve efficiency. Maverick buying is eliminated in this area of development, as there is an acceptance that the category manager is the best person to lead procurement control.

Key suppliers work actively to collaborate and help the firm develop benefits that make sense to both buyers and sellers. Technology features and applications, in particular, are embedded throughout the sourcing process, as agreement is reached on the systems and software that will enhance the processing. Visibility of historical and future spending data is easily accessed, total cost of ownership is understood and used in evaluations, and market response data and supplier performance are used to sustain relationships. The procurement organization is now firmly established as integral to the firm's business strategy.

The most critical part of this phase of the progression is working with suppliers to integrate features of the communication system so a network advantage is achieved. The number of sourcing organizations playing such a key role in this area is small but growing and proving the validity of the concept. A particularly difficult phase of this interaction is the integration of the buyer's and the seller's enterprise resource planning systems. A crucial element in network performance, this challenge becomes the Achilles' heel of Level 4 activities.

Interactive planning must be a network feature so there is a seamless system of supply and online visibility of what is taking place from end to end in the supply chain. That means design and planning are done collaboratively and interactively over an extranet of connectivity. From the standpoint of procurement, this means the sourcing strategy determines what will be purchased, from whom, and how the processing will be accomplished. Negotiations are completed and placed under long-term contract. The means of providing product and service, the communication flows, and the financial flows are all specific to the arrangements. Periodic reviews are mutually understood as a part of the relationship. Metrics are established to track and report total costs and supplier performance.

Level 5 is the next frontier, where network management is a reality and the new strategic procurement function is a central device in establishing global sourcing contracts that leverage the buying power and the capabilities of the suppliers across what has become the networked enterprise. All noncore activities are in the hands of the most capable constituent in the network, as best business unit category buyer has given way to best network member control. Technology is extended across this supply network. With so many different systems and applications in use, and so many players involved in a typical supply chain network, this need for connectivity is probably the ultimate challenge to supply management.

Figure 3.6 is a pictorial representation of full connectivity across a company, its suppliers, and its customers. The use of exchanges has been added as an enhancing feature. Having such network capability could be a differentiating factor in the market, where the key suppliers are now helping to build new revenues through total systems capabilities. Each nucleus firm must build its own network systems architecture and fill in the blanks with the help of willing and trusted suppliers. Cooperative network procurement will be a central feature of this most advanced level of supply chain progress.

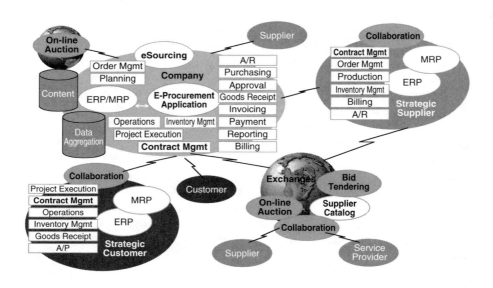

Strategic Supply Management must be supported by technologies that provide flexibility, high visibility into spend, process, performance and TCO information.

Figure 3.6 Technology Advances (From Commerce One, Pleasanton, CA)

OPTIMIZED CONDITIONS ENHANCE PROFIT PERFORMANCE

Advanced supply chain efforts only progress when there is documentation of the enhancements. Once again, the procurement function must play a vital role in that evaluation. With the help of the strategic suppliers and the firm's IT department, a system should be established to monitor the savings and report improvements to network executives. Figure 3.7 is just one model that has proven helpful for such tracking. As most firms recognize returns that enhance earnings or shareholder value, that objective is placed in the starting position.

Improvements that positively affect earnings and shareholder value come from three supply chain sources: cost and productivity improvement, better asset utilization, and profitable revenue growth. All of these activities must be accomplished, of course, while creating greater customer satisfaction. A system should be established to catalog and monitor the actual enhancements achieved in all three categories. The figure lists some typical factors that lead to tangible results. The firm is advised to work with key suppliers and business unit leaders to establish the parameters for listing specific factors and measuring the results.

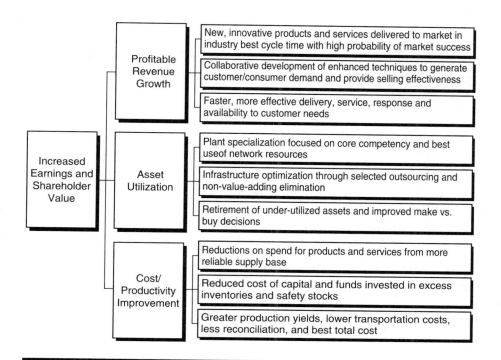

Figure 3.7   The Payoff for Optimized Procurement

SUMMARY

The functions of purchasing, sourcing, and procurement are essential to the success of a supply chain management effort. With an unrelenting emphasis being placed on an area that occupies so much space in the profit and loss statement, it is inevitable that the function evolves and provides greater benefits as the firm progresses with its supply chain initiatives. Using a matrix model to help define the appropriate strategies based on supply conditions and importance to the company is one way to enhance the effort.

Involving key members of the internal business units and other functional areas increases the importance and viability of such a matrix, which must also be matched with the tactics that are taken to achieve the intended benefits. Key suppliers must be in the center of whatever becomes the guiding instrument so valuable insights are not overlooked. Above all, collaboration with key constituents across the supply chain and the application of technology will become the factors that differentiate one network from another in the marketplace.

4

LOGISTICS MODELS, FROM MANUFACTURING TO ACCEPTED DELIVERY

After procurement and sourcing, the area receiving the most attention in supply chain management is logistics. Once again, the reasoning is directly related to the costs involved. For a typical firm, total logistics costs can be as much as 10 to 15%, or higher, of total revenues. This percent varies considerably by industry and the nature of the products being shipped, but remains a target for serious improvement efforts.

At one end of the logistics spectrum, bulk commodities, such as potash, salt, coal, and feed chemicals are low cost, stored in bulk, and moved in large quantities, with logistics making up as much as 20% of the overall cost. At the other end, high-technology products are expensive and the logistics cost, as a part of revenue, may only be 4 to 5%. The U.S. national average showing logistics costs, as a percent of gross domestic product (GDP), at 10% is not pertinent — only the average for a particular standard industry classification (SIC) code. In any event, the cost generally comes in right after purchased goods and services on the chart of expenses.

Transportation is the largest component of this cost segment, generally accounting for more than half, and receives the most attention. Included in that category are the costs of asset ownership, equipment maintenance, driver wages and benefits, fuel (a particularly troublesome issue in times of rising oil costs), and miscellaneous items such as tolls and insurance. Warehousing and storage follow that category, including the associated costs for space, taxes, obsolescence, depreciation, interest, and insurance on the inventories held in the system. Reducing these costs, just as in purchasing, is a never-ending business quest.

Most firms are successful in reducing these costs when they move through the early levels of supply chain. As efforts mature, however, a new level of sophistication enters the logistics discipline and companies move to more complex arrangements — network alliances and multiple business constituencies. These arrangements focus on all of the logistics costs that occur before manufacturing, including inbound freight and storage, unloading, and handling. They extend through the manufacturing processes, as logistics are involved in the movement of work in process and internal inventories, and then proceed to the final deliveries to customers and consumers. Should any materials or goods need to be returned, the function continues through reverse logistics and any return shipments until the cycle is completed. Hence, the area under consideration is from supply and manufacturing to delivery acceptance.

MODELS CHANGE WITH THE PROGRESSION

The logistics models being applied by businesses are also becoming more sophisticated. Early efforts were directed solely toward reducing internal costs, considering the many options to be used across multiple serving and receiving locations for a particular business or division of a large firm, and the use of equipment and facilities to make the necessary deliveries. Companies analyzed their distribution efforts by looking at specific internal facilities, perhaps at a divisional region, to determine where to locate a distribution center (DC), and how best to serve that division's customers. Interaction between facilities or across divisions and business units was difficult for these early studies due to limited cross-organizational cooperation, limiting the depth of the analysis and often restricting the improved service territories to county or state borders.

The prevalent thinking, moreover, was that all customer service needs were the same and a sort of one-size-fits-all mentality prevailed. With only a general idea of total transportation costs, those in logistics concentrated on filling the trucks, getting benefits from consolidating loads, and using transportation management systems (TMS) to improve outbound loading and create better backhauls. It took some time to move from a business silo view, and the idea that all customers were the same, to introducing intra- and inter-enterprise flexibility and adaptability into logistics thinking and the idea that service can and should be matched with the actual customer need.

Linear programming mathematical models were often introduced to find early, optimized solutions, typically considering only the shipment of finished goods to specific customer locations. Operations research techniques were alive and well during this phase as many algorithms were applied and heuristic programming used to sort out the best solutions, particularly as the complexity of systems became large and cumbersome. Some of these techniques are still applied, as firms build models to determine their costs versus those of major competitors, using industry data and customer site information to develop close approximations of the differences. With progress, the newer models employ the ability to incorporate additional factors, including nonlinear functions, allowing the models to consider elements from the extended supply chain, particularly those factors relating to end-customer satisfaction — on time deliveries, high fill rates, low returns, and so forth.

While the original models were primarily strategic in nature, more contemporary models are also used for ongoing dynamic tactical planning and execution. Simulations are applied to consider alternative approaches before adopting new strategies and systems. With business complexity now including multi-tiered suppliers, subcontractors and original equipment manufacturers, this advantage brings a new, higher dimension to the opportunities while lowering the risks inherent with new logistics systems. It also necessitates thinking well beyond the confines of internal logistics and considering external partners and network options in a quest to get closer to end-to-end optimized conditions. Entire extended enterprise networks are now analyzed to consider all aspects of transportation, warehousing, and delivery. These analyses are digitally based (on network extranets) and include the impact of inventory and the associated carrying costs. The effect of seasonality is factored into the newer models to create inventory-stocking rules. From a contemporary view, logistics has become a vital tool in extended enterprise efforts, from both a cost and satisfaction viewpoint.

This chapter considers this greater reach and sophistication as we explore the maturing of logistics as the second largest element of advanced supply chain management. We probe how firms are now reducing logistics cost as low as 4 to 5% of revenues while achieving higher customer satisfaction ratings. The leaders do this by taking advantage of network skills and the application of systems and software to create an adaptive logistics system, or what we call a *virtual logistics network*. A framework is used to follow the advancing sophistication through the five levels of supply chain evolution and to help position the models for use at the appropriate level. George Borza, Principal and Steve Goble, Peter Ilgenfritz, Steve Simco, and George Swartz, Partners at CSC, as well as David Durtsche, Tranzact, and Kevin Lynch, Nistevo, prepared materials for this chapter.

A FRAMEWORK DESCRIBES LOGISTICS ADVANCEMENT

As a firm progresses through its logistics effort, it generally follows the same kind of transformation described earlier and outlined in the five levels of supply chain evolution. Figure 4.1 presents a framework based on such a progression, from a company's initial position to the most appropriate advanced logistics level. This framework is followed throughout the chapter.

In Level 1, the firm typically focuses on its second largest element of cost and begins to work on reducing the overall costs of logistics from an internal viewpoint. This position is labeled *calibrate the beginning* to capture the need to know where the firm is starting and how far it might proceed. A company looks at its shipping and receiving costs, the techniques used for loading and unloading at various sites, how orders are managed, and how the firm could find better ways to control the amount of inventory used to support operations and customer satisfaction. This calibration is an essential first step in gaining an appreciation for the costs involved, how much might be saved, and how efficiency and satisfaction can be enhanced.

Ad hoc processing is popular at this level as nonintegrated models are used by separate divisions and business units, rather than pooling the total logistics costs across the firm. The use of these models is also sporadic, as the early gains are usually large enough to sustain the effort without detailed analysis. Typically, a firm initiates a call for information by separate business units or divisions and establishes a method to segment the costs by category — inventory storage, transportation, order selection, picking, packing, etc. Then teams are assigned to work through the categories, often from most to least costly, seeking new methods and systems to reduce these costs.

The early goals of the processing involve cost reduction in a functionally siloed orientation. The task is to identify and eliminate any existing supply chain *stress points*, process steps where problems occur with pickups, picking and packing the right goods for orders, having the right materials ready for transfer, meeting delivery schedules, eliminating duplicate handling, reducing driving time, and so forth. By streamlining or automating many of these steps, the firm enhances profits through reduced operating inefficiencies. Customer service levels may also improve, as the system becomes more effective in meeting plans and schedules.

Areas of consideration that typically come under early scrutiny include:

- Total logistics costs associated with the existing systems, including the inbound and outbound transportation costs, direct and indirect warehouse and distribution center operating costs, capital

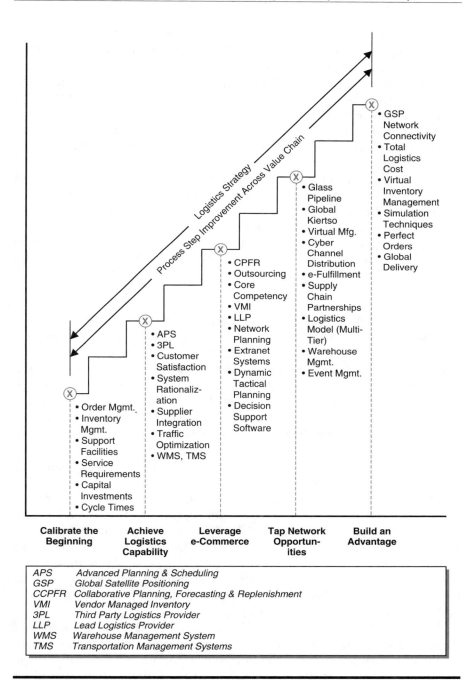

Figure 4.1   A Logistics Framework

investment, and relocation and severance costs. What is it costing to operate and maintain our logistics infrastructure and what would it cost to vacate a portion of it?

■ Number and location of facilities necessary to support current and projected business volumes. Do we have enough? Too much? Too little space to accommodate our needs?

■ Location, mission, and service area for each facility. Do we really need each site? Are the sites strategically located for our needs? Do we match with the locations of our key customers?

■ Inventory stocking policies and requirements for each facility. What do we have at these sites and why is it there? Will we hamper service levels by carrying less stock? What items can be reduced?

■ Impact on delivery cycle times (inbound and outbound) with the existing system. What are our lead times and cycles from order to accepted delivery? Is there an opportunity to increase sales by providing shorter cycles?

These and other aspects are considered as the Level 1 firm seriously evaluates logistics and starts to make improvements. From experience, virtually all companies make progress in reducing total logistics costs by constructing a map showing the delivery locations for key suppliers, the operating sites where deliveries are needed, and the location of key customers. Further analysis of this map leads to finding the best routing and working down the costs of fuel consumption, driver time, and waiting time. Finding backhauls to fill any empty vehicles is also an early consideration.

Unfortunately, most firms miss a critical element of this preliminary analysis. Great attention is paid to outbound freight — the cost of delivering the finished goods to customers — an element affecting customer satisfaction. The issue of inbound freight management, affected by suppliers, purchasing agreements, and handling at internal operations, takes a back seat and a major opportunity is overlooked. The problem occurs as the firm fails to isolate its inbound freight expense in the initial data collection effort, preferring to simply allow that expense to be added to the cost of the acquired materials and products. In this sense, a firm abdicates such responsibility to its suppliers.

Jack Ampuja and Ray Pucci, working with ten large companies in a study in this area, concluded "active management of inbound freight generates a savings of five to eight percent" (Ampuja, 2002, p. 51). George Borza, analyzing work done for clients of CSC, reported that: "based on actual improvements in shifting inbound freight from multiple modes to lowest cost could generate savings of 30 to 40% on this element of cost."

He offers, as one example, the shift from emergency airfreight to best LTL shipment.

The difficulty is usually born of the fact that Level 1 firms do not align purchasing with logistics. Content to allow inter-departmental and cross-business unit separation to thrive, the issue does not receive the attention it deserves. Outbound freight is larger and far easier to isolate (with this element of transportation making up as much as 40% of the distribution costs) and so it gets the attention. Inbound freight may only be ten percent of material or product cost and gets lost in the consideration. A smart, early step is to assign responsibility to a small team to analyze this facet of logistics and establish techniques that reduce the inherent costs. This team should be reactivated and carry forward its efforts in higher-level applications as multiple constituents and more opportunities are considered. Ampuja and Pucci offer some helpful recommendations for such actions.

> Although there are many facets to good management of inbound freight, there are six key areas of concern: freight terms, rate negotiation, effective communication of routing instructions, routing compliance, controlling premium freight, and private fleet utilization. By paying attention to these concerns, managers will see a marked increase in cost savings (Ampuja, 2002, p. 52).

There is another early complication. A special problem is encountered as the firm considers factors related to the assets being employed, especially tractors and trailers used for over-the-highway delivery and ownership of warehousing and distribution facilities. Most Level 1 companies are far more concerned with this aspect of logistics as a matter of *control* rather than a cost-improvement opportunity. That is, controlling equipment use, dispatching vehicles, overseeing receipt of materials and supplies, and directing shipments of finished product is the first concern, rather than optimizing costs. Under this perspective, companies overlook the advantages of placing logistics in the hands of the most competent constituent. One Level 1 company owner with whom we worked refused to accept an opportunity to save 30% of his logistics cost by turning the responsibility over to a qualified 3PL simply because he would not relinquish what he considered first-hand control of the process.

Who could own and take care of the trucks and trailers the way we want it done? Who will hire and pay the drivers and get the loyalty we expect for our firm? Who will dispatch the equipment that makes the final delivery to our customers and meet their demands? How can we trust anyone other than ourselves to make deliveries when needed? These are questions the control-minded firm uses to slow advancement into higher levels. The tendency is to want to directly sustain that control, in spite of opportunities to place such matters in the hands of more capable supply chain partners.

Patience is often the only solution. As the calibration uncovers baseline opportunities and savings develop, the resistance to outside help tends to break down. The alignment of shipments from suppliers and to customers leads to selecting the best traffic routes. Truck utilization comes under intense scrutiny to determine how investments in such equipment can be enhanced through fuller loading. Taking advantage of the total space within a vehicle improves cube utilization, while combining loads can result in more full truckloads. Use of external firms to make less-than-full-truckload (LTL) shipments becomes a viable option. So does becoming *mode agnostics* and evaluating mode shifting to make certain opportunities to use train, sea, and air alternatives are not overlooked and the best total solution is applied. Today, there is still a lot of open capacity on most equipment and the firm is advised to search for alternative solutions, particularly as this can be done electronically.

The traffic department rises in importance as solutions are discovered leading to better yard-management systems (often leading to the need for less equipment), pooling freight for pick up, and balancing the miles-per-week with needed pieces of equipment. Operational metrics such as cost per mile, back-haul percentage, percent of trips out of route, and number of empty miles all move in the right direction. A side benefit is that the amount of nonproductive time is minimized. Common carrier opportunities are investigated as most large firms combine the control of freight to a central position, measure the performance of many carriers, and consolidate their orders with strong regional companies. With central control comes the desire to consider external partners that can reliably handle the delivery requirements without disruption to customer satisfaction.

CROSS-COMPANY ACTIVITY MARKS LEVEL 2

In Level 2, dubbed *achieving logistics capability*, firms establish a *logistics center* where the total organizational costs are evaluated. As the firm begins to consider its ability to leverage transportation and storage in the same way as purchasing volume, it moves closer to traffic optimization turning attention to how the overall capability can be improved. Service requirements are examined, on both the inbound and outbound side of manufacturing, to determine if another supply chain partner can make the deliveries on a more economical and efficient basis. Leasing equipment to keep maintenance costs fixed and conserve cash becomes an option.

Dedicated carriers with responsibility for heavy traffic routes are used. Work is most often performed in this level as a special *study*, frequently done with the help of a third-party advisor. Significant, more comprehensive data collection typically accompanies these studies.

Attention is paid to where the key suppliers are and how they make shipments to the firm's operating facilities and storage depots. This focus is intended to ensure a reliable flow of incoming materials and supplies, while minimizing the inbound freight costs and handling. Where trucks can be sent to a supplier as part of an empty back haul, pickups become a viable alternative to having the supplier ship directly. As the analysis extends to the firm's total system, involving intra-company transfers and shipments to customers, the potential to better utilize assets (with fuller loads) increases.

An early effort in this area proved what could be accomplished by coordinating communications and delivery between supply chain partners. Nabisco, the Parsippany, New Jersey-based manufacturer of the familiar Planters Peanuts, and Wegmans Food Markets of Rochester, New York, with the help of software developed by Nistevo of Eden Prairie, Minnesota, teamed up in the fall of 2000 to develop a new way of handling delivery service from the farming of nuts through manufacture and delivery to retail stores.

Under the new system, instead of the supplier deciding how much to ship to the retailer and pushing inventory forward in the system toward the retailer's distribution centers, the firms worked out an arrangement that was more contemporary and mutually beneficial. Nabisco and Wegmans now exchange sales forecasts via the Web and agree on the amounts to meet the retailer's needs. With a firm idea of what is needed, contact is made with the Nabisco offices in Brazil, for example, signaling the need for cashews. The nuts are picked and packed and shipments are sent to Jacksonville, Florida.

Instead of having many trucks only partially loaded and without any return loads, as was the case under the old system, shippers and truckers now have online information provided by the Nistevo real-time system. This collaborative logistics network connects multiple manufacturers and transportation companies through an exchange that matches orders and makes certain the trucks are as full as possible. With better loads arriving at the Nabisco plants, the nuts are roasted and packed and sent to a warehouse consolidator, which replaces the Nabisco DC. Because Nabisco knows Wegmans' needs, there is no shortage or oversupply of the nuts. The consolidator puts the right amount of product on trucks headed for the Wegmans stores with other products, including some from competing firms. Transportation, warehousing, and inventory costs all drop with this system (Keenan, 2000, p. EB114).

This type of investigation can extend beyond transportation and the use of trucks, rail cars, ships, and planes, as serious consideration is given to the total assets tied up in warehouse space and DCs. Now those in the logistics center question: Are the facilities in the right place? Do we have more space than we need? Are the facilities performing the correct function? Do we have the best total cost of delivery and storage? Would we do better to turn over this part of the function to a more-qualified partner?

Most firms find ways here to significantly reduce these investments without harming delivery capability. Software programs are applied to determine where the warehousing should be located, how much space should be involved, and which company should own the facility. Using data on where suppliers are located, where the manufacturing plants are situated, and where key deliveries must be made, this analysis includes how much inventory is required to meet demand, as well as how the goods should be stored and retrieved, and often leads to rationalization of the total system and the installation of a warehouse management system (WMS) where it is deemed important. Working with many firms through this level, warehouse space reductions of 30 to 50% were not uncommon as the software revealed more economical alternatives.

Third-party logistics providers (3PLs), companies skilled at taking over the responsibility for equipment, maintenance, and drivers, and arranging transportation across the system, are brought in to discuss transferring ownership of this function. Advanced planning and scheduling (APS) begins to occur at this time, as these providers are given access to actual planning schedules so they can have the right equipment available at the right point of need. In short, the logistics function becomes a serious part of the firm's strategic framework. As supply chain strategy is fused with the business strategy and operating plans at this level, the elements required in order to attain logistics excellence are fused to the supply chain strategy.

The firm begins to factor the benefit of reducing total network cycle time as a sales advantage into its plans. Supply chain partnerships are given much greater consideration, especially as they relate to finding logistics savings and cycle time reductions from order to delivery. Performance metrics that track these elements also begin to appear in the progress reviews. The crucial step is to develop a deeper understanding of the existing conditions and how they affect the business strategy and then identify the opportunities for making as much progress with logistics as has been made with purchasing and sourcing. Typically, the beginnings of a network model appear and supply chain partners discuss how improved lead times and cycles can result in getting new business.

DIGITAL COMMERCE ENTERS LEVEL 3

When the firm crosses over the cultural barrier and moves into the third level of the evolution, it enters the area termed *leverage e-commerce*. The intention is to use Internet technology and cyber-based tools, internally and externally, to enhance logistics processing. Now the company takes advantage of its internal data analysis and, with the help of external advisors, starts its move toward the virtual logistics network. With some of its trusted allies, a firm develops the end-to-end visibility so important to a contemporary logistics model. The logistics function considers decision support software that includes real-time data transmission on order and shipment conditions and requires the involvement of supply chain partners to coordinate shipments and deliveries with demand data. Internally integrated modeling pulls the total needs together in a manner that allows the firm to consider many more options than previously accessed. Event tracking of shipments versus what the business plan called for becomes an attribute.

Unilever plc, the consumer products giant with such brands as Dove soap, Close-Up toothpaste, Q-tips, and Helene Curtis hair products, introduced such a Level 3 system when it linked subsidiary companies with contract manufacturers. Unilever places orders electronically and the contractors use the Unilever extranet to update order status, make changes, expedite orders, and review shipments. "Status reports are fed into Unilever's internal warehouse management and logistics systems in real time so Unilever can quickly coordinate the delivery of goods to retailers" (Semilof, 2001, p. 1). This system replaces a legacy system that entered orders piecemeal via the phone, e-mail, and fax, and where all transactions had to be entered manually into the firm's supply chain management applications.

Consistent with the need for both internal and external integration in these advanced network systems, this e-logistics system uses McHugh Software International's DigitaLogistix connected to Manugistics' demand forecasting applications and SAP purchasing and materials management applications. The software runs on Windows NT and 2000 servers. The firm expects to use the system with 40 contract manufacturers, but initiated the effort with only five.

This type of automation is especially beneficial as it reduces the time required to get packaged goods to retail customers, which typically give better consideration for shelf space to those manufacturers that can make products available quickly and accurately. Fred Berkheimer, Unilever's Vice President of Logistics, predicts, "When Unilever adds inventory management and forecasting applications to the integrated package, the company expects to remove up to ten days from that cycle, shortening order-to-delivery cycles to 48 hours by 2003" (Semilof, 2001, p. 1).

Dynamic tactical planning tools are applied in Level 3 to match manufacturing and delivery schedules with actual consumption and come up with executable plans. This planning is set up on a quarterly, semi-annual, or annual basis, and allows the firm to track results against a more reasonable budget. As implied, the tactics are adjusted as market conditions change and special needs with key customers arise. Extranet systems come into existence as the firm begins serious collaboration with its best suppliers and customers, often including some key distributors. Together, these partners look at network planning and delivery as a means of distinguishing the collaborating firms in the eyes of the final customer or end consumers.

Use of the Web allows anyone in a supply chain to share information and better coordinate product movement, make changes, and better react to current conditions. Ace Hardware, the Oak Brook, Illinois-based retailer, found substantial savings when it persuaded its retailers and suppliers to deliver forecasts and orders to an Internet online system. Suppliers now make instant recommendations on shipments to take advantage of efficiencies for ordering, for example, "210 cases of wrenches rather than 200 because the larger amount means a full pallet and a lower price." Because the supplier does not have to break up a pallet, pull out ten cases and wrap the short pallet for later use, this change saves time at the warehouse. On the delivery side, there is less chance for loose cases to be misplaced or lost requiring the reissuing of paperwork for missing items. The results for Ace have more than paid for the effort. "Transportation costs are down 18% and warehouse costs have been slashed 28%" (Keenan, 2000, p. EB116).

Applying these tools is not confined to manufacturers and retailers. In an effort to keep pace with the movement toward e-logistics and virtual logistics systems, trucking, logistics and service companies are taking the initiative and building digital supply chain solutions. Challenger, the Cambridge, Ontario-based firm serving Canada, the U.S. and Mexico, decided it needed to cut costs and enhance its services to customers. The firm selected a business analysis tool and a suite of transportation optimization tools from Logistics.com.

Before 1997, Challenger was using an internal system that could not keep up with its needs. Following a decision to move away from the in-house system, the company adopted a new technology infrastructure and a *business intelligence* software package. In February, 2001, after the infrastructure was in place, Challenger began installing Logistics.com's version of its OptiYield suite, eventually including all five modules — Driver & Load, Drop & Swap, Fuel & Route, Load Analyzer, and Profit Analyzer. The Driver & Load software recommends "optimal driver-load combinations," giving the planner a best choice with four alternatives.

Profit Analyzer "looks at all the costs and revenues that go into making an order profitable" and allows the firm to conduct what-if scenarios to "determine how pricing structures will affect the company's bottom line." Drop & Swap recommends "where to swap a driver mid-trip if there will be problems for the driver getting home or for an on-time delivery" (Hickey, 2001, p. 21).

LOGISTICS OPTIONS INCREASE WITH THE LEVEL OF PROGRESS

How far a firm should go with its logistics function and e-commerce becomes a critical question as success stories are evaluated and enabling applications are considered. A third-party logistics study conducted in 2001 by Georgia Institute of Technology, Cap Gemini, Ernst & Young, and Ryder System, Inc. generated the chart in Figure 4.2 (Cottrill, 2001, p. 17). This model can be useful in establishing what occurs as a firm moves toward the higher levels of logistics interaction and decides what might be the highest level appropriate. As indicated in the first or base level, the firm is working on improving its *insourcing* activities, applying resident knowledge to positively impact the infrastructure through many of the efforts described. When the firm moves to the second level, it considers lead service providers (LSP) with the focus being on cost reduction and location-specific analyses.

In the next area, third party logistics (3PL), providers are consulted to determine where enhanced capabilities might be found. This step requires the firm to downplay its insistence on controlling the assets being used while gaining assurances of service necessary to meet its planning and delivery needs. Broader service offerings become a part of such arrangements as does the ability to access multiple locations without having the need to own warehousing and distribution facilities.

It is generally in this area that the firm realizes that e-logistics systems are becoming a business imperative as the cost of doing business with suppliers the old way is too expensive and the demands of customers are forcing them to adopt more effective arrangements. Internet-based logistics systems help firms cut costs by automating processes — order entry and management, supplying customer information, and assuring good levels of service. Hon Industries, a Muscatine, Iowa furniture maker, came to this conclusion when it decided the company's lean manufacturing model should be integrated with a Synquest Inc. APS system. Deployed in March 2001, this system "manages a wide range of business processes, including customer orders, plant and production scheduling, and logistics" (Konicki, 2001, p. 64).

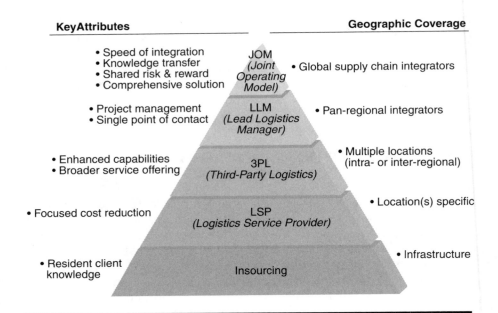

KeyAttributes
Geographic Coverage

- Speed of integration
- Knowledge transfer
- Shared risk & reward
- Comprehensive solution

JOM
(Joint Operating Model)

- Global supply chain integrators

- Project management
- Single point of contact

LLM
(Lead Logistics Manager)

- Pan-regional integrators

- Enhanced capabilities
- Broader service offering

3PL
(Third-Party Logistics)

- Multiple locations (intra- or inter-regional)

- Focused cost reduction

LSP
(Logistics Service Provider)

- Location(s) specific

- Resident client knowledge

Insourcing

- Infrastructure

Figure 4.2 Moving Logistics to Advanced Levels of Interaction (From Cottrill, K., *Traffic World*, 2001, Third-Party Logistics Study 2001, Georgia Institute of Technology, Atlanta, Cap Gemini, Ernst & Young Ryder System Inc.)

The system proved its value following the September 11 catastrophe when Hon needed to reschedule plants and change delivery schedules to meet an emergency 20-truckload order from a customer badly affected by the World Trade Center attack. With plants running at near capacity, it was a formidable challenge, but the new system helped Hon and its customer as plants and schedules were altered to make the required shipments.

In a move typical of this level of progression, electronic logistics applications are being moved away from proprietary systems and onto the Internet by an ever-increasing number of firms. General Motors Corporation's replacement parts operation applied such a technique to its link between suppliers and the automaker's 9,000 car dealers. 3PL provider Schneider Logistics developed a system with GM that was deployed in April 2001. The Internet-based format replaced a system of EDI transactions and telephone calls among GM and its suppliers and dealers. The system, according to Jerry Goilebiewski, Process Manager for inbound logistics at GM's Service Part Operation, "has made it simpler to prioritize the shipment of out-of-stock parts and reliably predict when they'll arrive at the dealers who need them" (Konicki, 2001, p. 64).

In Level 4, lead logistics managers (LLM) may be utilized. These organizations have little to no assets, but digital access to a wide variety of carriers, warehousing sites, and alternate modes of delivery. Now project management becomes the focus as a single point of contact is used to administer the firm's storage and transportation needs. In the highest level, joint operating models (JOM), virtual logistics become a reality and the firm can access online open capacity through hundreds of firms participating in a collaborative form of logistics.

Vendor-managed inventories become a feature of this type of advanced collaboration as the appropriate supplier, manufacturer, or other partner takes responsibility for having the right inventory at the right place, including stocking shelves in the retail stores, if appropriate. Applying the concept of core competency, loads are aggregated so the best constituent does the pick up and delivery. Where it makes better sense to do so, asset ownership is outsourced so the best firm assumes responsibility for warehousing and delivery. In the most advanced segment of Level 3, firms work diligently on collaborative planning, forecasting, and replenishment (CPFR).

A CASE STUDY ILLUSTRATES THE SAVINGS POTENTIAL

As a firm looks outside its own organization to consider how logistics costs can be reduced, a new realm of possibilities emerges, particularly those offered by what we term *virtual logistics*, or the ability to use Internet communications to gain access to a large number of possible freight carriers with open space on their equipment, often moving in the same lanes as those being studied for improvement. Minnesota-based Nistevo, Inc. offers software and assistance in this virtual logistics arena and has turned in some impressive action stories. One in particular involves International Paper Company, the world's largest provider of forest products, with $28 billion in sales revenue.

IP decided to drive part of its business process improvement effort across its visible, decentralized enterprise, hoping to improve freight carrier management and compliance. Although the shipments were being made, there was evidence that they were not being done under the contracts that had been painstakingly negotiated and included special values for the full leverage of the firm's traffic.

The IP transportation system covers the needs of the paper mills, where the paper is produced and wound into huge rolls, through its delivery to distribution sites, where sheeted stock is packaged and delivered to customers. Its annual transportation spend is $1.3 billion, of which $400 million is spent on full-truckload shipments and the balance on less-than-full loads and rail transfer. At the beginning of the effort with its distribution systems, IP projected a possible $20 million savings from off-contract buying by maverick buyers within that system. The planned solution included a command and control system to facilitate movement of the paper products through its supply chain and distribution network.

With the help of Nistevo, the firm went live in the summer of 2001, beginning at five locations. Through the system, the firm could access 120 carriers to handle their 200 daily shipments. By December, IP had expanded the program across their entire organization, with a total of 84 locations being deployed, accessing more than 250 carriers and handling 2,000 shipments per day. IP stores its contracts in a Nistevo module and leverages these contracts to ensure on-contract buying across its distribution network. Using the Nistevo system, the paper company projects it can eliminate the maverick buying and save most, if not all, of the $20 million.

A MODEL HELPS DEFINE FURTHER PROGRESSION

To capture the progression being considered, Figure 4.3 illustrates the elements of an advanced logistics model. Beginning with the supply phase, with its internal logistics house in order, the firm considers the design-source-buy-store sequence of improvement. This means the company is taking both an internal and external view of logistics and making certain it extends upstream to those firms involved in designing products and innovations. A cooperative internal arrangement between logistics and purchasing involves key suppliers in the designing and sourcing process, while determination of storage and deliveries are done in an optimal manner. With all the complexity of today's business networks, a series of Tier 1-n suppliers could be involved in this activity.

Depending on the network and its products and services, there could be other players active on the supply side. Wholesalers for beverages and spirits, distributors of food products and supplies, and logistics providers might be very helpful in bringing the necessary upstream materials and products to a manufacturer. In the contemporary view, all of these constituents must be operating with some form of online order processing and tracking technique and doing planning interactively.

In the next phase, inbound logistics is considered for all the reasons cited. Dispatching signals are sent to the key suppliers electronically. Transportation and distribution are coordinated to meet manufacturing schedules and match delivery with actual consumption. Tracking of inventory and shipments is online and diversions are made, often in transit, to meet emergency needs. Expediting will always be a part of any model and can be accommodated to meet real emergency needs. Special shipments can be arranged, accessing virtual networks to find open capacity on transportation equipment.

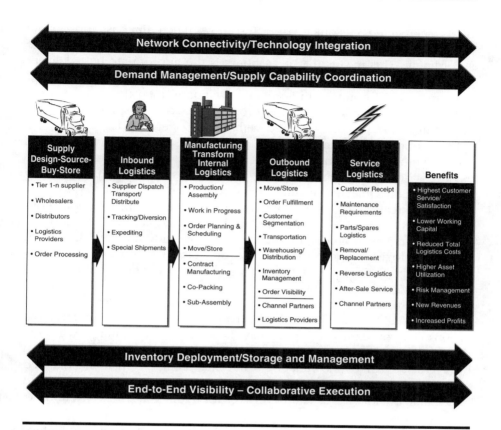

Figure 4.3 An Advanced Logistics Model

At the manufacturing or transformation site, internal logistics takes place in an optimized manner. Now the idea is to match the flow of incoming materials and supplies with the manufacturing schedules. Work in process could be a very important feature as it is in large steel and other metal-making operations where huge coils of semi-finished materials are transferred between operations. Order planning and scheduling is shared with key upstream and downstream partners so all parties are aware of the flows and disruptions that may be part of operations. Movement and storage are tracked and signals sent to important partners such as contract manufacturers, co-packing operations, and subassembly partners.

Once the products and goods are ready for transfer downstream, the firm and its allies work on outbound logistics. Here the emphasis is again on efficient movement and storage, but a closer look is given to order fulfillment. With many channels of distribution being considered today, the advanced firm is matching the best delivery method with the needs of its segmented customer base. Just how much time is appropriate between order and delivery, for example, is defined and execution done accordingly. This means that if 24 hours is the appropriate best delivery cycle for the highest priority customer group, all systems work toward that target. If 72 hours is an acceptable standard, then that becomes the target. The concept is to keep the promises made so customers can plan accordingly and not be burdened with excess safety stocks.

Transportation systems, warehousing and distribution considerations, and inventory management reach very sophisticated levels in the model, as order visibility — the ability to view and track shipments, make delivery promises, and manage inventories through an electronic system — becomes a reality. Important channel partners and the providers responsible for outbound logistics are key users of this system.

In the advanced model, the firm and its allies add another phase, that of service logistics. Now the focus is on customer and end consumer receipt of the flow of goods and services. The model questions how good that receipt has been and whether maintenance needs products delivered. Parts and spares logistics could be a part of the model, particularly in industries such as automotive and aerospace. Removal and replacement of obsolete or damaged parts may be a requisite feature. With the development of cyber-based ordering and shipping, reverse logistics can be a crucial part of the model, as Internet orders seem to be plagued with a high rate of return, often reaching as high as "40% compared to an average 8% for catalogs and even less for traditional stores" (Neuborne, 2001, p. 12).

After-sale service could call for special shipments and pick-ups. Once again, key channel partners must be a part of this phase to take advantage of open space on carriers moving in either direction in the supply chain. Outsourcing the entire reverse logistics function to more capable partners becomes a viable option. Sincerely Yours, a Lewisville, Texas home-décor business, made that decision when it gave the handling of returns to Newgistics, an Austin, Texas, reverse-logistics specialist. EZiba.com, a North Adams, Massachusetts seller of gift items, chose Client Logic, a Nashville-based specialist. These outsourcers handle all aspects of the return process, typically charging a fee per return.

Across the top and the bottom of the model there are requirements for success. There must be some form of network connectivity through which communications are channeled. That stipulation demands a compatibility of systems and software making technology integration a key element. Demand management, or the better analysis of actual replenishment needs, must be coordinated carefully with supply capacity and withdrawals from storage made in synchronization with current planning needs. Inventory deployment, storage, and management must be a network responsibility with each player managing its part of the sequence, from supply to final delivery. And above all else, there must be online end-to-end visibility of what is going on across the extended enterprise. That leads to collaborative excellence, a mark that will distinguish the network in the eyes of the final customer or end consumer.

The benefits from executing such a model have been clearly documented. They include:

- Attaining the highest customer service and satisfaction ratings
- Reducing the need for working capital through lower investments in inventory and capital equipment now shared or outsourced with supply chain partners
- Reducing total logistics costs through much greater efficiency in storage, shipment, and use of equipment
- Achieving higher asset utilization by aggregating the total needs across the network, taking advantage of the most useful facilities and gaining higher utilization metrics
- Gaining a better measure of risk management, as the network partners are online working real time to reduce the aberrations and emergencies that plague supply chains
- Developing new revenues as the superior performance leads network partners into nontraditional markets and increasing business with existing customers
- Bringing greater profits to the operating statement by virtue of being the best and lowest cost network of choice by the best customers

An example of the last element of benefit can be given through a look at what one major firm did to enhance logistics excellence and make more money for itself and a key partner. The technique of advancing through what amounts to multi-player outsourcing can bring significant improvements and savings to a firm if it works closely with a logistics partner and allows that partner to reap higher benefits as well. Whirlpool Corp., the Benton Harbor, Michigan appliance manufacturer, learned this lesson as it advanced through a series of logistics efforts.

Back in 1998, Whirlpool used multiple carriers and providers and managed the logistics function and assets internally. According to Tom Wright, VP of Supply Chain Operations, "the company's relationship with providers was based on complete cost pass through with a small freight fee tied to it" (Cottrill, 2001, p. 17). After a series of investigations and evaluations, Wright decided to outsource the business to lead logistics provider (LLP) Penske. This LLP now supplies manpower and assets to match the demands placed on the Whirlpool system. As part of the agreement, Penske agreed to deliver an annual cost reduction of 5%. After that amount, a gain-sharing feature kicks in and the firms split any further cost reductions evenly. This is the kind of incentive that drives a 3PL to seek the maximum benefits.

The firm plans to expand this venture and the inherent concepts as it moves toward a joint operating model and is pursuing such a move in Europe and Latin America. Bob Bos, Strategic Account Executive for Penske explains, "outsourcing relationships are multi-layered and become more strategic in nature as the partners achieve higher degrees of integration, ultimately leading to some form of joint venture." These joint ventures and the more advanced logistics models will be seen ever more frequently as the logistics effort continues to mature.

NETWORK OPPORTUNITIES BECOME THE LEVEL 4 OBJECTIVE

In Level 4, logistics strategy truly becomes a network experience with integration of efforts extending to multi-tiers of partners. Now the firm enters an area called tap network opportunities. With the assistance of key allies and data readily accessed internally and externally, the focus moves to the extended enterprise and the shipments and storage occurring across many organizations. The major feature of this level is the "glass pipeline" that develops through which the partners can view the entire supply chain flow, from the earliest important supplies to final consumption. Global satellite positioning (GSP) devices are used to track shipments and stored products. Radio-frequency equipment is mounted on warehouse trucks to link the communication right to the point of picking the correct items for any order. All inventories of merit are online, accessed through an extranet on a 24/7 basis. Virtual inventory management becomes a reality rather than a dream as the partners operate closely to meet delivery needs without excess inventory. The overall focus is on the *perfect order* with all partners working back from consumer and customer needs to provide the best possible solutions. Metrics are established to measure these perfect orders and used to solicit new business from other customers.

A key element in this level is jointly developing an analytical framework to guide the building of the network supply chain model. Using key data inputs from suppliers and distributors, the nucleus firm begins constructing a supply chain model to represent the existing and possible future (enhanced) state of conditions. This model could be very complicated for a large-scale operation such as automobile and aerospace delivery. It must include quantitative and qualitative data to evaluate performance and include service maps covering the entire enterprise. Figure 4.4 describes a useful analytical framework to facilitate the building of this model.

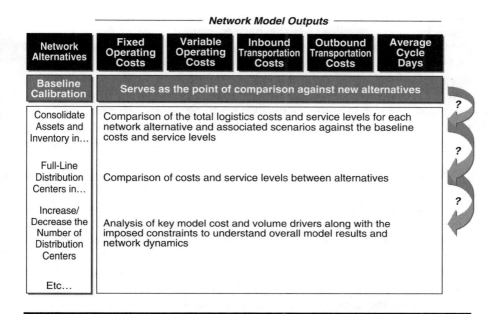

Network Model Outputs

Network Alternatives	Fixed Operating Costs	Variable Operating Costs	Inbound Transportation Costs	Outbound Transportation Costs	Average Cycle Days
Baseline Calibration	Serves as the point of comparison against new alternatives				
Consolidate Assets and Inventory in...	Comparison of the total logistics costs and service levels for each network alternative and associated scenarios against the baseline costs and service levels				
Full-Line Distribution Centers in...	Comparison of costs and service levels between alternatives				
Increase/ Decrease the Number of Distribution Centers	Analysis of key model cost and volume drivers along with the imposed constraints to understand overall model results and network dynamics				
Etc...					

Figure 4.4   Analytical Framework for Tapping Network Opportunities

With the help of a few key suppliers, distributors, and customers, the firm considers network alternatives, beginning with a baseline calibration that evaluates fixed operating costs, variable operating costs, inbound transportation, outbound transportation, and average cycle days. Other factors can be added to the model to meet specific industry or organizational demands. With this framework, the supply chain partners begin to discuss alternatives such as consolidating assets and inventories to minimize investments in equipment and working capital. Together, they compare total logistics costs and service metrics for each alternative against credible baselines. The need for full-line distribution centers is evaluated, as is the need to either increase or decrease the number of such centers.

The framework essentially moves from a view of multiple network alternatives to a quantitative model where outputs are combined with business judgment to reduce the options to those making the most sense to the network partners. Further refinement occurs as the highest priority alternatives are tested and additional constraints considered. A sensitivity or *what-if* analysis is then applied to a select group of alternatives to choose action initiatives and a recommended supply chain network design. This modeling approach typically moves through a stepped procedure to ensure an effective and timely completion. The steps include framing the analysis to suit the participants, collecting pertinent data, constructing and validating the model, determining the future-state design and advantage to the network, and building the path forward.

A major food service co-op provides a case study illustrating this procedure. This firm set the objective as defining the appropriate number, size, and location of its distribution facilities across its supply chain network to minimize logistics costs while enhancing customer service. Among the issues identified with its partners were to separate operations by different divisions, reduce the high inventories supporting slow-moving products, and deal with seasonal demand patterns that required an inventory pre-build.

The data collection included listing the basic network characteristics, determining product demand, and reviewing outbound transportation rates. The model building and validation step employed special software to design the least costly, most flexible and efficient distribution network. An operational analysis step was added to test several network alternatives to determine their relative benefits in terms of operating costs, investment requirements, and service performance. Strategy development led to the selection of the best alternatives and development of a high-level plan to migrate from the existing distribution system to the network solution.

Specific recommendations included co-location of two divisions to enable the firm to achieve economies of scale from third-party providers, consolidation of multiple Midwest facilities into a single location, consolidation of slow-moving product into a single site, and concentration of any additional facilities near processing plants. A review of results indicated that the variable operating costs had been reduced by 15%, capacity constraints had been alleviated resulting in significant inventory savings, and customer service levels had improved.

Activity between partners occurs more frequently in Level 4 with planning being done as often as weekly across the network activities affecting all key trading partners. Output is linked both strategically and tactically across these partners. For those firms involved in international shipments, a global kieretsu emerges, taking a page from the Japanese technique of combining many firms in an effort to optimize application of total assets. The logistics pipeline is a major support mechanism for the virtual manufacturing systems that have developed across the partners and their use of core competencies to have the right parts and products made by the best firm with final assembly and production done by the final shipper.

Companies shipping directly to stores or companies and consumers, which have placed order electronically, introduce what amounts to a cyber channel of delivery. Here, e-fulfillment, or the delivery, tracking, and assurance of proper receipt, all done on a cyber-based system, is an element that differentiates the network from other groups. Supply chain partnerships are extremely important in this case, as the delivery system is only as strong as the weakest element in the chain and delivery tracking is a full-time effort. Logistics models tend to be multi-tiered in this level as warehouse management systems are integrated to make certain high levels of satisfaction are attained by having the right product available and not introducing stock-outs of popular or fast-moving items.

THE GREATEST ADVANTAGE OCCURS IN LEVEL 5

Not all firms need to progress as far as Level 5, which has been termed *build an advantage*, but the opportunity to achieve more benefits, particularly in terms of customer and consumer satisfaction, occurs in this level. This area is for the most sophisticated of networks, requiring the formation of joint logistics models and involving full connectivity across the extended enterprise. Total logistics costs are evaluated through the connecting extranet communication system. Since the firms have applied activity-based costing and balanced-scorecard techniques to determine the costs per unit across the end-to-end network, they work together on the most cost-effective methodology while keeping customer ratings at industry best standards.

A robust, integrated, multi-tier capability is what distinguishes the linked players, as all key members are working together online on a real-time basis to match deliveries with actual demand. Simulation techniques are applied to study, evaluate, and test alternative delivery scenarios, and alert partners of relevant changes occurring within the system. Tight upward and downward propagation with regard to plans and changes are an element that brings further advantages.

In this highest level of progression, the logistics flow is viewed in a reversed order from the normal modeling. With the emphasis now definitely on a *pull* versus a *push* system, and many supply chain partners working in concert to meet the needs of the end consumers, Figure 4.5 describes the future model. The first demand signal that instigates movement begins with consumer data — actual store purchases, catalog orders, Web site buying, or return shipments. This information flows to the retailers that could include stores (Wal-Mart), outlet centers (Donna Karan), catalog providers (Land's End), or Web site suppliers (e-Bay). With so many options, the model could include anywhere from one to n possibilities.

Actual signals for required replenishment are now matched with what has been removed from the network so the next data flow is to the warehouses holding goods for delivery. This warehousing could include regional distribution centers, such as those set up by Wal-Mart on a territory basis to ship loads to individual stores or Sam's Club outlets. It might also include a distributor's distribution center, such as those owned by Fleming

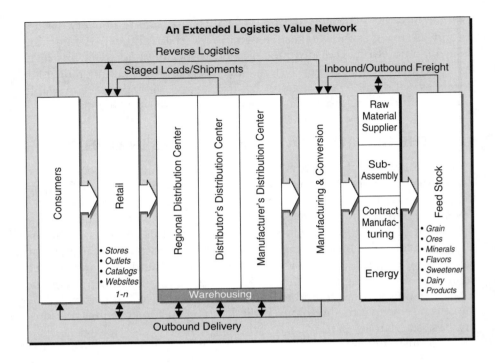

 *Demand signal*

Figure 4.5   The Future Logistics Model

and SuperValu, for delivery to independent food stores and some grocery chain outlets. It can also include a manufacturer's distribution center, such as those operated by Procter & Gamble. Returns can flow back to these locations for replacement and new product can flow forward to meet the demand signals. In the center, we show staged loads and shipments as some retailers, such as Wal-Mart, Target, and Sears, like to stage loads for multiple deliveries to many of their stores.

The next demand signal is sent to the manufacturer or converter to establish what needs to be pulled into the system to keep the flow balanced. These manufacturers can respond with shipments to one of the DCs or directly to the stores and, in the case of cyber orders, directly to a home or business location. From these manufacturers, the next signal is sent to one or more of the suppliers — raw materials, subassemblies, outsourced contract manufacturers, and possibly energy providers. From there, the signal proceeds to the suppliers' suppliers of such commodities as grain, ore, minerals, and dairy products. Inbound and outbound freight are considered from a network perspective as the partners are working under a joint modeling concept and considering virtual logistics opportunities.

Together the partners view the model as an extended logistics value network and optimized conditions are the objective as each player sets aside the need for control and uses the most effective system from beginning to end of the supply chain, even when it means one player incurs an extra cost in the process. Balanced scorecards become the means of analysis and assignment and the technique for allocating costs across the extended enterprise.

This model may not be applicable for all firms, but it is a harbinger of what is occurring as firms sit down with supply chain partners and design a differentiating logistics system, with the focus on achieving the highest levels of satisfaction with the most important customers and consumer groups. Any firm interested in such a situation is well advised to begin some form of partnering with a few trusted supply chain allies to determine if such a model has merit.

SUMMARY

Logistics is maturing as a business technique, especially as a key element of creating the most effective supply chain network. Most firms progress through five levels of improvement, although not all firms need to achieve the highest level of that progression. Models help guide the progress as firms carefully put the internal house in order and then select trusted partners to build advanced systems. Overall logistics costs decline in the process and customer satisfaction increases as the linked partners find the way to best any competing network in meeting actual delivery and replenishment needs.

5

MODELS FOR FORECASTING, DEMAND MANAGEMENT, AND CAPACITY PLANNING

Once a firm has paid adequate attention to sourcing and logistics as key elements of its supply chain improvement effort, attention typically turns to matters of customer service, inventory management, planning, and scheduling. As these processes are considered — the how of determining what should be created and shipped — it quickly becomes apparent that inherent flaws inhibit the potentially efficient processing that could occur. These flaws are endemic to most systems, but often are a part of the poor source information and the personnel issues that plague smooth and efficient supply chain procedures.

At the root of the problem is the unavoidable uncertainty in predicting future demand. This condition generally manifests itself in the unreliable sales forecasts that form the heart of the inventory management and planning system. Contributing to this uncertainty is the distortion of facts as the usual communication platforms, which include telephone, mail, fax, some EDI processing, and a bit of e-commerce, are often rife with mistakes and manual overrides. It is not uncommon to find multiple, conflicting accounts of past periods' actual sales activity across a single enterprise as a result of these data discrepancies. These problems lead to a significant amount of extra work to clean up the bad data and perform reconciliation.

Often, what goes into the upstream side of the chain is quite different from what is needed at the downstream side. In the early levels of the supply chain evolution, this complication leads to allowances being made for forecast error, additional buffers to inventories to cover contingencies, change schedules, and heroic efforts to respond to special customer conditions. Manual processes and overrides work but are extremely cost intensive and inefficient, as they require multiple transfers of order information throughout the end-to-end supply chain to get things right. The results are higher administrative costs, excess inventory and/or poor customer service levels, as well as higher costs of goods sold because of the instability in planning and scheduling systems.

Process control and some form of formal performance management are also generally lacking in the beginning, but become crucial in the advanced supply chain levels, particularly as network partners start planning together. At that stage, the members of the extended enterprise come to realize that, without a formal control system, mavericks in any one of the linked firms can upset an efficiently designed process flow. Buyers who refuse to accept the standard and centrally negotiated contracts order supplies from favored sources rather than those designated as part of the network plan. Sales personnel skilled at working the system to get orders moved ahead for their favored customers mangle efficient schedules. Pampered customers that are allowed to make schedule changes, rather than working on greater efficiency within their own perimeters, upset the balance in what could be a finely tuned manufacturing system. In the name of flexibility and customer service, well-developed systems are allowed to become inefficient.

The complications associated with these weak practices have a great effect on supply chain operations and the financial results that accrue as firms increase safety stocks to meet many contingency situations and cycle times are extended to accommodate information variability and inaccuracy. The advanced players do not accept this situation and expend time and effort to eliminate the problems and introduce new processes and systems that bring greater accuracy and efficiency to entering, planning, and fulfilling orders.

In this chapter, models that assist firms in improving further supply chain process steps, starting with forecasting and progressing through demand management and capacity planning, are considered. A framework for extending these models and the solutions they bring into the balance of supply chain processing is also introduced and used for the balance of this book. Particular thanks must go to Charles Troyer, Partner at CSC, for his invaluable help with this chapter.

A MODELING FRAMEWORK GUIDES EXECUTION

Figure 5.1 is used to illustrate the typical process steps that occur after sourcing and logistics in a supply chain management effort. A firm may wish to develop a customized list of specific steps for its own purposes

Process	Functions	Advanced Capability
Supply Chain Management End-to-End Product/Service Delivery	• Order processing • Design, plan, buy, make, sell, deliver, collect	• e–Business • Full network connectivity
Procurement Sourcing Material/Service Acquisition	• Supply base • Enterprise leverage • Strategic sourcing • Key suppliers	• Auctions • JIT scheduling • Network collaboration
Logistics Transportation, Storage, Delivery	• Enterprise leverage • Selective outsourcing • Asset utilization	• Virtual systems • Global tracking and delivery • Consortium distribution
Demand Management Forecasting, Planning and Order Management	• Sales forecasting • Order processing • SKU consolidation • Replenishment	• Consumption trigger • Higher turns • High forecast accuracy • Low forecast bias
Capacity Planning and Inventory Management	• Supply capability • Core competence • Cycle time consistency • Inventory, buffers	• Flexible response • Lower variability • Constraint elimination
Sales and Operations Planning	• Matching supply and demand planning • Performance review • Strategic use of resources	• Value chain planning • Synchronized material flow • High service/fill rates
Advance Scheduling and Planning	• Manage volatility • Available to promise • Distribution planning	• Balanced costs • Lead time reduction • Integrated work processing
Supplier Relationship Management	• Key supply arrangements • Standards, protocols • e-Procurement • Partnering in trust	• Network visibility • Revenue development • VMI • Joint strategies/planning
Customer Relationship Management	• Customer segmentation • Customer analytics • Data sharing • Joint business goals	• Network market knowledge • Joint technology adoption • Database marketing
Collaborative Design and Manufacturing	• Selective supplier assistance • Product lifecycle management • Time to market	• End consumer satisfaction • SRM/CRM convergence • Collaborative product design • Higher success rate
Collaborative Planning, Forecasting and Replenishment	• Channel partner cooperation • Technology application • Material/product visibility	• Automatic replenishment • Joint sales forecasting • Action matches with variance • Network management

Figure 5.1   Modeling Supply Chain Transformation

and develop the requisite enabling models, but this figure will guide what is presented in subsequent chapters of this book. Elaborations on the models and details will also be presented in those chapters.

Once a firm's supply base has been reduced, a cadre of key suppliers identified, and the logistics system moved to some form of external network arrangement, the focus generally switches to demand management. Now the firm pays attention to the weaknesses in sales forecasting and begins to establish better methods and procedures for order entry, order planning and order management, and supply planning. The number of items or SKUs offered is typically reduced to those on which the firm can make a profit or those needed for an acceptable offering in the market.

Processing is oriented around how to replenish those items under optimized conditions. In the advanced levels, consumption triggers this replenishment, often through an active, online network that transfers cash register data to planning systems, a key element in a true *pull* system. Higher turns in the most profitable items are experienced because of high forecast accuracy and a low bias in the forecast, which helps the firm avoid having too much or too little inventory to meet actual demand.

With a better handle on what is happening with internal order processing, attention moves to capacity planning — to match what can be produced with what is being demanded, essentially balancing the supply chain with the demand chain. Here the issue of inventory management is faced, not as a means of foisting inventories upstream in the supply chain to willing suppliers, but as a way to reduce the need for the extraneous inventories in the supply chain system and to utilize capacity to the highest degree possible. The results are a matching of just-in-time deliveries with actual manufacturing needs, and reduction of the buffer stocks by virtue of knowing what is truly being taken out of the system at the customer end of the chain.

Supply capability is reviewed in the advanced levels with respect to the firm's core competencies and its value chain partners, and decisions made as to which partner should perform which process steps. In the most advanced levels, flexible response systems that do not interfere with overall supply chain efficiency are created. There is much lower variability in the network as all parties work together through an online extranet to instantly review what is occurring and where changes must be made. Constraints in the system are eliminated or under control as the end-to-end partners link their ERP systems in order to make visible what is occurring across the full network.

This capacity planning has two subcomponent parts — sales and operations planning (S&OP) and advanced planning and scheduling (APS). The former is a well-established process and is complemented by the capabilities that the latter brings. Attention is given to both subjects in the following chapters as models are used to illustrate how a firm moves from whatever forecasting input it has to create response systems that guide the manufacturing and conversion operations and delivery to customers. Beginning with S&OP, the firm matches supply and demand planning through a rigorous system of meetings, reviews, and discussions that lead to strategic use of resources. In the best of these systems, value chain planning extends across the network to achieve synchronized material flows with high service and fill rates at the customer end.

APS is a more contemporary version of what takes place as the firm works with its key suppliers to establish standards on the products being created and protocols for their communications systems. available-to-promise (ATP) becomes a reality in this phase, as a company finds it can show customers what the firm is capable of producing and delivering and can fulfill these commitments with a high degree of accuracy. Distribution planning now extends from incoming supply to customer delivery and any return shipments. In the advanced levels, network partners use balanced scorecards to allocate costs across the full system and bring a degree of optimization to the total effort. Lead times are typically reduced to industry best levels and work processing is integrated as the firms link their ERP systems and software in a meaningful manner.

With better internal processing, attention once again focuses on the upstream side of the supply chain and the firm works on Supplier Relationship Management (SRM) with the key suppliers on which it depends for most of its operations. Arrangements are made with these suppliers, guaranteeing not just material and product supply, but help with strategic planning and advice on business plans. E-procurement features enter the picture as the partners seek the most efficient system of communication and begin partnering in a more trustful environment. In the advanced levels, these partners have full network visibility of what is occurring, from the customer purchase back through the need for incoming supplies. Vendor managed inventory (VMI) systems flourish and the thrust is to pull new revenues that benefit all parties in the network into the system.

ATTENTION MOVES FROM SUPPLY TO THE CUSTOMER

With the supply side better enabled, the firm next turns its attention to the downstream side of its supply chain. From an advanced viewpoint, the firm builds on its improvements and looks at customer relationship management (CRM). The concept is to mine databases to better enable the sales and service forces to respond properly to strategic customers and end consumers. The information that the firm and its key customers are willing to share is used to develop knowledge that leads to creating new revenues for both parties. Working with a customer segmentation that defines the importance of the customer and its need for attention and service, the firm shares important information and even makes joint business calls where appropriate. The more advanced firms employ a form of network market knowledge as a competitive advantage by virtue of sharing what was previously sacrosanct data. That data now helps the partners respond more effectively in target situations. Joint efforts are also made to adopt technology enablers beneficial to both parties.

Collaborative design and manufacturing enters the picture next, as the network relationships are flourishing and partners across the end-to-end value chain become willing to exchange more information. Now they work together to create the products and services most likely to succeed in the targeted markets and with specific customer and consumer groups with which the network wishes to establish strong market positions. With the aid of the most trusted suppliers, the firms work collaboratively on product lifecycle management, paying attention to the factors that will increase the likelihood of success with new products and offerings, while greatly reducing the time from new concept to market acceptance. In the advanced levels, SRM and CRM converge as the partners collaborate on new product design and determine how to introduce greater efficiencies into the process steps, linking the firms while assuring high market acceptance of the products created.

This cooperation extends, finally, into collaborative planning, forecasting, and replenishment (CPFR), an ambitious goal for advanced supply chain management in which the network partners work together to establish material and product visibility and the most efficient and optimized replenishment system. Channel partner cooperation peaks with this effort, and technology is mutually applied to introduce an automated replenishment system that is seamlessly integrated. Joint sales forecasting is at the center of this type of cooperation, as actions are matched with the variability in the system. It becomes a form of true network management.

FORECASTING IS THE ACHILLES' HEEL

Throughout this progression, supply chain efficiency is inexorably linked with a better understanding of exactly what is being demanded of the system. All of the process steps mentioned are affected by what is needed, when it is needed, and where it is needed. And forecast error often becomes the scapegoat for lack of an efficient response. Accurate forecasts are an oxymoron. The fact of the matter is that forecasts will always be inaccurate. In advanced supply chain, the challenge is careful management of this inaccuracy and balancing the incremental cost of producing higher accuracy versus the gains in service, processing costs, and inventories that accrue from additional accuracy.

The first issue that a firm must address in moving to more advanced levels of supply chain management is producing measurable and meaningful definitions of forecast accuracy. Using these measures, the impact of the current levels of inaccuracy can be weighed against the costs. This weighting must be in the context of other actions that impact the same set of costs. Inventory levels, and specifically safety stocks, are dramatically impacted by forecast accuracy. But they are also affected by replenishment lead times and lead-time variability. Only when the impact of all these factors are measured and evaluated can it be said with certainty that improved forecast accuracy is the most cost-effective culprit to attack in order to improve business performance.

Over the years, companies have spent considerable time and effort working with their historical data to project incoming orders, often sending approximations of what they believe to be current demand to planning. For those who persevere, mathematical models and algorithms are applied to match the educated guesses with actual data trends to keep the forecasts synchronized with what is actually taking place in the market. Combining history with the present, adjustments are made that should bring a closer congruence between what the firm thinks should occur and what really takes place.

Nevertheless, forecasting will remain an inexact science. In general terms, the most common mistakes interfering with the development and deployment of a successful forecasting system include:

- Unclear definition of forecast accuracy — Forecast accuracy should be defined and measured at the level that is meaningful to the physical decisions that are required within the unique context that each company's supply chain represents. A measure of forecast accuracy based on a forecast one period in the future is meaningless to an organization with a four-period supply lead time. Equally irrelevant are measures of forecast accuracy based on aggregates of demand in monetary units (e.g., total company sales in dollars).
- Lack of an ongoing and rigorous process of forecast error measurement — The only way a process can improve is to measure the results and make appropriate changes. This is also true of the forecasting process. If managers cannot measure, on a routine basis, the results of their work, there will be no improvement. Often, forecast error analysis is done as a special project and produced as a snapshot in time. Advanced firms have automated ongoing processes that measure forecast accuracy using meaningful and accepted definitions.

- Lack of organizational acceptance of the need for accurate forecasts — So long as everyone is skeptical about accuracy and there is no concerted effort to improve the inaccuracy, the information is rarely used to drive the operating system. Personal instinct and heroic service tend to dominate such systems.
- Forecasts are developed at a level of detail that is not actionable — This is a complementary point to the first one. That means the information is at too high a level, too broad in scope, or just plain not directly related to what must go into a master schedule. The result is a high-level forecast that gets modified so much it becomes meaningless for the needs of factory planning.
- Lack of clear organizational ownership of the forecasts that are generated — Without an obvious responsibility, everyone can run for cover and use weak forecasting as an excuse for all the poor processing and extra inventories. Some part of the organization must assume responsibility for forecast accuracy if this condition is to improve.
- Lack of clear rewards and incentives for forecast accuracy — The persons or organizational units having responsibility for forecasts should be rewarded based on their results as measured by forecast accuracy. Tying forecasts to sales quotas, for example, can produce some very bad results, as salespeople low-ball forecasts to ensure they beat their sales targets.
- Failure to understand the underlying patterns and the reasons for variances — Business people generally do not make enough use of the information they have in collective databases to improve the accuracy of sales forecasts. In a typical retail firm, for example, there is data on trade sales and marketing results, retail store transactions, warehouse and distribution center releases, and promotional results, all of which could span five or more years, only a portion of which is integrated into the forecasting process.
- Failure to involve senior executives in the forecasting process, while pushing responsibility to lower levels lacking the ability to work effectively with key customers — Often, senior executives have the strongest relationships with the key customers that drive most of the forecast, but they are reluctant to engage these customers in discussions that could lead to greater accuracy and benefits for both firms.

Finding solutions to these impediments and eliminating what becomes the Achilles' heel of supply chain management requires a rigorous effort to improve sales forecast accuracy. That starts with the realization that most sales forecasts are based on history, adjusted by sales predictions, and only occasionally matched with current consumption. This past information is further adjusted for current market conditions, seasonal alterations, special conditions, market changes, unforeseen events, and expected changes in buying and supplying arrangements. And recently, these factors have come under extraneous market influences that have changed much of the reliability of the inputs.

The need to integrate judgment with mathematical techniques has become a critical issue for improved performance in the area of predicting what any system should plan and produce. The reality is that forecasting consists of equal parts modeling and sound management.

Forecasting starts with asking the right people the right questions. The particular problems occur, not just around determining the direction of demand based on this input, but with the magnitude of the demand in a particular time frame. Forecasters can generally react well directionally. They tend to fail in knowing how much is needed for an adequate response, typically predicting higher sales than actual, and they tend to be slow in stemming the tide of extra inventory. One solution requires balancing forecasts by averaging multiple inputs — from sales, marketing, and operations. If housing starts are predicted correctly, that's step one. The second, crucial step is determining how many appliances or how much new carpeting will be needed. Rules-based forecasting is another technique that takes the judgment of the best experts, codifies their conclusions and uses this data to drive a mathematical model, resulting in a much more accurate forecast than one produced through data extrapolation.

FORECAST ACCURACY CAN BE IMPROVED

With a determination to overcome all of the obstacles cited, and to bring greater accuracy to the incoming data driving most planning systems, advanced supply chain firms find it is feasible to dramatically increase forecast accuracy. That effort starts with a realization that forecasting is a key component affecting information strategy across a firm and its network partners.

In Figure 5.2, we see that information flows among many components of a business, all of which are necessary for a firm to do business and all of which derive data from the forecasting process. Demand forecasting is directly linked with supply chain management and the enterprise data warehouse. It also links less directly with consumer relationship marketing, trade sales and marketing, retail operations, and the information infrastructure, but is used for virtually all planning steps and financial analysis. Within any firm, such a relationship diagram should be drawn and used to determine whether the necessary levels of accuracy are being achieved.

Figure 5.2   Forecasting Is a Key Component of Information Strategy

Without accuracy, optimization becomes a very elusive possibility. It starts with the understanding that better incoming forecasts for those customers that generate 75 to 80% of the business will drive improved decisions throughout the entire organization.

Another useful tool at the start of an effort to improve forecast accuracy is shown in Figure 5.3. The matrix is simple to establish and very beneficial in guiding implementation. It measures efforts on a scale that goes from low to high on "economic value added through higher forecast accuracy," and from low to high on "strategic imperative and competitiveness of the initiative." The elements from the previous figure can be moved to this matrix to establish the priority that should be given to the ensuing improvement plan. Improving demand forecasting generally receives the highest status but, with the rest of the array, priorities can be attached to the elements that will benefit from greater accuracy. The idea is to move the firm to a *single forecast* where the accuracy of retail sales, operations, and finance forecasting increases and more reliable figures move through the overall forecasting and planning process. Clear ownership for accuracy across these processes ensures that any change processes and revised reporting are also done with high efficiency.

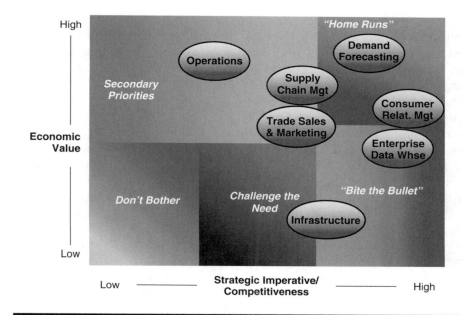

Figure 5.3 Organization Capability — Priority Setting

No effort is going to be effective and receive the support it needs without some documentation of the benefits. This axiom is especially important when pursuing forecast accuracy, as the area is surrounded by so much apathy as to the chances for significant improvement. To help assure endorsement for an improved forecasting system, the benefits of an integrated approach fall into four primary areas:

- Forecast creation and accurate maintenance means less time is spent on massaging the system, as redundant efforts are eliminated. The firm capitalizes on the entire organization's knowledge and time spent reconciling decisions based on differing forecasts from various sources will decrease dramatically.
- Executive management is facilitated as all functional decisions are aligned around a common set of demand expectations. Early warnings can be reviewed when current projections fall below the plan and the capture of new growth increases as the firm learns to stay in sync with current business conditions and activities.
- Customer service and operations benefit from a higher performance inventory that is more closely matched with actual withdrawals.
- Asset utilization improves as the need for creating unused inventories decreases and customer service gets better with inventories more accurately buffered against uncertainty in the forecast and uncertainty in the production process.

With this understanding, the firm moves to its flow charts and determines how the incoming forecast information affects processing. That means the analysis moves from forecasting to inventory planning, deployment planning, production scheduling, and purchase planning. The idea is to seek an integrated system. The flow chart must include how withdrawals are made from what is in current inventory, including work in process, material at co-packers or subassembly operations, product in transit, and materials and product on hand with suppliers and customers. In short, all of the linkages need to be identified so you can ask where it is working and where it is broken. This usually results in an understanding of where the firm begins to guess at what is needed, what to make, and what must be added to inventory to cover uncertainty.

An example from an actual firm helps illustrate these points. Figure 5.4 considers the flow of forecasting through the linkage for a large national manufacturer and retailer of a recognized consumer product. This firm worked hard to improve and integrate its forecasting and planning processes with excellent results. The system developed now reflects, with more than 80% accuracy, the demand by brand, size, and item.

In this system, the incoming forecast data flows to a demand by region, serviced by a specific shipping location, which flows to an inventory plan at each shipping location to meet predetermined service levels. The plan is further integrated to a deployment schedule at each shipping location to meet targeted deliveries. From this plan comes a signal to transportation

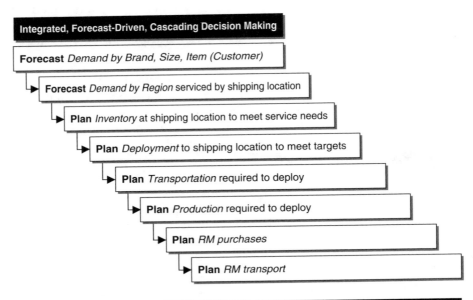

Figure 5.4   Linking Forecast Decisions to Operational Actions

on what is required to deploy, from which a signal also goes to the production plan on what's required to deploy. At the upstream side of the process, purchasing gets a signal regarding what must be procured and a plan is established for incoming transportation needs matched with receiving capacity.

Using this example as a guide, a firm can decide on the dimensions of the forecast by considering several elements:

- Geography must be settled to determine if the forecast is to be global, country-specific, regional, market, distribution center coverage, or submarket oriented.
- Customer segmentation comes under consideration to determine what categories to include: all customers, business unit customers, channels, corporate accounts, customer distribution centers, stores, demographic segment, consumer groups, and so forth.
- Product comes next as the firm looks at total sales, product attributes, product lines, color and size, items, demand type, or any other consideration having meaning to product segmentation.
- Time is an important consideration but must include granularity by year, quarter, month, week, day, or hour, depending on what the system requires. It also must include a horizon by years, months, weeks, or days, and also by events. A decision must also be made as to whether the horizon will be fixed in time or rolling to include updates from current events.
- The firm must settle on the units of measure. That means the forecast is based on consumer units, cases, equivalent cases, retail sales dollars, wholesale dollars, cost dollars, pounds, or some form of standardized sales currency.

FORECASTING IS A CIRCULAR PROCESS

An important realization in the development of improved forecasting is that it is a circular process. That is, the firm plays a proactive role in creating self-fulfilling prophecies. If forecasts based on the best available analysis fail to meet financial objectives, then product plans, advertising, and marketing programs can be instituted that have a proactive effect on future demand. In Figure 5.5, showing a forecast creation process, it can be seen that any such process begins with whatever information is available to the system — orders, point-of-sale data, and shipments, for example. From there, a demand history is maintained on a perpetual basis. Some scrubbing or adjustment can be performed based on market and customer intelligence. A variety of statistical forecasting tools are available

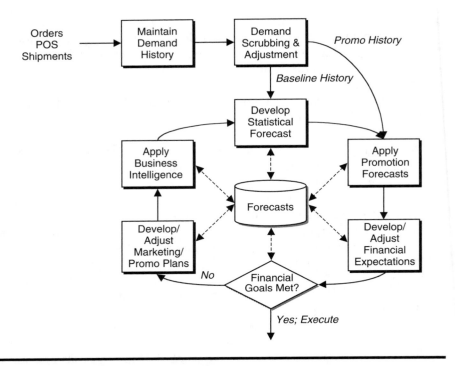

Figure 5.5 Forecast Creation — A Circular Process

in this area, from simple averaging smoothing methods and regression analysis, to Pareto analysis, frequency analysis, and econometric models.

The point to bear in mind is that forecasting should involve analyzing data and selecting tools that effectively improve accuracy at a reasonable cost. A fundamental element of any good forecast is the ability to apply business intelligence and manage uncertainty through effective use of the available information. The flow around the chart is impacted by a total organizational effort, including the need to meet financial expectations.

Figure 5.6 describes how the forecasting system for the manufacturer-retailer mentioned supports decisions across time and the various operations between the purchase of ingredients and sales to customers. A firm needs to determine the detail necessary for its processing and a similar chart developed. With this chart, the firm can track the flows and determine where forecast inaccuracy is causing problems or creating the need for excess inventory and safety stock. It can also pinpoint areas needing an improvement effort to increase overall customer satisfaction — internally and externally. Particular attention can be given to any bottlenecks or constraints in the system.

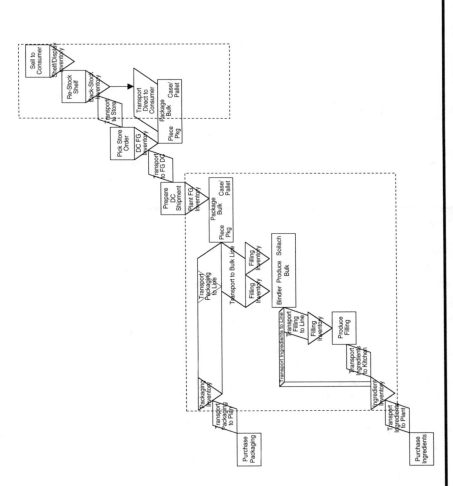

Figure 5.6 Forecasts Must Support Decisions Across Various Time Horizons and Levels of Detail Throughout the End-to-End Supply Chain

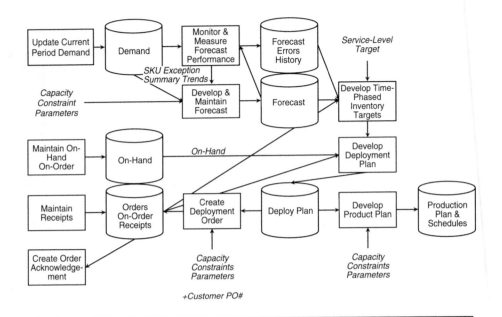

Figure 5.7 Integrating Forecasts into Operations

Next comes the issue of how the forecasts should be integrated into operations. That includes determining what level of forecast accuracy can be achieved, and what to do about the difference between what that level will introduce to the system and the desired optimized conditions. For the manufacturer-retailer, this is the point at which to decide just how high to raise forecast accuracy and what to do to allow for the difference between that level and total accuracy. Note in Figure 5.7 that demand is entered, monitored and measured for performance accuracy. Business and market intelligence enter the picture to help maintain forecast integrity. Time-phased inventory targets are made based on service-level targets. This information is then sent to the deployment plan. The entire process leads to a production plan and schedule, but at each step some form of analysis is applied to keep the resulting plan as close to actual needs as possible.

A checklist is helpful in an integrated approach to forecasting. The following elements should be included:

- Details of the organizational need for forecasting — why is it important and what can it do for us
- A common forecasting *level of details requirement*, something that receives general agreement throughout the company and does not place inappropriate demands on people

- A forecasting data model that makes sense for the business
- Definition of data, event, and decision inputs into the process
- Design for the total organizational forecasting and planning process
- Integration and leverage of information technology enabling tools — data warehouse, software from Manugistics or i2 Technologies, Excel/Lotus spreadsheets, and so forth
- Forecasting roles, responsibilities, and ownership

As the forecast becomes more accurate and is integrated into planning, inventories are managed to more closely track with actual withdrawals. The firm can then move to practices that will help develop more revenues. Vendor managed inventory (VMI) systems can be organized and integrated into the overall distribution system. That means the supplying firm takes responsibility for re-stocking its customers. These features will be discussed in subsequent chapters.

DEMAND MANAGEMENT EXTENDS THE PROCESSING

With improvements to forecasting and a reliable level of accuracy as deliverables, the firm looks next at its demand management and capacity planning systems. For any such system to work effectively, the firm must meticulously collect the necessary data from everyone who can generate valuable information about demand — internal sales representatives, customer service personnel, channel partners, distributors, customers, and consumers. This data must then be refined frequently and updated to match actual consumption and replenishment needs. Any alterations to changing consumer preferences, customer needs, buying patterns, competitive moves, and market conditions need to be part of the input to a dynamic system of analysis, direction, and response. The process is continuous and requires maintenance to keep the demand plan as close to actual consumption and replenishment needs as possible.

The idea is not to massage the forecast so participants feel better, but to increase its accuracy and to use it more effectively across the value chain. That starts by introducing an important measure — accuracy of the forecast versus actual demand. As this effort is assimilated and faithfully tracked, we find the added value of the forecasting effort increases. Michael Gilliland, director of demand management solutions for Answerthink, Inc. has introduced some worthwhile suggestions in a *Supply Chain Management Review* article to guide such an effort (Gilliland, 2002, p. 16). He discusses a format, termed forecast value added (FVA), that helps reduce the nonvalue-adding activities surrounding most forecast adjustments while bringing greater accuracy and usefulness. Additional suggestions are made in this chapter.

With increased forecast accuracy and less forecast bias as the objectives, the firm sets about considering the alternatives to accepting poor incoming information, including working closer with key customers to determine actual needs, performing deeper supply chain analysis, applying demand smoothing, and collaborating with those network partners that have useful information in their databases. In the first instance, the firm typically encounters the problem that most customers do not know much more about their current needs than the supplier. By working the data together, and analyzing trends and histories from a mutual perspective, accuracy generally climbs, often doubling. The key element, of course, is having a high degree of trust in the relationship as this information is shared.

The second key is to make the effort as active as possible. That means the partners should be less inclined to accept the customer demand pattern as sacrosanct. Demand smoothing requires the partners to look for ways to minimize the variability, or the volatility, of the accepted forecast. That requires them to separate the inherent demand variability, caused by natural consumption factors, from the artificial variability introduced by supply chain practices. Promotions, sales contests, and all of the end-of-the-period pushes contribute to unnatural variation. Encouraging demand patterns that are smoother and more reliable can lead to better accuracy and much higher efficiencies in the resulting processing. Working closely with key customers to plan the promotions and special events and maintain a flow of information on how the event is progressing by sector or retail store is one step in the right direction. With this cooperation, supply can be balanced with actual activity and inventory flow matched with consumption. This technique is now an accepted practice with such leaders as Nestlé and Sainsbury in Europe and Wal-Mart and P&G in the U.S.

THE KEY IS BALANCING DEMAND AND SUPPLY

The real purpose of this advanced collaboration is to bring a balance to *demand management* (caring for what is really needed in the supply chain) and *capacity planning* (making sure the right goods and services are available to meet the true demand). Figure 5.8 illustrates how this technique can be managed. Beginning outside the model, consumer demand becomes the key driver. What is actually needed is what should trigger the supply chain capability. This information comes from cash register entries or actual consumer purchases. Working backward from that driver, the key business customers become the first step in the process.

Demand forecasts can be generated in the usual, but preferably enhanced, manner. VMI requirements should also be considered as those doing the actual restocking record what is moving and what is still there. Replenishment information, based on actual cash register records or store-

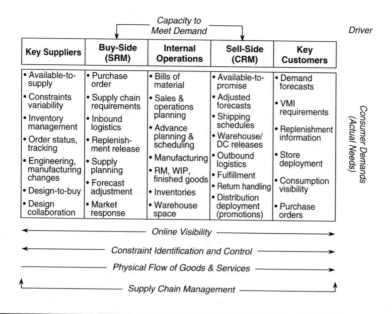

Figure 5.8   Inter-Enterprise Demand Management and Capacity Planning

planning systems, should be fed upstream. Deployment needs throughout the stores should be recorded. Any factors relating to consumption visibility that reflect what is actually occurring at the consumer level are also valid data for planning purposes. And certainly, the purchase orders reflect what the customer thinks is necessary.

Moving to the internal sector, firms must establish what capacity is needed to meet demand. That requires a strong coordination between the buy- and sell-side activities, something that is usually not done efficiently in most organizations. From the sell side, the firm compares what it said was available-to-promise with the adjusted forecasts, trying to bring closer synchronization and accuracy. Shipping schedules are reviewed to match the incoming customer data. Actual warehouse or distribution center releases are considered, as well as the outbound logistics requirements and delivery reports. Any special fulfillment needs become a factor, as does any return handling. If promotions have been involved, distribution deployment to meet those needs is another important factor.

As the firm analyzes its capacity to meet demand, it considers internal operations. Now the way that bills of material have been filled is discussed, the results of the sales and operations planning activity are considered, and advanced scheduling and planning results are reviewed to make sure out-of-balance conditions are not occurring. Adjustments are made, if necessary, to raw material, work in process, and finished goods to determine that the right amount of the right inventory is readied to meet the anticipated demand. The inventories and the warehouse space they occupy are reviewed to make sure high levels of order fill and on-time delivery will be maintained at the key customers.

Moving to the buy side, the firm reviews its purchase orders and supply chain requirements, basically to match forecast and demand against plans. Inbound logistics are considered to determine that shortages will not occur. Replenishment releases with key suppliers are adjusted where appropriate. Supply planning documents and forecasts previously sent to key suppliers are also adjusted to have a dynamic relationship with what was anticipated as demand and what is actually occurring. Marketing information, which could signal a demand change, is vital to good processing on this side of the supply chain.

In terms of the key suppliers, an analysis is made of what was received from them and matched with what they said was available. Any constraints that have entered the system or any problems that developed are considered as impacts on ability to fulfill orders. Constraint variability is fed into the network system by virtue of the partner-accepted software to identify and eliminate any current or impending bottlenecks. Order status and tracking procedures are investigated to again discover any problems before they inhibit efficient processing. In advanced relationships, the supplier provides engineering and manufacturing help and works on collaborative new designs. Inputs from all of these sectors are valuable in balancing the overall demand management and capacity planning system.

A simple procedure helps improve conditions across this system. An early step should be to form a partnership between purchasing and sales as they pursue higher forecast accuracy and try to enhance demand management. Since procuring the correct amount of raw materials at the right time is critical to meeting any forecast, it is only reasonable that the firm should begin by providing its key suppliers with better information on what will be needed. By systematically accumulating information on the sell side and sharing it on the buy side (with a few key suppliers), the firm increases the likelihood of being correct as it enters orders into planning. Visibility regarding customer requests, design activities, requests for samples, and request for information and quotations are helpful to any important supplier. Matching this data with sales histories, current market knowledge, and life cycle conditions moves both parties closer to understanding what will really occur.

TECHNOLOGY SOLUTIONS ARE AVAILABLE

Technology applications enhance the balance between supply and demand, with one caveat — there is no single cure for all the ills of inaccurate forecasts. A firm's forecasting needs are typically unique to the firm's situation, its supply base, product line, and customer base. Typically, multiple forecasting tools are necessary to cover all aspects, such as historical trend analysis, promotion planning, new product introduction, and key account planning. These tools must be assembled based on a firm's unique needs, and integrated across the planning process.

Sell-side solution packages are available from a variety of sources to help automate sales and marketing efforts. Many of these packages are also valuable in assisting demand management and capacity planning and supplier response. There has been a proliferation of software, for example, intended to consolidate supply chain requirements with demand planning and logistics needs. Later-generation software takes greater advantage of collaboration and extends what were typically point-to-point transactions to enterprise-wide solutions that enable multi-point and multi-level cooperation across a supply chain network.

Hunter Douglas, a supplier of window treatments and architectural products in Europe, is applying such collaboration. In the first stage of its effort, the firm enters historical shipping and inventory data into a forecast engine to create a demand plan across its full enterprise. This data is refined and finalized as various internal departments collaborate to make the forecast more accurate. In the second stage, the firm collaborates with key customers. "If we can involve our customers, we will get more up-front sales commitments from them, and we'll make sure that the inventory they need is available," says Michael Tonino, director of European Logistics for Hunter Douglas. Sharing that information with key suppliers brings greater reliability to the overall effort. "If there are supply problems," Tonino adds, "we'll have more objective discussions about what's happening and why" (Forger, 2001, p. 91).

Most suppliers are very aware of their role and the contribution they can make to better demand planning. The problem is that they are seldom consulted. The software that will emerge as the dominant enabler in this area is classified under the term *demand-chain management*, and that revolves around how well a firm manages its channel relations on both the upstream and downstream side. It requires uniting sales and supply chain information with demand planning and customer replenishment. This, in turn, requires analyzing the data generated on everything from initial forecast to actual shipments and returns and warranty to improve what is happening.

Lincoln Electric Company in Cleveland, Ohio, applies its demand planning tools as a means to get its salesforce to "spend more time working with end customers — showing them how to operate the company's welding products — and less time checking the status of orders." E-business manager Jim Appledorn estimates the company's system will let its 180 sales representatives spend 10% more time on meaningful customer relations. This could result in a 5% increase in annual revenue. "We can take those highly trained technicians and have them focus on technical relationships rather than answer simple questions, which now can be handled on the Web," Appledorn adds (Gonsalves, 2001, p. 51).

Some firms, disappointed with the results of their forecasting system, turn to Web-enabled systems. Gulistan Carpets Inc. did so when it moved away from its traditional system of manually reviewing past orders received from dealers and using that information to determine manufacturing schedules. In 2001, Gulistan installed Demantra Limited's Demand Planner at its Aberdeen, North Carolina headquarters, integrating this application with an existing Oracle8i database. Demand planner uses "a proprietary forecasting algorithm to analyze sales data, factoring in quantity, seasonality, and the purchaser's geographic location" (Moozakis, 2002, p. 1).

Gulistan's dealers electronically input their sales data to the headquarters' order management department where it then goes into an ERP system. The information then flows automatically to Demand Planner. Accurate forecasts are then created, based on actual retailer sales. With the new system, the firm has been able to reduce inventories by more than 30%, while forecast errors have been cut in half. According to Richard Witt, vice president of materials management, "Demand Planner has enabled Gulistan to align production throughout its three plants with demand, thereby replacing traditional manufacturing with a leaner production system" (Moozakis, 2002, p. 2).

ACCURATE CAPACITY PLANNING COMPLETES THE LOOP

As the interaction between demand management and capacity planning is better understood, and techniques are in place to tap all valuable data inputs, the firm and its partners set about to match capacity with better knowledge of what is really in demand. Figure 5.9 illustrates such processing. Beginning with the input from the stores, catalog sales, Internet purchases, or telephone and fax orders, the consumption data triggers the required response. This demand is fed first into the business customer's database to determine store and replenishment center availability. That means store sales and consumer orders are matched with the forecasted demand and any necessary adjustments are made.

Before sending another demand signal upstream, retailers answer the questions: Do we have enough current capacity to receive and store supplier deliveries or are there current receiving constraints? Do we have enough storage space to hold any increased inventories? Safety stocks are

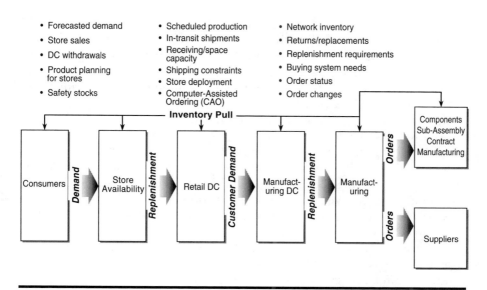

Figure 5.9   Matching Capacity with Consumer Demand

analyzed to make certain they are still synchronized with the actual pull out of store supply. Product planning for the stores should be reviewed and revised for any noticeable change in demand pattern. The basic idea in this area is to determine that there are no capacity constraints affecting the efficient deployment and delivery of goods to the stores needing replenishment based on the consumption data.

As the store stocks are drawn down, a replenishment signal is sent to the appropriate retail or manufacturing distribution center. Here the scheduled production is viewed against actual withdrawal needs. Any in-transit shipments are factored into the analysis, so excess stocks are not dispatched. Receiving capacity at the stores is matched with the most economical shipping quantity and multiple store deployments are considered to optimize the delivery space in the truck or other carrier. Any other shipping constraints, especially related to having the correct number of trucks available at the right time, are considered before dispatching the vehicle to the stores. In some advanced systems, computer-aided ordering (CAO) systems are used to match store needs with distribution and manufacturing capacity and place accurate orders. Once again, the basic idea is to match demand and capacity at every key link in the network.

On the manufacturing side of the picture, the replenishment signal is now forwarded to the appropriate manufacturing site. Inventory in the network should be online and analyzed to determine what needs to be produced in addition to what is available in the system to meet the incoming demand signal and satisfy actual replenishment needs. The manufacturer answers questions such as: Do we have sufficient capacity to meet the incoming signals? Do we have enough space to put away any inventories, especially for large promotional demands requiring product storage? Do we have enough delivery equipment to get the products back to the retail DC or stores in time to meet demand?

Any returns or necessary replacements should be added or subtracted from the demand. If there are any buying system requirements, such as minimum order quantities or lead-time factors, they should be considered before making changes to planning and scheduling. Status of orders and any changes to blanket orders should be processed at this time. Finally, new orders or adjustments to orders are sent to suppliers and subassembly manufacturers or contract partners.

A particularly strong tool to apply at the manufacturing node in a supply chain is called time-phased planning. Andre Martin and Daryl Landvater offer especially good advice in this area (Martin, 2001). These planning veterans have moved from MRP and MRP II to distribution resource planning (DRP) and beyond as they have helped innumerable firms come to grips with how to match demand with capacity in an effective manner.

As indicated, any special event planning should be done across the end-to-end network, as well as coordinating any changes with the financial planning system affecting all constituents. Credits, consignments, payment terms, and invoicing are checked against actual transactions and shipments. In this way, an accurate accounting of what is taking place occurs, and all firms get a better handle on the economic impact of any significant changes. Throughout the processing, lead times are studied to make certain there are no undue constraints entering the system that create a disadvantage for the customer or end consumer.

SUMMARY

An effective supply chain effort moves from the early savings made in sourcing and logistics to improving inventory management, planning, and scheduling. The accuracy of the sales forecast, and the proper handling or mishandling of market data and information on actual consumption, dramatically affect these process steps. While most firms suffer from low levels of forecast accuracy and often fail to take advantage of what is known about demand and supply, improvements can be made. By applying the models described, forecast accuracy can be increased to 70 or 80%, and beyond for advanced firms. With better incoming data, all of the subsequent process steps improve. Then the firm can move to balance demand management with capacity capabilities by taking advantage of shared market and production information with selected business partners. Numerous techniques have been reviewed to help at each step in this overall processing, all of which require bringing greater rigor to an often misunderstood and maligned effort.

6

MODELS FOR ORDER MANAGEMENT AND INVENTORY MANAGEMENT

Every business firm is looking for ways to increase the number of incoming orders, but not all have spent the time and effort necessary to make the processes of order entry and order management more efficient and effective. Although customer orders drive what happens across a business supply chain, they tend not to receive the kind of attention afforded to other supply chain management (SCM) functions, particularly sourcing, logistics, forecasting, and inventory control. The concept of customer order management (COM) as an important function of supply chain management remains elusive and is generally given second-priority attention. This is a mistake as attention to COM and the related issue of inventory management will have a high business payback.

Included in the contemporary concept of supply chain order management are the process steps of error-free order entry, credit management, order processing, pricing, available-to-promise, tracking fulfillment, billing, invoicing, accounting, and accounts receivable processing. When the orientation of these steps is toward achieving greater customer satisfaction, as well as profit improvement, the idea of customer order management emerges. Those who then pursue improvement to COM find the mundane but critical tasks included in the concept have a much greater impact on customer satisfaction and financial results than most firms realize, often adding or deleting two to three points of profit from a P&L statement. Unfortunately, many companies simply do not have a solid handle on their order management processing or the inherent costs.

The output of good COM processing reduces the costs of cleaning and resolving mistakes, doing reconciliation, having to expedite orders, making reshipments, and providing emergency deliveries, while creating a much happier customer and a reasonable funds transfer system without excessive days outstanding waiting on payments. Leading systems also include pricing mechanisms that assure the setting of price levels commensurate with customer status and market conditions without unwarranted discounts. Under best-case conditions, the processing occurs in a *lights-out* environment (i.e., with automated credit checking preapproved for key accounts and no human intervention and review) unless the system indicates an alert. A successful system is also an asset for planning and scheduling and a source of valuable information for a customer relationship management (CRM) system. Simply put, most functions within an extended enterprise either improve or suffer as a direct result of the efficiency of COM. In this chapter, we consider the process steps involved in COM and present models that lead to more effective order management. The best practice metric under these models becomes the perfect order — complete in every important aspect and leading to the highest fill rates, on-time delivery, no damage, and so forth. We also consider how effective COM can positively impact other functions and especially improve inventory management.

Rob Guzak and Steve Simco, who are CSC partners and order-management specialists, developed this chapter.

THE PROBLEM STARTS WITH A POOR UNDERSTANDING OF ORDER PROCESSING

The difficulty with order management begins with the general weak understanding of and attention given to an aspect of business that has a direct impact on what occurs across an extended enterprise. It continues with the poor realization of the inherent costs and overall effect on the organization and its business partners. When we surveyed a large number of firms, for example, to determine what they thought the cost of processing an order might be, we received answers that varied from a low of $30 to $50 per order to a high of $250 to $300. More disappointingly, over half of the sample did not know what that cost might be or failed to have any tangible basis for making an estimate. Some appeared unconcerned about the cost as they told us any savings would be spurious. They believed that, if the processing could be improved, there would be no real reduction in the number of people involved and, therefore, there would be no tangible savings. When we pursued the issue to discuss the number of errors occurring in the orders, there was a similar opinion that it was not generally a problem.

As we continued to discuss how these orders were eventually tabulated and transferred into planning and scheduling, the responses indicated a great use of ad hoc communications, manual operations, much changing, and generally weak systems trying to support lean and effective manufacturing. Most systems were characterized by heuristic processing based on gut instinct as opposed to automated systems responding to reliable and concrete fulfillment needs. These are not the traits of an advanced supply chain management operation.

The first step in establishing the cost and opportunity of COM is to organize a central order database from which to extract and assess pertinent information on the actions and costs associated with entering and processing orders, tracking order progress, and delivering valuable insights to the rest of the network. This database should be an integral part of any intra-enterprise communication system. This process step also requires the defining of each action taken in COM. Next, you need to accumulate the relevant cost elements related to how the orders are received and processed, including transfer to planning, fulfillment, tracking, invoicing, and accounting with some form of a scorecard to evaluate performance. With this data in hand, the firm is positioned to improve its processing while establishing the objectives of gaining better customer satisfaction and lowering costs. From our research, we find that those firms consistently placing emphasis on good order management are among the leaders in advanced supply chain management (ASCM) and show the highest customer retention rates.

The next step is to move the order system to a higher level of accuracy and automation by taking advantage of cyber technology. In spite of the advances made in e-commerce and digital communications, our research indicates most firms today still enter the majority of orders by telephone and facsimile machines. A small percentage of mail orders also continues to be a part of the processing. EDI transmissions probably amount to no more than a third, at best, of order entry and have been limited because of the cost incurred by small- and mid-size firms. The amount of e-commerce ordering is less than 10% of the total and tends to be most prevalent in high-technology industries. While there are exceptions, a rough alignment for a typical order entry system would be: mail, phone, or fax, 60%; EDI, 20%; e-mail, 15%; and e-commerce, 5% — where e-commerce is an online system that transfers orders directly into planning.

The problem with these systems and their dependence on manual processing from telephone or fax entries starts with the errors in the incoming orders. Having conducted many tests with a variety of business firms where we analyzed the accuracy of orders for a 60- to 90-day period, we consistently found that up to 40% of the orders contained one or more mistakes. These errors included the wrong customer name, location, quantity, specification, date, or packaging details. More importantly, most of the errors were in pricing and terms, detracting directly from company profits. The problem continued as we tracked how the day proceeded and found the mistakes exacerbated when there were multiple transfers of the data. As manual processing continued and fatigue became a factor, the number of mistakes increased. It generally resulted in a very weak system that required much reconciliation, expediting, and problem solving to get things right. That is a large, hidden cost endemic in most supply chain systems. Working with one large consumer goods firm, where an automated system virtually eliminated all errors in order entry and the processing was automated with correct pricing and terms, an additional 1.5% of profit accrued.

DETERMINING THE ELEMENTS OF GOOD COM BRINGS PROPER ORIENTATION

In order to establish an effective COM system, the firm is advised to begin with a determination of what a good system will provide. The questions needing to be answered include:

- Can the firm, through its order management processing, respond quickly and accurately in a manner acceptable to its best customers? Are there any measurements that validate high performance with the system?
- Will the customer receive a good response, regardless of the channel through which the order was received — sales representative, telephone or fax contact, EDI, Web-based ordering, or store purchase?
- Is there credibility in the promises being made? Do false expectations get entered before processing begins? Are tools available to determine an accurate and reliable commitment is being made?
- How many errors and mistakes exist in the current system? How much time is spent cleansing these problems and reconciling them within the organization and with customers?
- Is the cost to accept and fill an order documented? If the costs are reduced through automation or e-commerce, will the savings be real or will the process simply be improved?
- Is there a profit in each and every order? Are there parameters to determine how to link pricing to customers and orders?

For the companies in the lead in this area of SCM, COM has become a mission-critical function as they discovered that answering the questions in a positive manner led to more orders with higher profits and better-satisfied customers. As they further realized through analysis and improvement efforts how COM touches most other functions in the business and affects the ability to perform at optimum levels, the order management role began to receive the attention it deserved. The ability to better manage orders and inventories, both internally and externally, to achieve greater cost-effectiveness and provide data that assists in creating real-time visibility across the enterprise network were among the rewards.

AN ACTION PLAN GUIDES GOOD CUSTOMER ORDER MANAGEMENT

Order entry and order management are functions that truly impact everything that follows in a supply chain system. For that reason, it is imperative that proper attention be paid to all process steps and the output from the effort is integrated across the end-to-end supply chain. Figure 6.1 is a worksheet that can be used to determine a firm's current position with respect to the linked process steps to define the required procedure to achieve high performance and decide on the priority that should be assigned to each of those steps. A firm should prepare such a worksheet, listing the key process steps in its customer order management system, and then conduct an analysis to determine where improvements can be made.

Each of the *principles* on the worksheet should be considered as an effective step in the processing, beginning with whatever technique is used to configure orders. It progresses with quotation systems that optimize the ordering process, allowing for order entry through alternative channels. It must include how the output of the system is used as a key input to forecasting and scheduling. As the order-to-receipt-of-payment processing is identified, the worksheet proceeds to integrate those functions, making certain regulatory requirements are met. Since customer satisfaction is of paramount importance, the process continues into improving accuracy and shortening cycle times. As the figure shows, the steps continue through the front- and back-office functions and culminate with integration across the supply chain. It may or may not end with training to assure success, depending on what management believes are the post-sale activities that should be included, such as handling returns, issuing credits, and so forth.

The *key learnings* are based on an analysis of high-performing companies and the steps taken to achieve above-average conditions. The columns left blank are to be completed by an analysis team working with the members of the order processing group, beginning with the *current position*. The idea is to complete a reasonably good listing of the as-is conditions, with particular emphasis on where the system is weak, where the points of pain occur, and where a better technique would yield better results. The *next steps* portion is where the team establishes the basis for an improvement plan by listing steps that will lead to an improved condition. The *priority* establishes the sequence of the improvement steps and should have assigned responsibilities and a timetable for implementation. This worksheet should then be used as a checklist as the firm proceeds to improve its order management systems and methodology.

Principle	Key Learnings	Current Position	Next Steps	Priority
Employ Configuration Tools	• Use configuration tools that provide a seamless user interface • Select configuration tools designed to meet the specific challenges posed by your company's business processes • Employ standardized question sets to improve the order entry process • Combine order configuration and back-office applications to respond more quickly and effectively to customer requests • Identify point solutions that can be integrated into existing systems to minimize expenses			
Incorporate Quote Optimization and Point-of-Sale Support	• Employ electronic quote system that integrates the quote process with the order entry process • Improve sales performance by increasing the sales team's ability to configure and price new or complex products • Enable sales people to perform complex pricing calculations in the field • Incorporate product visualization tools to enhance the selling process			
Develop Alternative Order Entry Channels	• Provide alternative channels for order entry to reach a wider customer base • Create global order entry stations to allow customers to place orders around the clock • Deploy Internet-based order entry technologies that allow for configuration checks and supplier links • Consider scanning technology for an easy, low-cost order entry alternative			
Utilize the Order Entry System for Scheduling and Forecasting	• Integrate production planning and order entry systems to provide accurate scheduling information • Employ real-time, Internet-based order entry programs that allow configuration, constraint verification and production scheduling • Align the order entry system with customer service and forecasting to ensure customers receive optimal service • Enter orders into a relational database to improve forecasting systems			

Figure 6.1 Order Management Action-Planning Worksheet

Principle	Key Learnings	Current Position	Next Steps	Priority
Integrate Order Processing Functions	• Employ systems that tightly integrate each step of the order-to-receipt process • Link service order reports, processing and invoicing to reduce cycle time • Tie sales, support and service into one system to maximize customer value			
Deploy Systems to Fulfill Regulatory Requirements	• Employ software that automates the documentation and foreign regulatory process			
Improve Scheduling Accuracy and Cycle Time	• Drive customer loyalty by accurately anticipating order delivery dates • Build on supply chain and vendor scheduling technologies to improve delivery time quotations and performance			
Streamline Finance and Credit Approvals	• Employ order processing systems that include credit verifications, accounting, and other financial capabilities • Deploy systems to bridge currency and language differences • Streamline the purchasing approval process to improve speed of transactions • Employ an order entry system which automates the customer credit check • Use rule-based processes to improve the accuracy and consistency of credit management • Streamline processing and billing to enhance competitive position			
Manage Workflow to Drive Improvement	• Employ or design solutions to streamline and direct processes • Employ messaging systems to link internal and external customers • Use groupware solutions to improve workflow and internal communications			
Integrate the Supply Chain	• Catalog and maintain supplier information on a real-time basis to improve the quality of purchasing decisions • Employ pre-negotiated agreements with suppliers to improve outsourcing performance • Streamline the payment process to free resources and reduce costs			
Employ Integrated Technology Solutions	• Integrate technology solutions across the supply chain for maximum return on investment			

Figure 6.1 (continued) Order Management Action-Planning Worksheet

Principle	Key Learnings	Current Position	Next Steps	Priority
	• Develop a technology infrastructure that supports seamless outsourcing			
	• Practice integrated order fulfillment to streamline the "virtual enterprise"			
	• Employ Electronic Data Interchange (EDI) systems to improve supply chain management			
	• Work closely with suppliers and customers to promote EDI implementation along the entire supply chain			
	• Identify and hold to standards when selecting EDI vendors and applications			
	• Use the Internet and intranets to link suppliers and manufacturing facilities			
	• Employ security measures to improve the reliability of Internet commerce			
	• Employ a Wide Area Network (WAN) to provide a dedicated, secure communication link			
	• Enable electronic purchasing to reduce costs and ensure accuracy			
	• Employ MRPII to streamline the processing of customer orders			
Link Front-and Back-Office	• Tie back office and customer support systems together to deliver integrated services			
	• Link installation and assembly with other systems to enhance control			
Plan for Successful Implementation	• Carefully detail the hidden costs of implementation beyond hardware and software purchases			
	• Design implementation schedules to provide an orderly transition to new systems			
	• Carefully evaluate potential vendors and system integrators to ensure a correct "fit"			
Train for Success	• Take a collaborative, team-based approach to ensure system implementation proceeds smoothly			
	• Set realistic expectations for training requirements to avoid surprises			
	• Select software vendors with a proven commitment to providing user support			
	• Train "super users" within the company to ensure continuity of expertise once the consulting engagement is over			
	• Employ dedicated support staff and trainers for new order entry systems			
	• Anticipate and train to minimize the fear of change			

Figure 6.1 (continued) Order Management Action-Planning Worksheet

CUSTOMER ORDER MANAGEMENT SOLVES MANY OF THE BUSINESS PROBLEMS

As the firm proceeds through its order processing analysis, it generally finds that providing delivery through multiple distribution channels can make order promises, order tracking, and fulfillment a complex, confusing, and labor-intensive issue. With orders coming in by telephone, fax, EDI, e-mail, and the Internet, and being received by different parts of the firm and at different locations, providing a customer with solid information is often an elusive process. Moreover, if orders and commitments are not properly balanced against the company's forecasting and replenishment activities, serious problems in meeting actual demand occur.

Today, a business firm needs to be prepared to make decisions on a real-time basis while managing and controlling multiple tasks linked in a continuous process. The end result of this processing must be to satisfy a typically diverse customer base including individuals and firms that often have little understanding of the actual needs and circumstances surrounding current activities. Many are also reacting to short-term imperatives brought on by unexpected market conditions. These factors drive the need for order management control in an environment characterized by changes in the selling process, greater customer expectations, and a demand for ever-shorter cycle times. The historical order processing systems have evolved into something much more complex that requires taking incoming data from many sources, managing thousands of purchase documents, and dealing with multiple supply chain partners in order to achieve efficient results.

Most large-scale firms with many recognized brands, many separate and nearly autonomous business units, and many channels of delivery, have accumulated large databases with enormous amounts of data. The task is to sort through these multiple systems, deal with the inherent inconsistencies, and aggregate the critical information in a usable fashion. Then the data needed by various supply chain constituents can be shared electronically. This task can best be accomplished with an effective order-management control system, the elements of which are described in Figure 6.2.

Order management control begins by establishing one methodology for handling the order-entry channel. In today's environment, where a firm is expected to have multiple options, these orders must be received in an error-free manner, whether they come by telephone, mail, fax, or some form of electronic entry. The system established for this step must be studied and moved as close to full automation as possible. In any event, the number of errors should be determined, the root causes of the errors analyzed and resolved, and a fail-safe system installed to spot these

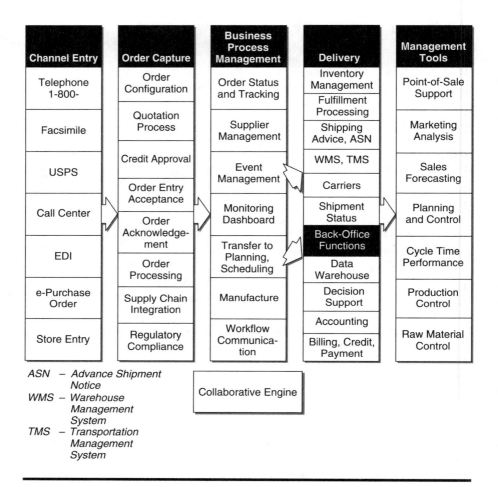

Figure 6.2 Elements of Order Management Control

errors and remove them before the orders move forward. In addition, any customer service representative tracking any progress or problems will need access to the order history. Questions regarding order location, expected delivery date, and changing orders require access to data on a real-time basis. Regardless of the type or point of channel entry, the system must be put online.

The next segment is order capture. Once the method for order receipt is established, the firm has to clearly set up how the order will be configured to meet all downstream requirements and regulations. The quotation process has to be equally clear as our research shows a lot of profit can be lost in poorly designed systems. This process should be reviewed at least quarterly to determine that all parameters are current and are being observed as orders get priced. Credit approval is generally handled as a matter of course in this segment, but again must stay in compliance with predetermined decision rules.

Order entry acceptance comes next, as the system determines all factors are within acceptable parameters and the order can be entered. An acknowledgement is sent when required, preferably electronically and only when requested by the customer. Details from this step then proceed to order processing and other functions needing data on the current level of orders. Certainly, this data is important to the supply chain integration intended with the planning and scheduling process steps. A check should be built into the system to make certain all pertinent regulatory conditions are being met.

Business process management is the next area of good order management control as the firm now provides a system to observe and track order status through the supply chain network. The idea is to create a thread of knowledge following order processing. Supplier management enters the picture in that bills of material must be completed, critical supplies must be on hand, and any replenishment needs are communicated in time to make efficient delivery possible. Where event management is a factor in the business, another signal must be sent from the incoming orders to those constituents needing advance notice. In short, a monitoring dashboard has become a feature of advanced supply chain systems, providing online access to important data on order progress. Users are then able to monitor the order management processing, track any problems, automatically manage necessary exceptions, and take the required corrective action. Planned and *blanket* orders from key customers can also be set up for better management and control.

The information that is transferred to planning and scheduling can also be useful to other parts of the organization — sales, marketing, accounting — and provision should be made for rapid and accurate transfer of this data. The orders then proceed into manufacturing and a workflow communication system is set in place so those observers needing information can access it through the company's intranet. Note that a collaboration engine should also be added to the system so external parties needing updates and actual processing information can find what the firm determines is accessible to them.

Now the flow moves in two directions. In the first instance, it moves to delivery of the finished products or services. Fulfillment processing takes place in accordance with the delivery channel set up by the customer. Shipping advice should be available and an advance shipping notice (ASN) sent to the customer at the appropriate time, advising of the proposed delivery schedule. This data should also flow to the warehouse management system (WMS) and transportation management system (TMS) set up by the firm to handle post-manufacturing operations. The idea is to integrate the front-end information — on purchase orders, call center data, and such — with back-end solutions, including enterprise resource planning (ERP), CRM, WMS and TMS, coping with any legacy systems being used. The carriers selected for the actual shipments will need advice on what is coming from manufacturing, but they also benefit from knowing what is in the order-processing stream. At all times, shipment status should be available to answer the inevitable requests for status from customers.

The second flow is to the back-office functions where the data warehouse is replenished with current order information. Decision support needs are met here, as authorized parties can access what is happening and react to any unusual pattern changes. Accounting picks up what is needed to make sure that billing, credit, and payment requirements are met within established parameters.

The final movement is to the area of management tools where control is really exercised. Here, point-of-sale support can be initiated to help with unusual customer requirements — shortfalls in capacity, current or expected bottlenecks, or any other problem that needs special attention. Marketing needs the data to analyze and compare with plans established many months before. Adjustments can be made, promotions planned, or changes made to products in development. Sales forecasting should also be adjusted based on what is actually occurring at the front end of the system versus what was expected. Planning and control must be made aware of current order status, particularly to track and anticipate any surges or shortfalls that will impact capacity requirements.

From a broader perspective, if cycle times become an issue, the need to match performance with promises is considered to make certain customers will be satisfied by getting their orders completed in the time frame set up before order entry. A caveat is in order here. Our research has shown overwhelmingly that it is less important, in most business situations, to promise extremely short cycle times than it is to make reliable commitments. While 24 hours or less seems to be a goal for many delivery cycles, getting the goods within 72 hours with 100% accuracy can be very acceptable to most customers and their planning systems. The problem always occurs when the goods are not at the point of need at the time promised and the customer must take alternative action.

Production control enters the picture, as any dramatic changes to what was expected must be viewed as early as possible without requiring a large chain reaction effect when schedules are altered. Finally, the information must be relayed to those responsible for making sure the correct amount of the right raw materials are flowing into the system to meet downstream manufacturing and delivery needs.

Packaged software applications are available to cover many parts of this control system. Firms interested in having an effective order management control system should evaluate these solutions and decide on an architecture that ensures adequate end-to-end control while providing a level of flexibility that matches its current market conditions. Any system selected must also resolve all of the problems cited in the earlier part of this chapter. Any comprehensive order management control system will have an order engine that supports the end-to-end business processes that need accommodating. Complete processing requires easy management of the order complexity across the various types of orders, customer variances, and difficulties encountered from unforeseen events. Done effectively, the orders move smoothly from process to process and any constituent needing accurate data on progress will find it quickly. Only a unified data model will aggregate this information into a single database.

Supporting this database will be a common definition of how the information is to be arranged and defined across the enterprise. A robust order management control system, moreover, includes an integration framework that facilitates order information exchange across the extended enterprise. An integration layer also supports monitoring what happens in the system. This integration framework will be in compliance with industry standards and support multiple protocols and file formats. Business process management (BPM) techniques become especially useful in this area to institute the required visibility of the threads of information. Order management control ultimately means the necessary tools are in place to seamlessly automate the previous manual operations, eliminate inherent errors and mistakes, and minimize call center complaints and customer order problems while better aligning payment and invoice processing.

DuPont offers an example of a successfully automated process. Two years ago, the Performance Coating business unit, a $3.8 billion automotive paint supplier, embraced an e-commerce order management system based on its existing SAP-developed ERP system. Essentially, they began by converting a static catalog into an attractive and easy-to-use means of interaction between the business and its paint distributors. Using software from Comergent Technologies as its order portal, the firm also had Bowstreet, Inc. "automate and assemble a business-to-business portal that could be customized so distributors using Web services would have a personalized experience" (Colkin, 2001, p. 1).

Since the portals were launched, distributors have been able to log on and access information on their accounts, place and change orders, and check an order status, all of which is integrated to the back-office ERP system. Customers have two choices for order entry. They can access DuPont's Order Management System, a private marketplace, to shop via the catalog. Their orders are converted to a cXML message and forwarded to the SAP system via middleware that handles the exchange between the cXML and SAP formats. They can also enter an order into the proprietary point-of-sale system, where the order is converted to cXML and sent via the Internet to DuPont to be received by Commerce Manager. DuPont is pleased with the results and is now looking to tighten relationships with its distributors' customers — the body shops that actually buy and use the paint. That means, "offering online access to safety manuals and instructions on paint use" (Colkin, 2001, p. 2).

PRICING IS A SPECIAL PROBLEM

Absent from the model illustrated in Figure 6.2 is the process step of pricing. While it is subsumed under the quotation process, it deserves special attention, as it can be the difference between profit and loss. Manugistics has a software package, Profitable Order Management (POM), that provides quotations to customers while capturing the orders and including time-phased product availability information and optimal pricing. If a quotation is for a customer or product for which there is no existing agreement, the price is determined by balancing potential profit from winning the order with the probability of winning the order.

Pricing optimization algorithms produce quotes and pricing that are optimized to win desired business and generate price lists that are optimized while meeting contract obligations. For standard price list products, POM can create and update optimal prices for thousands of products for multiple channels and market segments reflecting the company's goals and factors in a changing market. The software also allocates inventory and production capacity while automating workflow across the entire order management system. The system consolidates orders into a single interface for submission, tracking, routing, fulfillment, and status inquiry.

i2 Technologies offers a similar package through its Order Management program. Theirs is a service-based architecture designed to leverage existing infrastructure while better enabling operability. It offers a capability to quote, capture orders, manage orders, provide online visibility of order status, and fulfill orders across multiple channels and business units. A key feature is the ability to synchronize many back-office transactions in a matter of hours.

The framework is also designed to meet the needs of a distributed order management solution through these features:

■ Capturing and managing orders across multiple interaction channels — making reliable promises and keeping commitments

- Managing and fulfilling orders across multiple enterprises — coordinating and ensuring delivery and execution across multiple companies and systems
- Deploying through a service-based architecture — freeing organizations to operate at a pace suitable to capability while meeting service requirements

INVENTORY MANAGEMENT IS ENHANCED WITH BETTER ORDER MANAGEMENT CONTROL

With the fundamentals for efficient order management in place, the firm is now prepared to consider how to use this tool for more effective inventory management. The full scope of such an effort requires the thorough review, analysis, and establishment of control procedures, most of which is not within the scope of this study. What we will consider is how the impact of better order knowledge and an effective COM system can be factors in better inventory management.

Contemporary thinking schools that this management begins with a classification of the inventory needed to support the orders, not just by category or value of the goods, including the risks and potential returns on the inventory. Inventory management is a process step basically oriented around decisions on when goods should be available, in what specification, and in what quantity. The return on holding goods in inventory becomes a function of the sales volume eventually derived and the profit margin received, allowing for the cost of carrying the inventory. The risk is a function of carrying too little or too much stock, which can result in back orders, emergency shipments, lost sales, and price discounts. Under best-case conditions, where the demand is well known, these costs are minimal. Under conditions of uncertainty, they can be the difference between profit and loss for small-margin businesses.

With such a view of risk and return, a company can make better decisions and use its COM to track results from beginning to end. Apple Computer, for example, made some bold moves when Steve Jobs returned to a floundering company and introduced the iMac. At the same time, the firm established an array of supply chain initiatives aimed at better managing product demand, inventory investment, channel distribution, and supply chain relationships. In the area of inventory management, Apple reduced its product line by almost half, began forecasting sales on a weekly basis (instead of monthly) with daily adjustments sent to production, and requested suppliers to manage inventory for standard parts and components. "Apple also formalized a partnership with a supplier to build components close to its facilities with just-in-time (JIT) delivery, created a direct-ship distribution network through the Web, and simplified its finished goods distribution channel" (Trent, 2002, p. 28). The firm now operates with six days of inventory, compared with the previous 23 days. Turns have gone from 10 to 180 and gross profit margins have increased almost 40% in two years.

Robert J. Trent, Professor at Lehigh University, has presented a very useful model to help any firm view and manage its inventory. According to Trent, "Companies that are serious about managing inventory must visualize how their practices and approaches will affect the three Vs of inventory management — volume, velocity, and value of inventory." Figure 6.3 describes his model, including key objectives, measures, and examples of activities, that relate to each dimension (Trent, 2002, p. 30).

Per Trent, volume relates to the amount of inventory a company owns at any time and key indicators will relate to total units on hand, including safety stock levels. Velocity refers to how quickly raw material and work-in-process inventory is transformed into finished goods that are accepted

Volume pertains to the amount of physical inventory a company owns at any given time across the supply chain

Key Question: How much and what types of inventory do we own?

Key Measures: Total units, total pounds

Activities Affecting Volume: Improved forecasting techniques, supplier-provided consignment inventory

Value pertains to the unit cost and total dollar value of inventory

Key Question: What is the unit cost and total value of the different types of inventory we own?

Key Measures: Total dollars, period-by-period unit value changes, ratio of sales to working capital

Activities Affecting Volume: Product simplification and standardization, leverage purchase agreements

Velocity pertains to how quickly raw material and WIP become finished goods that are accepted and paid for by the customer

Key Question: How fast do we move inventory toward the customer?

Key Measures: Inventory turns, material throughput rates, order-to-cash cycle time

Activities Affecting Velocity: Lean supply chain practices; make-to-order production

Working Capital Reduction	Increased Profitability	Increased Customer Satisfaction	Improved Asset Return
Performance Results			

Figure 6.3 Three Vs Model of Inventory Management (From Trent, R.J., *Supply Chain Management Review,* 2002 With Permission)

and paid for by the customer. Under his conditions, as the rate of inventory movement from suppliers through operations to customers increases, the average amount of inventory being held is reduced. Higher velocity then results in a lower commitment to working capital and improves cash flow. His key measures of results are material throughput rates, inventory turns, and order-to-cash cycle time. Value becomes the cost of the inventory, with key measures being standard costs and the total value of the inventory. Organizations, to be effective, must pursue activities that positively influence all three factors.

Beyond these parameters, the firm must diligently work at keeping track of its inventory, particularly as it ages. Our research is full of examples where inventory was carried well beyond its prime and ended up not being related to current order management needs. The subsequent write-offs were often delayed as long as possible, but inevitably resulted in periods of very poor performance and, occasionally, some career adjustments. With the models and systems described, a firm will be much better prepared to match orders with inventory needs and keep the system online and prime.

SUMMARY

Order entry and order management are not the highest priority issues in most supply chain efforts, but they deserve sufficient attention to assure problems are not created across the enterprise and for the firm's partners because of shortcomings. In this chapter, we considered some of the fundamentals for getting this task done correctly and more effectively. The end result is a much better flow of crucial information that creates a thread of connection across the extended enterprise and results in better customer satisfaction. The returns to the firm include lower costs, better pricing, and an online system to view just what is happening in the network. Another valuable assist occurs for all downstream functions, including better back-office applications, by virtue of the ability to access reliable information that affects the holding and delivery of inventories.

7

MODELS FOR SALES AND OPERATIONS PLANNING

In most supply chain efforts, the need to cope with how orders are received and passed into the planning process and on to manufacturing or production was dealt with early in the improvement process. In most instances, the participants found there was an absence of solid methodology for accomplishing this task in an efficient manner. Although data was passed forward, there were always questions concerning the accuracy of the demand figures, the confidence in the inventory data, the reliability of production schedules, and so forth. Then sales and operations planning (S&OP) entered the picture and became a staple of supply chain efforts beginning in the early 1990s. With maturity of the supply chain efforts, many firms have made strides in this area while others have gone well beyond this type of effort. As a result, most organizations have progressed to a form of advanced planning and scheduling (APS), which will be explained in the next chapter.

Nevertheless, some of the old complications linger, and certainly the concepts of forecasting and planning in isolation are still alive and well in some organizations. In this chapter, we will consider a bit of the history leading to S&OP and the models that have emerged. We will also describe this tool as it is being used in most supply chain efforts today, generally as a precursor to an enterprise-wide resource planning (ERP) system. Particular thanks for assistance with this chapter go to Brad Barton and Steve Simco, partners at CSC Consulting, and to Jeffrey Sica.

A PLANNING PROGRESSION HAS BEEN UNDER WAY FOR SOME TIME

The process steps of planning and control in business organizations have gone through several metamorphoses over the years. First, we had some form of statistical order point analysis to drive planning, or an economic order quantity (EOQ) that would be reached and a trigger signal sent to manufacturing to begin replenishment. The data used consisted of quantity on hand, average time to replenish, and the demand history. These techniques became categorized and progressed to material requirements planning (MRP) — where demands were entered, bills of material exploded, and supplies matched with manufacturing needs. MRP planned subassemblies and purchased items so they were matched with the need for finished goods. Gross requirements were netted against what was on hand and what was already on order to determine net requirements to complete the orders. The planners then had a more realistic picture of what needed to be done to support actual demand.

Unfortunately, MRP does not specify the capability of internal resources to accomplish the plan in the specified time period. It also caused much confusion as it provided help, because most business plans lacked the element of achievability. With typical MRP systems, there was a disconnect between what people driven to show increasing sales thought would happen and what people who were charged with having the machines and people ready to meet expected demand thought would actually occur.

Then we saw Manufacturing Resource Planning (MRPII), an advancement introduced by Oliver Wight, which was intended to create a capacity-balanced master schedule before the firm went to bills of material and beyond in the planning and delivery cycle. MRPII was meant to add the use of resource dependencies to the item's routing. After determining the material net requirements, production quantities would be multiplied by their resource usage specified on the routing to determine the capacity requirements. The problem now was that, although the master schedule was a great foundation, operations still tended to do what they deemed best, often in response to bonus features that favored productivity rather than meeting actual customer needs. Salespeople still tended to inflate the possible level of demand and manufacturing people continued to set schedules based on historical conditions. MRPII also relied on sequential planning of materials first and then capacity, and made little distinction between order quantity and transfer batch size between operations in that sequence.

S&OP ENTERS THE PLANNING PICTURE

With the recognition that the problem was more people and process related than it was systems or software, S&OP appeared as the means to force the players to consider and discuss what was happening between orders and planning and take action before the plant or firm got into trouble. Figure 7.1 outlines the intended processing. Past performance would be brought forward into a demand and supply planning sequence that would develop a planning consensus and end with an execution plan that met the firm's strategic intent and marketplace realities. One game plan, according to this concept, should be reviewed and revised frequently in the face of market conditions. Similarly, one group working to execute that plan, based on reality linked with business objectives, should determine the intended actions.

According to the thinking at the time, S&OP was to represent a single, integrated plan created and monitored frequently, and revised based on actual operating conditions and evidence of shifts in market and customer demand. The actual schedules sent forward, or amended in midstream, would be based on a timely and accurate evaluation of available data. With the schedules better linked to real conditions and connected tightly to business objectives, performance to plan would be more likely to occur than the typical wild fluctuations encountered before S&OP.

The supply chain Level 2 planning and scheduling weaknesses that were to be addressed with this tool included:

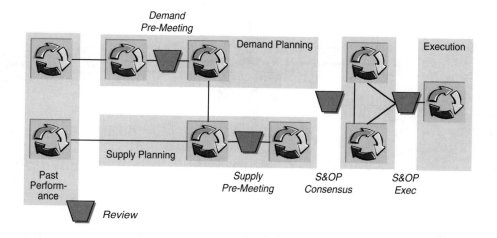

Figure 7.1   Sales and Operations Planning Process

- Poor forecast accuracy — based on history and not consumption, and often being as low as 40%
- Manufacturing inefficiencies, which needed to be improved while retaining flexibility
- Measurements that were unit based with a direct link to budgets and not customer demand
- Little to no customer input, except from pertinent complaints for nondelivery or pointing to an important root cause
- Poor integration systems and data hand off between internal functions and personnel
- Preponderance of legacy systems that do not interface

S&OP BECOMES A CROSS-ORGANIZATIONAL EFFORT

With the new viewpoint, illustrated in Figure 7.2, sales and operations planning became a process step that utilizes cross-functional resources, accurate information, and expertise in an attempt to synchronize supply with demand in a manner that takes best advantage of the firm's resources. In the figure, we can see the basic processing involved with S&OP, which includes receiving inputs from operations, sales, marketing, finance, and strategic planning — all intended to bring better definition and resolution to an age-old problem while making optimal use of the firm's resources.

To begin this processing, those involved must understand that S&OP is to be driven by what is happening in the market and with key customers. Customer demand should be the ingredient that drives the manufacturing

Figure 7.2   Sales and Operations Planning — A Cross-Functional Process

process, not the desires of the operating managers. The integration of supply and demand should be at the center of the effort. The format should be to create a 12- to 18-month rolling evaluation of what is happening and what should take place to maintain a proper sequence and coordination between planned and actual events. Under these circumstances, the first requirement is a set of objectives oriented around synchronization with the marketplace.

These objectives should include, but not be limited to:

- Supporting and managing the business plan
- Ensuring plans are realistic
- Providing a means to effectively manage change
- Better managing the level of finished goods inventory and backlog to support customer service
- Establishing a system to measure performance in close coordination with the firm's strategies
- Building teamwork among functional activities

The second requirement is to have a concise written sales and operations planning policy that covers the purpose, processes, and participants. Three core processes must be involved:

- Those charged with the responsibility for supply-demand management become responsible for developing the forecasts and loading the plant in line with demand, capacity, inventory policies, and service level requirements.
- Those taking care of product provisioning or materials management schedule the work in detail and make products and materials available to replenish stocks and meet requirements defined by the demand.
- Those responsible for customer order fulfillment take orders and arrange shipment. They also manage back orders and inform customers of current state conditions.

The prerequisites include having each department or function understand the meaning of the process and the need for each area to devote time and resources to making the effort a success. Adequate planning horizons need to be established and time fences defined so participants can manage to a reasonable schedule. Generally, participants then come together in prearranged monthly meetings, review the information, and conduct an overview of major activities. Figure 7.3 details the typical activities in the S&OP process. The meeting dates are set well in advance to avoid schedule conflicts. A formal agenda is circulated before every meeting, ownership for the S&OP process is established, and all participants

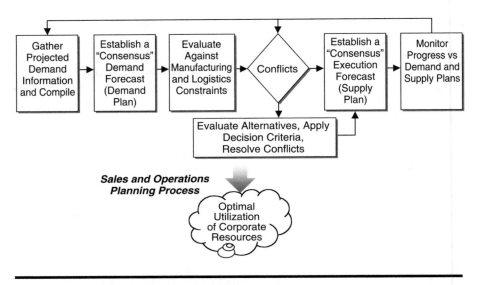

Figure 7.3 Overview of S&OP Activities

come prepared. Before the actual meeting, projected demand data is gathered and compiled in a format to be used by the meeting attendees. During the meeting, the members then establish a *consensus* demand forecast or demand plan. Next, they evaluate this plan against known manufacturing and logistics constraints (i.e., what we need to make and ship is compared with what we can make and ship). Conflicts are resolved and a consensus execution forecast or supply plan is established. This plan is then used to monitor progress by tracking actual conditions versus what the demand and supply plans predicted. Adjustments are made and the process continued at the next meeting.

GROUND RULES ARE IMPORTANT FOR SUCCESS

Each participant is expected to not only come prepared, but to actively engage in the discussion. They should come with the pertinent information from their areas of responsibility and an open viewpoint as to other functional requirements. Figure 7.4 captures the typical input data brought to the monthly meeting. Operations personnel bring their constraint data; sales discusses demand forecast and any special intelligence from key accounts; marketing is prepared to discuss new product information and any special promotions or market trends; finance keeps part of the discussion centered on meeting the firm's fiduciary objectives and matching

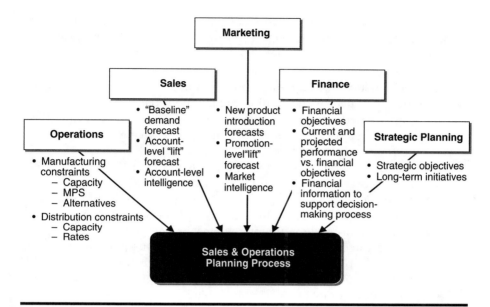

Figure 7.4   Key Inputs to S&OP

projections against those objectives; and strategic planning keeps an eye on how current performance is matching long-term initiatives and the firm's strategy.

Product family units responsible for parts of what needs to be manufactured review the plans with the help of the other parties. The presentation of information includes a review of both past performance and future plans. Inventory and delivery lead times are reviewed each month as part of the process. At all times, the group keeps an eye on the assumptions about the business and what is happening in the marketplace. This facet has the effect of enhancing the understanding of actual conditions and becomes the basis for making projections. Mechanisms should be put in place to ensure aggregate sales plans agree with detailed sales plans by item or family units and by market segment or geographical area. Time fences should be established as guidelines for managing necessary changes. These fences should always be under review with an eye toward reducing them. The production plan then becomes the driver of the master production schedule and is supported by a procedure that assures these plans are in agreement. As a matter of detail, the group makes certain all measurements are in the appropriate form — units or dollars — for the various parts of the organization needing feedback from the meetings.

S&OP meeting dates must be established well ahead to avoid perceived or real conflicts. Sessions should be conducted monthly and each department should have a representative in attendance; stand-ins should be designated early in the process to be ready in case of complications. A typical agenda will include:

- Special issues needing attention, including a summary of particular issues or concerns that senior management has at the current time
- Company performance review used to gauge the health of the business and catch problems or deviations so corrective action can be taken
  - Customer service — service/fill levels, product availability, backorders, aging, quality, and warranty problems
  - Financial and business issues — bookings, orders, shipments, backlog, inventory, profit margin, cash flow
  - Department-by-department reviews in aggregate — sales plan, forecast accuracy, marketing plan, promotions plan, manufacturing and operations plans and outputs, productivity, costs, availability, engineering support needed, strategic planning updates
- Review of assumptions and vulnerabilities
- Review of product families being manufactured
- New product discussion
- Special projects being planned or implemented, especially promotions
- Review of meeting decisions
- Critique of process

Minutes of each meeting should be concise and circulated immediately after the sessions. Finally, there must be a general manager who is available and will make decisions at points of conflict. From past performance, data is searched, reviewed, and brought to a demand premeeting. In both sessions, the participants work over historical information with current data on sales, production, inventory, backlog, shipments, and special events to get a handle on just what is being demanded and what supply capabilities there are or should be to match that demand. In essence, it becomes an effort to match supply demand with what the supply chain can provide so the results are closer to optimized conditions. New product development and introductions are reviewed at these meetings to avoid later surprises. Inventory and delivery lead times are reviewed and new manufacturing conditions discussed.

With lots of concentrated effort, consensus is reached and plans are sent to master scheduling and on to production planning, where the final manufacturing schedules are prepared and executed. Tolerances are established to determine acceptable performance for sales, engineering, finance, and production. Accountability is clearly established throughout the processing. The production plan is the driver of the master schedule and is supported by a procedure that defines summary conditions to make sure they are in agreement.

Once the plan reaches the final step, timing is added to the effort so a period in which the plan is frozen is designated; the next segment to be frozen is identified and the time for a new plan period to be added is defined. The objective is to synchronize what happens within the four walls with what is being demanded in the marketplace. And the caveat is straightforward — the participants in S&OP must be convinced the plans are realistic. This is a crucial element as we move toward accurate available-to-promise conditions and other advanced techniques.

PLANNING BECOMES A MEANS OF VIEWING PERFORMANCE

As a firm progresses with S&OP, it finds there is a need to establish various levels of planning. Figure 7.5 details how to organize such activity. The planning horizons can be set at short-, medium-, and long-term. The corresponding frequency of updating the horizon can then be set at weekly, monthly, and quarterly intervals. In each designation, the team leader, team members, and those responsible for issue resolution should be established. For example, in the weekly short-term horizon, the operations planning group (OPG) leader can resolve issues, but the long-term issues are best taken to the presidential level. Then the process objectives for each type of meeting are detailed. Sample process inputs are accepted, and sample process measures set in place to monitor progress.

Based on the theory that what gets measured gets improved, the firm moves to an operations planning state where key performance indicators can be established and attached to each major function in the overall processing. In Figure 7.6, a future state planning scenario is illustrated where each function has received and accepted responsibility for what becomes the elements of good S&OP conditions. The marketing and sales functions are not only providing inputs to the demand planning portion of the process, they are responsible for the average inventory level, work in progress (WIP), and the customer service metrics.

Those who assume responsibility for forecasting (and its inherent accuracy) work on distribution planning and have metrics that cover forecast error, on-time performance, and number of changes made. They also coordinate with those in distribution on deployment and customer shipping, while looking at planned versus actual loads shipped and on-time delivery percentages. The people in distribution also become concerned with master production scheduling and manufacturing and, with the help of the production planning group, focus on a range of key performance indicators (KPI).

Planning Horizons	Process Frequency	Functional Team Members	Process Objectives	Sample Process Inputs	Sample Process Performance Measures
Short-Term • Weekly buckets for approximately 6 weeks • Daily buckets for first week, if required	Weekly	• Leader: Demand Planner • Team: Demand Planner; SMEs (as required) • Issues Resolution: OPG Leader	• Monitor progress vs. demand and supply plans (S&OP) • Resolve short-term/ interim conflicts	• Firm orders • Frozen production schedules • Current DC inventory • Deployment schedules	• Order fill rates • Extraneous costs
Medium-Term • Weekly buckets for 52 weeks	Monthly	• Leader: OPG Leader • Team: Demand Planner; OPG team • Issue Resolution: President	• Identify medium-term supply/demand imbalances • Evaluate performance of past short- and medium-term plans • Develop and implement corrective actions	• Demand forecasts - Baseline - Promotion - NPIs • Supply forecasts and constraints	• Customer service • Inventory investment • Asset utilization • Total supply chain costs
Long-Term • Monthly buckets for 2 to 3 years	Quarterly	• Leader: OPG Leader • Team: President, VP Sales, VP Operations, VP Marketing, VP Finance, Strategic Planning Representative • Issue Resolution: President	• Identify long-term supply/ demand imbalances • Evaluate performance of past medium- and long-term plans • Develop and implement corrective actions	• Long-term demand forecasts and trends • Long-term supply forecasts and trends • Strategic initiatives • Financial objectives and current performance	• RONA • Market share • Contribution • Profitability

Figure 7.5   S&OP — Various Levels of Planning

The combined skills are then brought to bear on following processing across the functional areas while maintaining the strategic orientation. The decision-making process becomes much more data driven and the ability to think and act beyond functional boundaries comes into play as the participants keep the focus on operational effectiveness, as well as customer satisfaction. Through their joint responsibilities, the participants synthesize the forecast data and create a statement of what is the consensus demand. They feed back information to sales and marketing as needed to help those functions carry out their work. Inventory target levels are established and matched with the master production schedule. At all times, there is an active forum for discussing issues and seeking resolution and action.

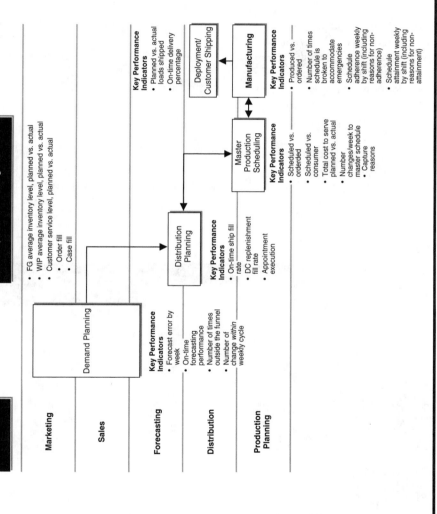

Figure 7.6 Sales and Operations Planning — Future State

CONCLUSIONS

To summarize, Figure 7.7 depicts the activities that occur across an S&OP effort. In Step 1: Demand Review, the goal is to create the most accurate estimate of demand and identify the critical situations needing attention and resolution.

The methods employed include:

■ Review outputs from the operations planning process and make necessary adjustments
■ Review the latest activities from sales, inventories, trends, and customer service performance
■ Review planned marketing and sales activities
■ Review key customers' marketing calendars
■ Highlight potential out-of-capacity situations

The outcome from this phase will be a review of the predicted results and any adjustments necessary to stay close to the strategic intentions. Any imbalance will be clearly identified and the group can publish and communicate what becomes the official demand statement.

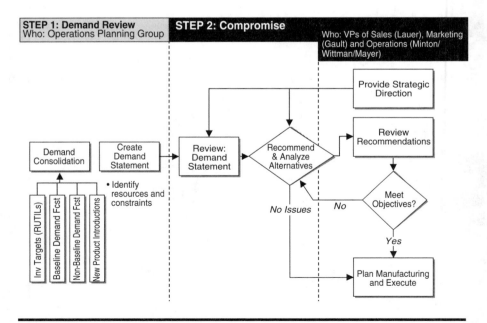

Figure 7.7 S&OP — A Series of Activities

In Step 2: Compromise, the goal becomes one of resolving any detailed imbalances between the supply and demand statements, to analyze the risks and costs, and then predict the results for executive review and approval. The methods involved include review of historic performance of the demand statement, review of the critical resource constraints, and an analysis of the impact of the decisions made to relieve constraints — from an economic and marketplace viewpoint. The outcomes will be an updated production plan, resource decisions that need to be made, and open issues directed to the executive team for approval, arbitration, and strategy decisions.

In Step 3: Executive Alignment Meeting, the goal is to review the impact of management decision for approval or adjustment and make further strategic decisions based on the inputs being received. The methods used will include a review of recent process performance, a review of customer service goals and results, a review of operating plans and progress against annual business plans, and arbitration of unresolved planning issues. The outcomes will be changes to the master production schedule, if necessary, and strategy briefings given to the appropriate senior managers.

As a firm progresses with S&OP, it reaches a point at which something more advanced is necessary, particularly as the company moves into Level 3 of the supply chain evolution. In Figure 7.8, the process reaches the point at which it becomes an important element in the senior management review process. A firm can expect that the level of detail requested will expand, as well as the elements included in the planning process.

These efforts typically peak with the kind of overview presented in Figure 7.9. At this stage, a vision drives the processing and all elements are linked to accomplishing that vision and its inherent purposes. The

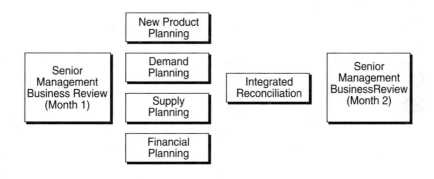

Figure 7.8 The Elements of Sales and Operations Planning

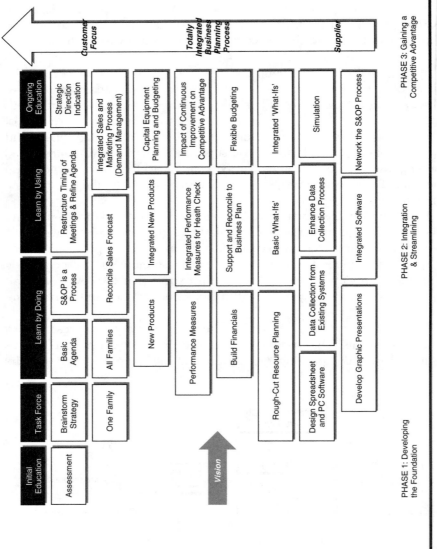

Figure 7.9 Sales and Operations Planning Implementation

entire effort is geared toward customer focus and objectives through a totally integrated business planning process. Key suppliers also become involved in the activity. In the next chapter, we explain the more advanced kinds of activities conducted under advanced planning and scheduling.

8

ADVANCED PLANNING AND SCHEDULING MODELS

In order for a business to meet the fundamental requirements to satisfy its customers in today's demanding environment, it must have an advanced planning and scheduling (APS) system. With the evolution of supply chain and the enabling technologies supporting advanced efforts, the building blocks are now available to construct such a system and extend its use to key supply chain partners. To appreciate the importance and advantages of such a capability, consider that everything in business starts with a plan — some quantification of what the business wants to achieve based on what it believes the future holds. Unfortunately, many business plans seem to contain equal amounts of hopes and guesses in combination with actual capabilities and customer needs.

Functional silos or stovepipe thinking contribute to the limitations of these plans. Purchasing thinks in terms of how to get the lowest price from multiple suppliers. Manufacturing worries about minimizing the number of changeovers and how to extend run lengths and create volume (inventories). Distribution wants low inventories and low transportation costs, usually with nothing but full truckload shipments. Customer service is looking for high inventories in regional warehouses to sustain high service levels, often accomplished through less-than-full truckload shipments. Finance wants low inventories to keep working capital costs down and eliminate excess carrying costs. When external partners are included in the planning, the private interests and spurious nature of the planning exchange only increase.

PLANNING IS AN ESSENTIAL BUSINESS ELEMENT

Plans are important to a business. They eventually lead to some form of scheduled activities. The schedule becomes an output of those plans, which include a commitment to create a specific amount of goods or services in a specific time frame, with detailed actions to be taken. But in an ASCM environment, the problems are exacerbated by market conditions. Today, ever-increasing customer demands introduce the need to include customization features to face shorter product life cycles, accept product proliferation, and consider outsourcing some of the manufacturing and logistics functions. In the ASCM world, it is necessary to include supply chain partners in planning to assure that what is being promised matches what can be delivered, and to do so ahead of actual production and delivery. The same kind of local and political considerations enter the picture on a larger scale as each constituent worries about its internal problems and not the extended enterprise situation.

With plans and schedules thus built on a weak foundation, matters can get worse as the firm uses whatever external information is delivered to its system and begins to answer questions such as: What will we produce and when will we do it? What ingredients do we require to make what we plan to produce? What do we currently have and what do we need to procure? When do we need the procured materials? When do we schedule shipments through our third-party logistics (3PL)? Who will have an impact on our success? In the current business environment, there is little margin for error; and to avoid lost orders most firms attempt to work in an arena where 95% or greater accuracy is the measure of good performance across the total planning and scheduling effort. In the beginning of most planning efforts, that likelihood is small, particularly on an inter-enterprise basis.

Hope for improvement comes when the firm moves into sales and operations planning (S&OP) and it increases as the firm adopts APS. With each step, the accuracy of the information and the connectivity between most desired conditions and actual performance converges. Eventually, APS becomes a part of a Level 3 supply chain effort and the forerunner to ERP-to-ERP (enterprise-wide resource planning) connectivity. The intention behind this progression is to apply Internet enhancements and go beyond the shortcomings of manufacturing resource planning (MRPII) and S&OP techniques. Taking advantage of the latest e-commerce technology, such as object-oriented programming and memory-resident processing, and the application of advanced algorithms (heuristic, linear programming, genetic), APS offers the ability to consider material availability and capacity issues simultaneously.

And the effort can be extended on an external basis, using the help of trusted allies, leading to more flexibility in customer response — from applying variable lead times and introducing variations in manufacturing capacity that match market needs. Knowing what the customer really needs and what the network can really supply makes for a much better business climate. With a solid model of how to involve participants in the end-to-end system, and with increased accuracy of the data being used, APS becomes the new tool that will bring planning performance to a level that meets the needs of the most demanding customers. It also becomes part of the network systems architecture delivering information that can greatly improve decision making inside the firm and with selected partners, while moving closer to optimum results.

This chapter focuses on this currently most advanced form of planning and scheduling and how it has become much more than a planning tool. It is at the heart of establishing an extended enterprise network for firms working for the same purpose — building new revenues among better-satisfied customers. Special thanks go to Larry Lapide, VP at AMR Research, and Jeffrey Sica for their help with this chapter.

APS EXTENDS THE S&OP EFFORT

As a supply chain effort moves into Level 3, and some form of network formation occurs with selected business partners, the application of APS on an inter-enterprise basis, built on shared data models, becomes an important factor to further improve efficiency and continue to drive costs down. Two aspects, the introduction of available-to-promise (ATP), or the ability to tell a customer (from its inventory status) what the firm can deliver and when, and capable-to-promise (CTP), or the ability to define what capacity is available to fill orders, become valuable tools. Because of previously gained improved abilities in forecasting, planning, and scheduling, these tools become distinguishing features for the firm and its business allies. Responsiveness and agility become added features of ATP and CTP, and are enhanced as APS emerges as the system used to manage across the entire supply chain.

To put this tool into perspective, we should begin by reviewing one aspect that occurs within most supply chains, a phenomenon originally noted by Professor Hau Lee of Stanford University. Lee called attention to the fact that a *bullwhip* effect can be observed as upstream partners in a supply chain experience erratic, volatile demand patterns brought on by consumer signals being passed through multiple links — retailers, distributors, wholesalers, and manufacturers — on their way to the primary suppliers.

When a consumer change occurs, it becomes like the crack of a whip and the effect moves through the linked partners. At each link, responses are made, especially to planning and inventories. Along the way, the response becomes greater because the involved firms are located further from the source. By the time the signal gets all the way upstream, it is like a bullwhip where all the action is at the end of the chain. Through the process, the result — in terms of inventory to meet the fluctuating demand — increases and always seems to be highest at the most upstream part of the linkage. This situation demands a system that more directly connects what is happening at both ends of the end-to-end processing. Better information and connectivity mean lower inventory needs.

As firms began to consider the need for such a connective system, attention moved to how the company can extend its S&OP activities from manufacturing facilities and warehouses to suppliers, distributors, and key customers. The historical tendency was to keep the focus on a make-to-stock orientation and use S&OP as the link between internal operations and finished goods in the warehouse. Suppliers were only considered in terms of lead times, filling bills of material (BOMs), and their ability to respond to emergency needs. In the new environment, the attention moves to how suppliers can play a key role in the overall efficiency of the inter-enterprise network and reduce the bullwhip effect.

Heavily influenced by the work of Eliyahu Goldratt and his constraint-based management thinking, a number of new decision support tools appeared and were bolted on to MRPII and S&OP systems. Now the firm considered the full range of supply-and-demand constraints with a focus on eliminating any bottlenecks that interfered with throughput. Consideration was given to customer demands and priorities and how material constraints, capacity limitations, setups, and changeover times could contribute to potential bottlenecks.

The principles were generally applied in the following manner:

1. Identify a bottleneck in the process flow.
2. Get to the root causes, eliminate them, and optimize the bottleneck, assuring high throughput.
3. Control the flows (product and information) from the previous bottleneck by pulling orders to the bottleneck.
4. Assure critical resources and materials get to the point of need so the bottleneck does not recur.
5. Search out the next bottleneck.

Organizations such as i2Technologies, Manugistics, and SynQuest offered firms software that could apply the inherent theories and go beyond S&OP. There was to be one integrated plan that managed demand, supplies, and constraints, went the thinking, giving the planners visibility into what takes place across the full network. In such a case, S&OP became more strategic in nature, requiring input and decision making

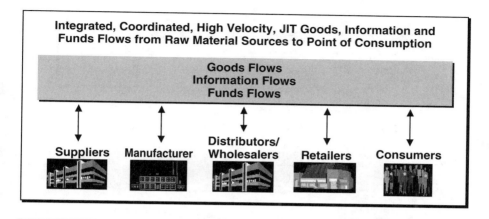

Figure 8.1   What Is APS?

across numerous external partners to that network so further decision enhancing information could be sent to the points of need.

With APS, illustrated in Figure 8.1, the concept becomes one of having an integrated, coordinated, high velocity flow of just-in-time goods and services, reliable information, and timely financial flows, all the way from raw material sources to the point of final consumption. This move expands S&OP as the firm considers supply and distribution constraints and how to employ concurrent sourcing, manufacturing, and distribution planning and scheduling. In these instances, i2 Technologies and Manugistics have been very effective in applying their constraint-based analyses to identify the bottlenecks and deliver the necessary information upstream and downstream to meet actual conditions.

If all of this is a bit confusing, let's put the matter in layman's terms. MRP attempted to answer the question, "What do we need to make?" MRPII dealt with "Can we actually make it?" S&OP forced people to discuss the realities of the system capabilities and come to grips with, "When can we actually make and deliver it?" APS brought on the consideration of "Can we make it and get it delivered to the right place at the right time?" while APS, in support of ASCM, revolves around, "What should we make and when?" This latter effort requires full planning and scheduling suites matched with better demand signals and synchronized plans across all functions and network partners.

In Figure 8.2, the question of what is involved in APS is answered. APS becomes the next step in order management and planning and should become a key tool in supporting supply chain management practices. As a firm progresses to advanced levels of supply chain, APS and ERP will converge and support supply chain practices across a business network.

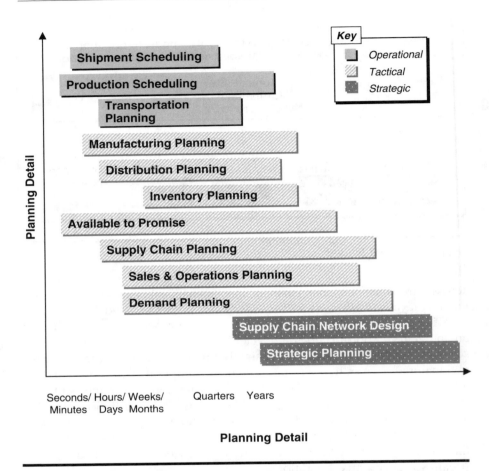

Figure 8.2 What's Involved in APS? (From L. Lapide, AMR Research, Boston)

To get started, however, it is necessary to identify 12 practices involved in APS, each illustrated in Figure 8.2. A firm begins with the first two strategic elements, taking input from its strategic plan, and moving the inherent requirements to meet strategy into its supply chain network design, which should have come into view as the firm progressed beyond Level 2.

Now the specific strategic intentions are turned into a vision to guide planning and scheduling, ideally focused on exceeding customer satisfaction requirements. The resulting network design will then reflect a means of accomplishing the strategy while optimizing use of resources. If the strategy, for example, calls for delivering all goods within a 72-hour time frame, the linked partners can develop a design that delivers on such a commitment. If the strategy calls for matching delivery lead times with needs determined by a customer segmentation analysis, then an alternate design will be created matching lead times with what is appropriate for each customer segment. In either case, the involved parties will understand their role and have decision rules that guide their actions.

Then the firm moves through a tactical suite of seven tools intended to culminate, as the company passes into Level 3 and beyond, with a capability to tell the customer, through an online connection, what is available to promise and what it has capacity to promise. The first step is to bring a high level of confidence to demand planning through many of the tactics described earlier. S&OP then transforms that information into an input into supply chain planning using the procedures described in the previous chapter. The planning detail must include visible access to information on supplies, inventory, distribution, and manufacturing planning. The result will be an ATP/CTP system that induces customers to buy from the firm and its network partners because they see what capacity can be made available and what inventory is available. They can also track progress and will learn that the information is highly reliable. The firm and its partners benefit because inventory levels shrink to those needed to support the actual demand, distribution has what it needs when it is needed to make deliveries, and manufacturing has a much better handle on what to put in the master schedule. Based on the understanding of material availability to meet demand, CTP emerges as a workable solution among the network partners.

ATP AND CTP BECOME DISTINGUISHING NETWORK FEATURES

A bit of clarification is in order regarding the two key factors being discussed. Capable-to-promise (CTP) is based on capacity, while available-to-promise (ATP) is based on inventory. CTP is a function of the structure of bills of material, routing calendars, and resources from which certain potential outcomes can be determined. ATP is a function of the schedule or a commitment to produce something in a given time period, resulting in a net balance of stock from which a promise can be made. The commitment behind the ATP is ratified in the master schedule. A level of rigidity or firmness is required in the master schedule for a fixed period in order to maintain commitments among the supply chain constituents. The linking is performed through the use of planning fences and multi-level master schedules combined with planning bills to compensate for any discretion exercised between levels in features and options.

The application of ATP was an outcome of the understanding of the structure used in the processing behind MRP. It is the result of linking bills of material, routing, and inventory with demand in the unified commitment that becomes the master schedule. This schedule not only drives the MRP process backward through supply, more importantly it provides for a commitment of service to the market and the firm's customers. CTP has grown as a solution most often advocated by the vendors of APS systems and leading theorists. Two primary drivers of this advocacy are data architectures, capable of modeling capacity with special features and options, and computer performance, which has increased dramatically, reducing calculation time. From the theorist viewpoint, the move to CTP is the outcome of advanced just-in-time (JIT); lean manufacturing thinking schools that inventory is negative and the firm should maintain ultimate flexibility in customer response. In that manner, the company commits from capacity with elements of mass customization. The customer response then becomes not "What do we have to offer?" but rather "What can we make for you?"

The CTP option does have practical obstacles to its implementation, regardless of its intellectually enticing efficiencies and technological foundation. The CTP option is most workable when the abstraction between what the customer requests and what the producer offers is the same. In other words, CTP is a good choice when the customer's demand unit of measure matches the producer's promissory unit of measure. This circumstance is most often found in the transportation of process-based goods. For instance, a freight carrier has capacity to transport so many pounds and freight customers want so many pounds to be delivered. In this circumstance, the CTP solution is relatively easy to implement. The APS system is a bit easier as it does not have to match the customer's abstracted demand, for instance, down to the level of an "each" with the supplier's abstracted potential to commit to that demand referenced in a bill of material and routing to calculate an answer. All that is required is the tabulation of what pounds are promised against what is requested.

The *each* request works best when there is agreement on what is available, as in the case of airline seats. Each passenger requires one seat. In the application of CTP, the problem of the unit of measure of *each* is a world filled with features and options, which implies there are many different interpretations between the potential requested *each* and what is modeled or structured by the producer as an available *each*. Under these conditions, it is exponentially more complicated —not only for the computer, but for the humans trying to model the amount of discretion in the system. When the product has any degree of variability in configuration and process, the result is poor capacity assumptions and lengthy system calculations from which a valid promise is difficult to make.

CTP is based on capacity, or a model of the capability of the system to perform work. Capacity is a function of structure, BOMs, routings, resources, and calendars, which provide for limits on the discretion the system has to make promises. For a large number of enterprises, to model a structure with enough flexibility is theoretically possible, but humanly difficult to maintain. This problem is significantly compounded when stretched across the supply chain as features and options are compounded. In a practical sense, the difficulty with CTP is one of not knowing in advance to what exactly you are being asked to commit.

ATP is again a bit more reliable as it is based on inventory, which is a function of the schedule or commitment to production. To handle the discretion applied to most demand, ATP relies foremost on what the system says is in inventory or stock buffers within the limits of the master schedule and not the flexible capacity of CTP. The problems with ATP are associated with the commitments or process difficulties. Externally, this implies that there is a potential problem with understanding the commitment of the buyer and matching it with the commitment to produce. The greater the uncertainty between the two factors, the more inventory or production is required for the producer. Internally, the ability of a company to promise from a schedule is quantified in classical measures: inventory, bills of material, routing and master schedule accuracy. Again, it is inventory that is required to compensate for the lack of ability in these matters in order to keep promises. To measure the level of commitment or the ability the firm has for keeping its scheduled promises, you need only to look at the quality of its processes from which those promises are made.

In most cases, ATP is the most practical technique to implement, although CTP should be held out as the ultimate objective for improvement efforts. When implementing ATP, the problems of commitment or lack of ability can be more readily overcome — through established process improvement efforts — than can the structural uncertainty problems associated with CTP. Externally with customers, this condition involves such things as collaborative planning and forecasting and, internally, such efforts as alignment of performance measures and design for manufacturing. With the proper alignment, uncertainty can be reduced and discretion classified in advance, thus reducing the need for extra inventory. At the master schedule level, ATP stock buffers can be expressed in days or even hours versus weeks or months of supply.

OPERATIONAL ISSUES ADDRESSED

As we return to the 12-step framework, the APS suite finally moves to operational issues, considering transportation planning and on to production and shipment scheduling. If the firm has a warehouse management

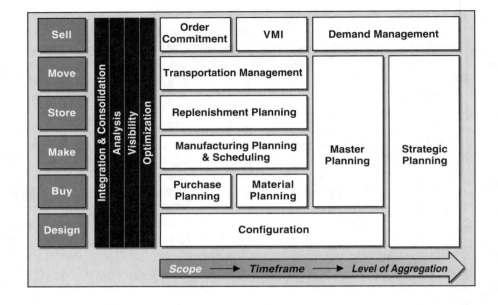

Figure 8.3 Manugistics NetWORKS (From Manugistics, Rockville, MD)

system (WMS) or transportation management system (TMS), direct links are made with those systems to keep the whole process in balance with what is taking place in the market. In Figure 8.3, we see one example of a suite covering all the segments mentioned. This on is from Manugistics and depicts that firm's NetWORKS solution, which is described by the company as being designed to "provide application portability and intelligence to transform the traditional supply chain into a trading community."

Another system is depicted in Figure 8.4. This one comes from Intentia International (www.intentia.com) and is dubbed Movex APP (Advanced Production Planner). This software supports planning over the tactical to operational horizon and scheduling over the operational to real-time horizon. The concept is to remove any constraints in the supply chain by hiring people, adding machines or machine time, or making changes to the processing. Then advanced planning proceeds from end to end across the network. A feature of the software is that it enables the firm to change the capacity loading on bottleneck resources and simulate the possible effects.

A firm might modify the selected suite for the particular conditions of its supply chain, but it is essential that the links between the three elements are established and carried out. As the house is put in order, it is also

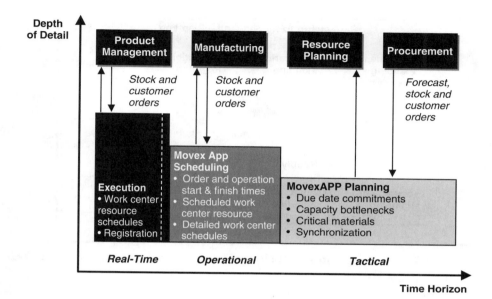

Figure 8.4   Movex APP System (From Intentia International, Danderyd, Sweden)

important that the key network partners come along for the ride. That means the company goes forward on an equal footing with suppliers, distributors, and customers that have also progressed through this part of the evolution and have the technical capability to interface with APS. Otherwise, the firm or one of its partners will become a bottleneck or link with poor information that introduces inherent delays. That is an unacceptable condition today with so much pressure on shorter cycle times.

When the partners have made the journey to the same level together, a variety of practices and positive developments appear. The focus on process improvement across the network will lead to much higher accuracy in the data supporting forecasting and planning. Supply-and-demand chain planning will be in closer synchronization. Planning cycles will be shortened, requiring less safety stocks and inventory. Co-management of inventory will lead to the elimination of unnecessary stores, and not pushing them upstream in the supply chain. The seeds of collaboration will begin bearing fruit as the focus moves from stovepipe thinking to improving process-oriented actions, such as reducing the order-to-cash and request-to-promise cycle times. As shown in Figure 8.5, the overall effect is to move from synchronized, sequential planning to synchronized, concurrent planning with many partners.

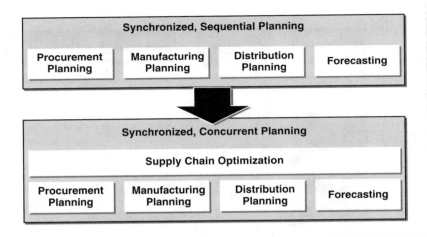

Figure 8.5   APS Brings Greater Ability to Optimize the Whole Supply Chain

GOOD MEASUREMENTS PROVE CONCEPT VALIDITY

With the design and framework in place, the partners turn their attention to measuring the results. Working under the idea that anything measured gets better, they work together to develop a set of metrics that will show APS is working and delivering benefits. This exercise begins internally and AMR Research created the measurement framework described in Figure 8.6 to help the effort. Starting with the purpose of improving planning inside the enterprise, the firm sets measures for purchasing, manufacturing, logistics, and customer service. The metrics listed can be amended to suit a firm's particular circumstances and other functions can be included. The concept is to have a scorecard showing the intended improvement and how much progress is being made.

Note that an overriding feature is to use cross-function, process-based measures to reduce the conflicting goals mentioned at the beginning of the chapter. Focusing on delivery of *perfect orders* — right in every aspect from the customer's perspective — helps assure that intention. The actual measures selected are meant to be a set of diagnostics that drive the desired performance. As skill is attained, these measures are extended on an external basis by determining the impact the suppliers and distributors will have on delivering perfect orders and further improving the metrics. The purpose becomes to assure APS is used effectively to support cross-organizational practices and instill the desired positive trends.

As a prelude to this external measuring, planning and execution suites are compared and integrated between key partners so planning is

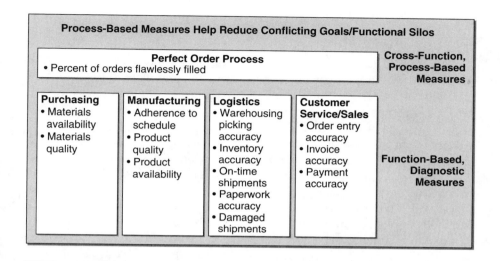

Figure 8.6 Measuring APS Performance (From L. Lapide, AMR Research, Boston)

approached on a concurrent, rather than sequential, basis. A collaborative attitude is essential, leading to proactive information sharing and enabling the workflow so there are no bottlenecks. Transfer of critical data in a real-time format is at the heart of this collaboration. The information, while coming from separate databases, will be intelligible and useful to support strategic, operational, and tactical planning through synchronized planning models. A feature of most systems will also be the capability to do *what-if* type of simulations so partners can test alternate market condition scenarios. Typical results will add incentive to the effort as partners find on-time information sharing between supply chain constituents increases forecast accuracy and the means to process more orders with less inventory.

When the partners have achieved these conditions, they develop graphical planning boards, or dashboards, tracking progress and introducing a means of representing network performance, such as cycle time from receipt of order to delivery, inventory requirements from end-to-end of order fulfillment, total cost of delivery, and the ability to meet commitments. Other measures include the means to evaluate vendor-managed inventory, customer replenishment processing, and category management commitments. To ensure compliance with the strategic intentions, planning parameters will be jointly developed so that when the customer is given a commitment, the partners know their roles in maintaining high performance levels. Eventually, the most advanced groups will progress to using a balanced scorecard technique to measure cost and performance on an end-to-end supply chain basis.

AN ACTION STUDY

TaylorMade/Adidas Golf offers an example of what can be achieved following that firm's decision to test the possibilities offered by APS. Beginning with a strategic imperative, the company wanted to extend the visibility of its supply chain from manufacturing to its offshore suppliers and sales representatives in retail stores equipped with wireless technology. The idea was to increase visibility and control while offering an advantage at the store level. Forecasting, planning, and collaboration tools from i2 Technologies were used to help the firm with another strategic intention — to move toward a made-to-order environment allowing consumers to get customized golf clubs delivered in a 24-hour time frame. Improved planning and inventory control had to be at the center of the strategic implementation. In a sense, the idea to use supply chain as a competitive strategy evolved. According to Mark Leposky, vice president of Global Operations, "Previously, TaylorMade has had some issues executing at the supply chain level. A few years ago it was a liability. It's our intent to make supply chain an advantage moving into the future" (Karpinski, 2001, p. 2).

TaylorMade runs the applications on Hewlett-Packard NT and Unix servers and Oracle databases on Unix. The first two modules installed were for handling demand planning and procurement collaboration with ten suppliers, mostly in Southeast Asia. The demand planner module lets the firm prepare collaborative forecasts based on inputs from internal data, retailers, suppliers, and third-party companies. The company uses this information to ensure that the parts necessary for the assembly of the golf clubs are made and delivered on time. Suppliers have been particularly pleased with the system as they can now view what is happening, particularly in terms of incoming orders, and plan accordingly.

The firm has plans to extend the effort by adding modules for inventory planning to help the firm assess the need for safety stocks; master planning, which will help optimize work schedules; allocation planning, intended to manage distribution of inventories to retailers; and order management, which will assist the company in its dealings with the demand pull from retailers. In addition to all the systems installation, the firm is developing a wireless strategy to put this information online for its sales representatives, for use when they are calling on retail customers. These representatives manage inventory and stocking in their customers' stores and the wireless connectivity will give them data that will enhance their efficiency and help keep their promises to customers. "Our ultimate goal," says Rob McClellan, TaylorMade's global eMarketing manager, "is to make retailers that sell TaylorMade more profitable than anyone else. We think we can really turn the industry on its head" (Karpinski, 2001, p. 3).

CONCLUSIONS

Let us now reconsider the underlying premises behind what has been discussed. First, a company is never going to leave Level 2 if it is still pursuing a *push* mentality. The culture must move to a *pull* mentality, where everyone thinks in terms of "Let's make what we sell." (or what the customer wants), and not "You better sell what we make." The latter orientation only leads to excess inventories, most of which are disposed of at discounted prices, and include high carrying costs. The former brings the supply chain in synchronization with what is happening in the marketplace.

Second, the firm needs an integrated planning and execution suite to match demand planning as closely as possible with forecasting, and then move to an available-to-promise (ATP) condition supporting the pull environment, followed by a capable-to-promise (CTP) functionality that relies on dependent material availability. At the time the firm is capable of supporting APS, inventory is under control, production capabilities are fine tuned to the market, and capacity is committed to orders as they are taken, thus providing for the most agility and responsiveness for a given infrastructure. With the correct suite installed and operating at the end of Level 2, the company will have a faster and more accurate planning engine that is real time and accessible online. Planning and execution will be synchronized across the internal supply chain resulting in the right deliveries at the right time to the point of need. During the final stages, sophisticated and imbedded optimization algorithms will become part of the planning suite with the capacity to do real-time analyses of various scenarios and even some fundamental simulations.

Third, this stage of development will position the firm to connect with suppliers and customers and share information over what becomes the communication extranet in Level 3. Then the firm gets into position to participate in joint trading partner functionalities, such as vendor-managed inventory (VMI) and customer relationship processing (CRP). As firms, particularly large ones, proceed with their planning and delivery process improvement, many move into an ERP planning system. Figure 8.7 illustrates such an advanced network scenario with connectivity from suppliers through retail operations. These are large-scale, integrated systems and require a very disciplined approach to business processing, and often the use of business process management technologies to proceed. They are the product of Level 4 and higher systems integration between partners committed to network performance.

In summary, lights appear at the end of the supply chain tunnel with the use of APS, as supply chain and demand chain information are linked to provide a much clearer picture of network needs. Constraints are eliminated through joint efforts, strategic imperatives are met through the

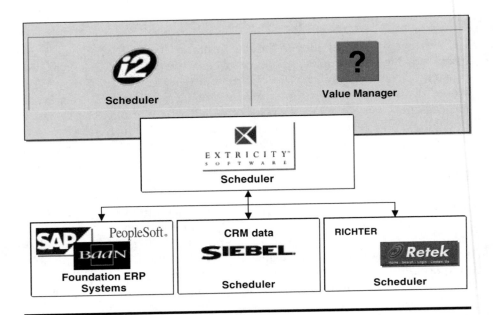

Figure 8.7   An APS Network Scenario

cooperation of many partners, and performance to business plans are aligned. APS takes a company and its best allies a long way beyond MRP. The results will include more accurate plans, better coordination of activities, and sharing of previously private information, which better supports supply chain management efforts. Typical benefits reported by leading firms include a 3 to 5% increase in revenues, 40 to 50% reductions in the cash-to-cash cycle, and a 15 to 17% improvement in meeting customer delivery dates.

9

MODELS FOR SUPPLIER RELATIONSHIP MANAGEMENT

Thus far, we have considered modeling supply chain in a sequential manner as described in Figure 5.1. Having progressed from order processing through procurement and sourcing, logistics, demand management, and capacity planning, with its subcomponents of sales and operations planning (S&OP) and advanced planning and scheduling (APS), we are prepared to enter the arena of advanced supply chain management (ASCM). Each of the areas covered in the previous chapters have been necessary precursors to taking the high ground in a market or industry — by getting the internal house in order before collaborating and applying technology in an inter-enterprise network. Now the focus moves to using the advantages gained internally to team with selected allies to make similar or larger gains through a networked effort.

This higher Level 3 and beyond effort begins with the supply side of the framework as the purchasing and sourcing function takes advantage of all the work that went into reducing the supply base, segmenting the suppliers in terms of importance, and beginning work with a few of those suppliers to build advanced level models that will be beneficial to both organizations. In this chapter, we enter the realm of ASCM and explain how the assistance of key suppliers is an absolutely crucial ingredient to success. The vehicle for funneling that assistance into a proactive and beneficial format is supplier relationship management (SRM), a keystone for constructing an ASCM system. Special assistance for this chapter came from Brad Barton and Chuck Wiza, partners at CSC Consulting, and Rick Zuza and Mark Stodola at Allstate Insurance Company.

PARTICIPATION IN VIRTUAL, NETWORKED ENVIRONMENTS BECOMES THE OBJECTIVE

The movement to a higher-level networked supply chain activity should begin on the supply side because that is where the greatest opportunity for financial improvement exists, and it fits the pattern of having the house in order before approaching key customers in search of new business and further savings. The process follows a linear pattern. The firm completes its work on internal excellence and then peruses its list of key suppliers to find those willing and able to help build a network architecture. Starting with a few trusted suppliers, the idea is to work collaboratively to construct a business model containing virtual liquidity of information transfer that will be compelling in the eyes of the targeted customers. Later, when we discuss customer relationship management (CRM), the concept will be expanded to include key customers whose help will be invaluable to completing the business model and moving the focus to targeted consumer groups.

The idea of moving from an internal perspective to an external environment, in which partners in an extended enterprise come together and plan their future has been intriguing to many companies and individuals for some time. Collaboration and technology are not new concepts; they are as old as trading chickens and building ships. Today, many purchasing groups are testing the collaboration/technology waters as they try to move forward with savings generated in the early levels of supply chain. For some, the idea of forming networks and then using the latest technology to enhance performance is simply an old trick brought up to date. What is new is the idea of collaborating across business entities and sharing information and practices so the constituents can all benefit. Another innovative feature is the concept that the purchasing function must rise in internal importance and become a vehicle for assisting the strategic intentions of the firm through inputs from key suppliers willing to help in that part of the relationship.

The advanced proposition begins with the idea that enterprises, buyers, and suppliers know how to collaborate. The problem has been that one or both parties think they must dominate the transaction. That is an aspect of negotiation. Each party believes he or she has taken better advantage of the other or something has been lost. Win-lose is very much a pattern in historical buy-sell relationships. In a modern enterprise environment, that concept loses its value as the constituents in the buying and selling seek a higher plateau and begin to focus on win-win, or how each entity can improve its position through collaboration with business partners. Working with a select group of suppliers, the advanced supply chain initiative is to find the hidden values, which have eluded the buy-sell relationship, and can lead to better profits for both parties and building new revenues with targeted customers.

Through the collaboration, one key feature will be the application of technology at the right points in the jointly developed business model. That requires answering the question: Why has technology implementation been so hard to achieve in a network environment? Generally, it's because of the lack of communications standards and common business processes recognized by all parties, and the inability to link disparate software and applications across an extended enterprise where each constituent is an expert on the one best way to communicate. It is also because of political considerations regarding who should dominate the relationship, who has the greatest experience, and who will compromise for the good of the alliance.

In spite of the Internet environment in which all forms of information can be shared at the click of a mouse, supply chain constituents will cling to their databases and only share what they think is inconsequential as they gather all they can to enhance their performance. The new thinking says that attitude prevents you from getting to the hidden values and savings that could come from a more open, sharing relationship. Select parts of the database that help both parties should be shared through an interactive extranet designed for such a purpose. That becomes a crucial element in SRM.

Supplier relationship management emerges from this difficult situation as companies seek the means to establish a more disciplined, honest, and strategically oriented environment around supplier relations — to ensure that the network effort is harmonized to bring optimum conditions to all participants. From a purchasing perspective, this condition goes well beyond strategic sourcing, e-procurement, and advanced purchasing techniques. It involves selecting a few key suppliers and working diligently with them to find the optimized means of collaborating for mutual advantage. From another perspective, it also involves an alliance between the chief purchasing office (CPO) and the chief information officer (CIO). With this internal collaboration, their two organizations seek out those suppliers with whom they can design, test, and apply the interactive communication systems needed for network cooperation.

Most importantly, SRM requires collaboration as a supplement to negotiation. As the participants to SRM move to a more disciplined, strategically focused, and technically enhanced relationship, the sourcing effort moves toward using the supply side to establish a meaningful business model that supports and enhances the joint business strategies. When this is accomplished, the distances between buyers and sellers will diminish and an integrated entity will be prepared to extend the network effort to the customer side. With the enhancements that come from IT and the application of technology to bring features of the relationship online — to speed cycle times and connect upstream activities to the downstream necessities — the budding network only gets stronger. Then the firm moves forward toward customers knowing the house is really in order.

SRM BECOMES THE ENGINE THAT DRIVES COLLABORATION

One caveat is in order before describing the models that assist the SRM effort. To begin, there must be a solid purpose or guiding mission jointly developed and understood by all parties to the exercise. The intention of that mission cannot be to find additional values solely for the buyer. If so, the effort will fail. Too much has been extracted from the supply chain efforts in Levels 1 and 2 through suppliers making concessions to maintain or grow volume. The next level of enrichment will come from collaborating on the means to find hidden values that benefit both parties, sharing the rewards, and determining how to build new revenues together. With a guiding vision capturing these thoughts, which both parties accept as meaningful, the business allies go into SRM looking for shared values. The next step is deciding how the process should work. A definition often helps this phase of the effort.

According to Gartner Consulting, SRM is defined as "a set of methodologies and practices needed for interacting with suppliers of products and services of varied criticality to the profitability of the enterprise" (Gartner, 2001, p. 2). In view of what we just discussed, we would add to the definition that SRM is *a means of building closer relationships with selected strategic suppliers, the purpose being to discover added features that could enhance the relationship while improving business performance as the firms work in a network environment for mutual benefit and increase the likelihood of creating profitable new revenues together.*

How important can this relationship enhancement be? Gartner further suggests that "by 2005, enterprises will move strongly to SRM methodologies or they will see profit reductions of close to two percent" (Gartner, 2001, p. 2). This firm lists some of the potential benefits of SRM in Figure 9.1.

- Optimize supplier relationships — treat different suppliers in different ways depending on the nature of the relationships and their strategic value
- Create competitive advantage and drive revenue by jointly bringing new, better, and more customer-centric solutions to market faster
- Lengthen and strengthen critical supplier relationships — integrate suppliers into your business processes
- Drive profit enhancement through reduced supply chain and operational costs while maintaining quality

- **Optimize supplier relationships** – treat different suppliers in different ways depending on the nature of the relationships and their strategic value

- **Create competitive advantage and drive revenue by jointly bringing new, better and more customer-centric solutions to market faster**

- **Lengthen and strengthen critical supplier relationships** – integrate suppliers into your business processes

- **Drive profit enhancement through reduced supply chain and operational costs while maintaining quality.**

Figure 9.1   The Benefits of SRM (From Gartner Consulting, San Jose, CA, 2001)

SELECTING THE RIGHT CATEGORIES STARTS THE PROCESS

With the mission resolved and a clear understanding of the purpose and opportunity, the next step is for the company sponsoring SRM (often a nucleus firm) to group its purchases by category of importance and complexity. This step includes the implicit requirement that the firm know all about its buy. How much of what is being bought, from whom, by which purchasing agent, at what prices, and with what results must be a part of the ante. SRM can only begin when the firm thoroughly knows its buy and has done the standardization necessary to make certain the categories of buy represent what they should contain. That means there cannot be a misunderstanding as to which category motors or pumps belong to, or confusion about whether a particular supplier is providing something that looks like a motor or pump. Standard nomenclature must be used and the purchases made part of a specific category in the total buy.

With these requirements in mind, the firm proceeds with its SRM effort by carefully separating the buy categories into some meaningful segmentation so sourcing and pricing plans can be attached to each group. A four-segment approach is illustrated in Figure 9.2. Another segmentation may be more appropriate for a specific firm, but this exhibit will allow us to draw out the salient points for the effort. Note that the scales vary. On the vertical axis of the matrix, the ranking moves from low spend volumes and low purchasing leverage to high positions. On the horizontal axis, the variation is from low to high product and service complexity.

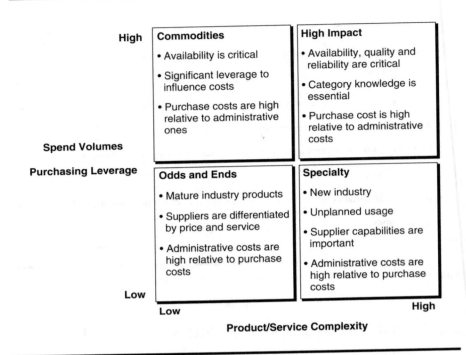

Figure 9.2 Purchase Categories

Beginning on the lower left side of the matrix, with the low volumes and low complexity categories quadrant dubbed Odds and Ends, the procurement objectives become something such as:

- Ensure getting the best price and service for volume tendered
- Provide users self-service capabilities, minimizing contact time with suppliers
- Reduce administrative costs through streamlining and e-procurement techniques, where appropriate

Moving up to the area of high volume and leverage and still low complexity, we find the Commodities quadrant where the objectives become:

- Leverage buying power to seek the best consolidated arrangement
- Rationalize SKUs to industry standards
- Manage contracts closely to obtain negotiated benefits

In the lower right-hand side, where we have high complexity and low volumes, the Specialty quadrant calls for these objectives:

- Gain access to cost and technology information from key suppliers
- Enable suppliers to provide value-adding features and services to internal customers
- Reduce administrative costs through improved online RFQ procedures

Finally, in the upper right, we see high product and service complexity matched with high spend volume and leverage and the category marked High Impact. Now the objectives become:

- Leverage buying power with limited suppliers
- Understand industry cost drivers, emerging technologies, and full capabilities of key suppliers
- Encourage supplier involvement in product development and the search for added features and values

A firm may care to add to the decision criteria, based on its internal needs, but it is in this last quadrant that the search for SRM candidates centers. If an effort is going to be made to find advanced relationships where the company will share very important information, it should be with suppliers in this category. What comes out of the eventual SRM effort will establish a framework, as well as decision rules for dealing with the other categories, but partner selection should start with the high-impact quadrant.

SELECTING THE RIGHT SUPPLIERS IS CRUCIAL TO SUCCESS

With a good fix on where the action should begin, the next element in the SRM sequence is to decide on a selection criterion that makes sense to the firm, its internal partners, and the few companies selected for a collaborative effort. That means the firm needs to apply a format for picking the names of the most likely candidates for SRM activities, such as that represented in Figure 9.3.

This matrix can be modified or extended to cover other characteristics that a firm believes will help segment its supply base. The idea is to move from the *basic* suppliers that a firm needs to get its work accomplished to those of *value*, those adding *special values*, and those that have *strategic importance*. Most firms can make this analysis intuitively, but the matrix approach helps establish the criteria for selection and enables the firm to cope with a large number of suppliers. The focus with this technique changes in each of these categories and, again, should reflect the distinctions the firm wants to bring to each segment.

Supplier Category/Focus	Basic	Value Added	Preferred	Strategic
Relationship	Product or service as commodity	Impacts operational efficiency	Process expertise valued	Unique advantage is valued
Operation Mode	Competitive bid	Performance incentive	Continuous improvement	Flexible, agile, collaborative
Capability	Fulfill to requirements	Deploy specific competencies	Customized expertise & skills	Ability to assist with market changes/demands
Information Sharing	Limited–electronic	Limited – tactical dialogue	2-way controlled	Direct linkage access to parts of company database
Risk Management	Contract penalties	Incentives and penalties	Incentives and information linkages	Process management, shared risk/reward
Planning Horizon	Current deal	Ongoing, near-term	Joint planning with end point	No end point, joint strategic planning
Nature of trust	Confident in ability to fulfill contract	Confident of execution performance	Confident in expertise; performance agility	Shared vision, ownership of intellectual capital
Metrics	Compliance tracking	Service level benchmarking	Best practice relationship	Business results; shared incentives
Customer Interaction	None to limited	Enabler of quality	Impacts individual customers	Impacts major number of customers

Figure 9.3   Supplier Relationship Attribute Model

Overall, the matrix should describe how a supplier moves through positions and provide a framework for selecting the key strategic suppliers with which it wants to embark on an SRM effort. Working with one major manufacturer of hand tools, we began with 3,500 suppliers. This group was reduced to 1,500 with 1,000 falling into the basic category, 250 into the value category, 150 into the preferred category, and 100 emerging as strategic suppliers. The last group becomes a manageable number from which two or three are selected after matching with the high-impact categories to begin an SRM effort.

This step in the SRM sequence requires some cross referencing between the lists of high-impact buy categories and the strategic suppliers. The intention is to find the small number of critical items and the small number of strategic suppliers where an advanced relationship effort will be most rewarding. That requires the firm to develop a complementary evaluation sheet that culls through the previous lists. A cross-functional team, which includes members from operations, finance, IT, and logistics, in addition to purchasing and sourcing, should come together and set up decision rules around how a supplier fits into selection criteria and attains suitability to help with SRM. The team wants to make certain the elected suppliers have characteristics that relate to achieving the business strategies, as well

Strategic importance	High	Medium	Low
Ability to collaborate electronically	High	Medium	Low
Ability to provide resources for actions	High	Medium	Low
Quality of past relationships	High	Medium	Low
Ability to add network value	High	Medium	Low
Alignment of business thinking	High	Medium	Low
Share the same values	High	Medium	Low
Length of relationship	High	Medium	Low

Figure 9.4   Supplier Relationship Matrix

as the ability to partner in the SRM process. We suggest a simple matrix similar to that shown in Figure 9.4.

Once again, the matrix can be modified, but it must reflect the factors of importance to the firm, as so much will be at stake as the effort goes forward. There will be a significant commitment of time and resources and a lot of eyes will be on the progress made. Therefore, the team should take the time to make certain the first two or three firms selected have the highest probability of being successful for what will become the initial SRM pilots.

When the names have been generated and reviewed with a cross section of senior management, a letter from the CEO is prepared inviting the selected firms to participate. This letter should include a statement outlining the opportunity to discuss the proposed vision or mission to guide the effort, the type of processing that will occur, a commitment to pursue joint benefits while using joint resources, and the preliminary list of areas of opportunity for both parties. The responding firm should also be allowed to suggest improvement ideas from its perspective.

IDENTIFYING THE TOTAL COST OF OWNERSHIP BECOMES A PRIMARY OBJECTIVE

When an agreement to participate is received from the invitee, the sponsoring firm's team sets up the logistics. The time and place for the preliminary meetings are arranged. An agenda that will kick off the joint discussions is prepared and the specific attendees chosen. Process maps, explaining how each firm believes the processing takes place between the partners, are prepared and brought to the initial meetings. This step is a crucial preliminary action. Most firms come to the first meeting with a decidedly different perception of how the products and services, information, and financial flows take place between the two companies. With flow charts showing each perception, the group has a means to get quickly into what are the actual conditions so they can then begin collaborating on a redesigned, improved state.

It is equally important in these initial meetings to have a cross section of functions in the meeting room. In addition to buyers and sellers, there should be representatives from logistics, IT, operations, finance, planning, engineering (where appropriate), and so forth. The idea is to give the functions that can benefit from an improved relationship the chance to discuss first hand what these improvements might be and how they would impact each organization.

Referring to Figure 9.5, we can see a model that will help initiate the preliminary conversations with the selected suppliers — the total cost of ownership. The usual focus with any buy-sell share session is placed on the invoice price and how it can be improved. Freight is separated from the part or supply cost so a focus can be placed on both of these elements. In SRM, the focus moves higher to measure the total value that suppliers provide. Above the usual base line, we find a category marked *execution costs*. Here attention is on the costs associated with making the purchases, handling the accounts payable, systems administration, and the delivery mechanisms.

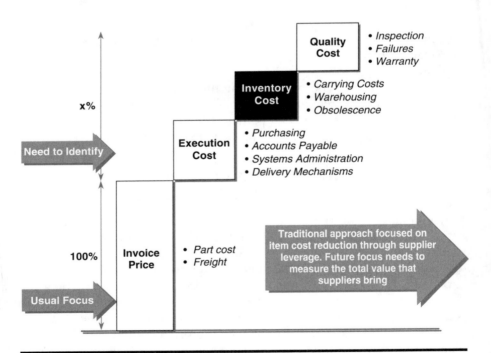

Figure 9.5 Total Cost of Ownership Model

Moving even higher on the chart, we encounter the inventory cost, a most elusive supply chain cost. The elements are clear enough — they contain the value of the inventory as it resides in working capital on the balance sheet, the carrying cost of holding the inventory, the warehousing costs, and the cost of any obsolescence. This is a very serious part of the effort as the joint intention must be to reduce the amount of network inventory needed, through visibility and just-in-time delivery techniques, without jeopardizing manufacturing plans. Traditionally, inventories are simply moved upstream and onto the books of the suppliers. The new thinking is to match demand with supply and have a flow that covers demand without excess safety stocks.

The highest block is called quality costs and represents the costs of inspection, failures, and warranty. Now the partners want to make certain there are no hidden costs in assuming the right goods at the right time and place do not have to be returned or discarded. There is generally plenty of historical information to identify these costs, but they lay buried in databases and must be rooted out and assembled in a meaningful manner, so the inventories can be reduced or eliminated, often through joint action team initiatives. As the partners unearth this information and begin using it, the supplier should be given a chance to add to the total cost of ownership any elements it believes are also of importance.

As the team looks at this total cost of ownership from the latter perspective, there is another format, supplied by Zeger Degraeve and Filip Roodhooft in their *Harvard Business Review* article, that will prove helpful. These authors point out that a systematic exploration of all costs involved in the relationships with suppliers will help the firm "make intelligent decisions about trade-offs using mathematical optimization models" (Degraeve and Roodhooft, 2001, p. 22). They offer the framework illustrated in Figure 9.6 as a means for the team to identify opportunity areas by focusing across various levels (unit, order, and supplier) and across activities (acquisition, reception, possession, utilization, and elimination). In the appropriate sectors, they call attention to costs that can be investigated to see whether they can be improved.

As the total cost of ownership becomes clear, the firm will also want to establish a system to assign weights to the elements pinpointed for improvement. This step involves identifying the improvement areas and weighing the importance of each area. Next, the team identifies what data will be used to measure the improvements accomplished and how this data will be obtained. Then they focus on how the data will be used, obtaining the supplier commitment to help, and making supplier responsibilities part of the SRM effort. Figure 9.7 outlines a typical weighting process.

		Acquisition	Reception	Possession	Utilization	Elimination
Supplier Level	Cash	• Total purchase discounts				
	Non-Cash	• Supplier vetting costs • RFP costs • Contract administration costs • Supplier follow-up costs (feedback) • Supplier change costs	• Litigation costs for breach of contract		• Engineering costs • Personnel training costs • System adaption costs	
Order Level	Cash	• Payment-delay savings or costs	• External transportation costs			
	Non-Cash	• Ordering costs	• Receiving costs • Invoice and payment processing costs • Quantity testing costs • Quality testing costs • Litigation costs for problems with quality	• Internal transportation costs	• Quality control costs • Production delay costs	• Waste collection
Unit Level	Cash	• Price • Production discounts				
	Non-Cash	• Service costs for installation and assembly • Testing costs		• Inventory holding costs • Order picking costs	• Production failure costs • Product failure costs • Maintenance costs • Installation costs	• Costs of removing obsolete materials • Disposal management costs

Figure 9.6 Uncovering the Hidden Costs of Procurement (From Degraeve, Z. and Roodhooft, F., *Harvard Business Review*, 2001)

FORMAL STEPS EXTEND THE SRM ACTIVITY

With the potential value improvement opportunities identified and the selected suppliers committed to providing resources for the selected SRM activities, joint teams are now dispatched to review the opportunities in a formal manner. The opportunity list should be divided so teams can be assembled with the expertise to tackle each major area. These sub-team meetings are arranged and comprehensive review formats established to monitor progress. Executive reviews should be overlaid on these meetings

Weight	Element	Measurement	Weight
25%	Quality	• Quality Performance	30%
		• Receiving Inspection	20%
		• Line Performance	20%
		• Reliability Performance	20%
		• Field Retrofits Required	10%
25%	Delivery	• On-Time Committed Receipt Date	30%
		• On-Time Requested Receipt Date	10%
		• Standard Interval Performance	30%
		• Delivery Error Performance	20%
		• Flexibility and Lead Time	10%
25%	Technology	• Access to Obsolete Technology	15%
		• Process Technology	25%
		• Early Design Involvement	20%
		• Long-Range Plans	20%
		• Technology Roadmap Match	20%
15%	Service	• Purchasing/Materials Support	60%
		• EDI Capability Support	20%
		• Leading-Edge Procurement Support	20%
10%	Environment	• Environment Policy	30%
		• Regulatory Compliance	50%
		• Conservation Program	20%

Figure 9.7   A Total Value Weighting Process

so participants can recap past achievements, report on progress status, and identify new opportunities discovered in the team interactions. These reviews should be structured to be as comprehensive as possible and to achieve a consistent and total category and supplier evaluation. Figure 9.8 depicts an example form that could be used so the opportunities are classified and progress rated versus the initial plans developed and the projected completion dates.

A BEHAVIORS MODEL TO GUIDE JOINT ACTIONS ESTABLISHES AGREEMENT

As the teams progress with their research to discover the hidden opportunities in their firms' relationships, evaluations and recommendations will emerge and a pattern will develop describing the enhanced relationship. For the product flow, new logistics systems will be found that take advantage of joint assets — warehouse space, distribution facilities, and trucks. Substitute materials will be recommended or the supply of larger subassemblies. Features of supply that enhance the machine set-up times and quality, the changeover process between orders, and manufacturing run capabilities will be discovered. The information flow will show new ways to bring visibility to the critical information — to better match actual demand with supply capacity and reduce the need for safety stocks.

Category: _____   Period Purchases ($M):_____

Review Period:_____   Year-to-Date Purchases ($M):_____

Key Organ. Contact: _____   Total Year Forecast ($M):_____

Phone/Fax #s _____   Prior Year ($M)_____

Key "Supplier" Contact _____ Phone/Fax #s_____

Organ. Site(s) Represented

_____

Review of Previously Identified Key Action Items

Action Item	Current Status	Remaining Action Required

Quality Performance (25 Possible Points)	Score: _____

Accomplishments
- _____
- _____
- _____

Issues
- _____
- _____
- _____

Actions
- _____
- _____
- _____

Total SRM Score:_____

Figure 9.8 Supplier Relationship Management Review Example

Algorithms and software will be selected to greatly improve the accuracy of forecasts and match demand planning with supply capacity. Cycle times will also shrink as non-value-adding steps are eliminated. In the financial flow, schemes will be introduced to speed payments and eliminate any errors and reconciliation. In short, the SRM results include a list of surprising means to add benefits for both firms.

From an IT perspective, some of the typical traits that come from SRM efforts and help drive success include:

■ Joint capability to resolve issues around disparate information systems and use an open Internet-based architecture for communicating vital data

- Agreement on translation engines that permit information sharing between heterogeneous systems and applications
- Online visibility of product, information, and financial flows across the full supply chain
- Ability to provide online collaborative support in the search for continuous improvement with further process steps across the supply chain

In some of the more advanced SRM efforts, the results from the effort will lead to a greater understanding and set of decision rules that can be applied by the sponsoring firm across its supply base. A behaviors model appears that summarizes the new actions and benefits while describing the intended rewards for both organizations. Figure 9.9 is an abbreviated version of such a model that has been extended to list the behaviors, not just for the strategic suppliers, but for each of the previous categories listed in earlier matrices.

BUYING ENGINES CAN FACILITATE LOWER PURCHASE CATEGORIES

As the firm builds its SRM relationships, it will find there are some ancillary benefits. When most firms progress beyond supply chain Levels 1 and 2, they invariably begin to consider e-procurement systems to simplify, control, and automate the purchase of goods and services from multiple sources. Software offerings are considered and used to aggregate needs, choose sources, and reduce transaction time and cost. Marketplaces and auctions are employed to find opportunistic savings. Buying portals are set up for sharing requests for quotations and to facilitate the bidding process with selected suppliers. Order placement, tracking, and payment can be handled with such portals. Many companies are now extending these cyber-based techniques from what were initially attempts to reduce indirect costs to more direct buying categories.

When the SRM effort is under way with a few strategic suppliers, the sponsoring firm can take a step back and apply the information developed during the selection and action processes to help its buyers with the lower echelon buy categories from the lower segmented suppliers by taking advantage of these e-commerce techniques. As the firm looks at its *odds and ends* and *commodities* categories, for example, and how they are sourced from *basic* suppliers, an automated mechanism might make good sense. The question becomes: How do we choose from among the many options available?

One answer lies in the application of a software comparison grid. That means the firm lists the various software providers it is considering

Rewards/ Value	Basic	Value-Added	Preferred	Strategic
Value and Compensation Supplier	• Supplier provides exactly to the contract agreement • Agreements are short-term transactions	• Offer improvement suggestions • Provide no special expertise; electronic purchasing	• Commit to cost improvements • E-Procurement • Non-traditional pricing	• Value added through expertise • Metrics-based agreement
Buyer	• Paid according to agreement and conditions • Short-term transaction	• Negotiate early payment options • Process orders electronically	• Direct entry of invoices • 2- to 5-year contracts for multiple transactions	• Bonus incentives • Open-ended contracts
Pricing/Volume Supplier	• Commit to competitive pricing • Supply not guaranteed	• Contract with fixed term and option to extend • Audit right to buyer	• Multi-year options with price guarantees • Audit right to buyer	• Most favored customer commitment • Supplier shares pricing model to establish profit margin
Buyer	• Commits to volume spend • Uses competitive bid for awards	• Awards business as back up to preferred supplier • Alternate sources may be tested	• RFP not required • Always in bid process • Evergreen contract	• Allows fair margins • Collaborates on requirements • Offers right of first refusal
Risk Sharing Supplier	• Accepts minimal risk based on contract	• Accept modest risk with allowed incentives and penalties	• Accept moderate risk with allowed significant incentives	• Compenstion tied to buying firm's successes; makes joint investments
Buyer	• Accepts minimal risk based on contract	• Accept modest risk with incentives and penalties	• Accepts moderate risk balanced with incentives for enhancements	• Shares documented successes; makes joint investments
Information Sharing Supplier	• Shares data as defined by contract	• Shares limited tactical data to better enable completed tasks	• Shares product strategy and best business process practices	• Shares business strategy and direction; facilitates sharing of improvement ideas
Buyer	• Shares data defined by contract	• Shares operational data to help planning	• Significant tactical data and some strategy to aid supplier	• Allows supplier to participate in strategy development and add value servicing

Figure 9.9   SRM Behaviors Model (From Allstate Insurance Company With Permission)

and develops a grid that shows the strategic focus of the offering, the maturity level of that offering, the positive and negative aspects of using the offering, and information on any installations in a similar industry that might be available for each company. The idea is to have the spending categories drive the assisting technology choices and apply a spend/supply analysis for prioritizing how the sourcing tools are selected and applied.

There is one complication. There are so many buying engines and software solutions being offered, it is often difficult to match the appropriate software with the appropriate category. In fact, the landscape has become almost littered with choices and, as much as we would like to offer help and advice, it is somewhat risky to list the current conditions as acquisitions and mergers are changing the landscape. A recent listing of principal vendors, including those performing auction services, would include: Agile, Ariba, Clarus, Commerce One, Diligent, Emptoris, Freemarkets, Healy Hudson, iPlanet, i2Technologies, MindFlow, MRO Software, Oracle, PeopleSoft, Peregrine Systems, PurchasePro, SAP, and Verticalnet. The recommendation is that these sources, or the shorter list of viable candidates selected by the buying firm, be placed on the comparison grid and the buyers match the capabilities of the various suppliers with the needs of the lower position categories in view of the engines' capability to automate and improve some or most of those categories.

While there is no definitive data available to determine exactly how much of the total buy these software engines have absorbed, reasonable estimates place e-procurement at about 15%. So, for most firms employing such techniques, it has become a significant part of the buying process. Such electronic buying has significantly progressed beyond the use of auctions and now includes an entire field of e-sourcing tools: spend analysis and planning, sourcing directories, direct materials sourcing, RFQ workflow, collaboration, bidding events, bidding analysis, negotiation, contract development/management, trading exchanges, and supplier performance management.

There are also category and industry specialists offering sourcing services such as ChemConnect for chemicals, Covisint for Automotive, GlobalSources for Retail, LifetecNet for Life Sciences, and ProcureZone for construction. There are, indeed, so many choices that it takes a special task force to sort through the options and complete the comparison grid. Moving e-procurement properly into these areas will require a penetrating analysis to make certain the chosen supplier can do more than bring an automation tool to the effort. It is equally important that the software works to support the overall trading relationship and delivers what the buying firm's internal constituents need.

Some e-procurement suppliers focus, for example, on the optimization of the relationship through strong transaction and decision supporting features. Ariba and Commerce One fit here as they provide products designed to manage many transactions. iPlanet's BuyerXpert and Clarus' eProcurement also provide transaction billing and settlement features. Peregrine offers help with asset management and assists MRO purchasing with maintenance schedules and product availability. i2 provides technology that covers the entire production cycle, including resource scheduling, planning, inventory management, and demand forecasting.

In short, there are a plethora of offerings and the firm is well advised to sort out those options against the needs of the categories for which they will be applied. According to experts at *Information Week*, the "key goal is to find the best deal, the right products, sufficient product availability, and acceptable prices. Businesses need, moreover, to evaluate not only prices, but also attributes such as supplier responsiveness, service levels, delivery history, and customer satisfaction ratings" (Foust, 2002, p. 1). These authors present a very good analysis of some major e-procurement suppliers that could be very useful as a firm builds its comparison grid (Foust, 2002, pp. 4–6). Similar information is available through Boston-based AMR Research.

Beyond the techniques and suppliers mentioned, all of the major ERP providers are working to help with SRM efforts. The idea is to assist companies as they design and manage end-to-end supply chain systems, beginning with data analysis and proceeding to real-time project collaboration. A firm with an installed ERP system is also advised to consider how this base can be used and extended into enhancing an SRM effort (Schultz, 2001). Visibility is the central issue as partners share more and make it possible to see what is actually happening in the supply chain while getting a view of performance across the spectrum of activities in the end-to-end processing. Increasing efficiency at lower costs is the usual result.

IMPROVEMENTS CAN BE SIGNIFICANT

Results from SRM efforts and the fall-off events that aid lower-echelon buying systems will vary by firm, partners selected, industry, and market conditions. Case studies are limited as the technique is new and still evolving. An example, however, points out the potential. One firm studied purchased 22,000 products from thousands of suppliers. Following a strategy that began with SRM efforts with the more limited group of strategic suppliers, and extended to "webifying" the lower buy categories through the application of some form of e-procurement, the firm documented the following improvements:

- Inventory turns went from 11 to 24.
- Procurement costs improved by 17%.
- Purchase order cycle time was reduced by 50%.
- Automation of purchase orders went to 70% of the total.

- Inventories identified as excess were eliminated.
- Suppliers rated the effort as good to excellent, particularly in view of the shared savings.

SUMMARY

As a firm's purchasing and sourcing function matures along the supply chain evolution, it moves to a position where it becomes more difficult to attain the kind of early savings that were generated. As this point of diminishing returns is reached, and the firm enters Levels 3 and 4 of the evolution, it makes sense to progress into a more collaborative environment with a few selected strategic suppliers. That move should begin after the internal house is in order. Concise spending visibility is a prerequisite with the total buy known and segregated. The supply base must also be segregated to determine the strategic suppliers on which the firm depends for most of its major purchases.

From this upper echelon list, the firm matches key suppliers with high-impact categories and chooses a small number of partners to participate in a disciplined, systematic supplier relationship management (SRM) effort. These partners meet with the buying firm and establish a mission or strategic purpose for the SRM effort. The focus then moves to analyzing the total cost of ownership (or total life cycle costs) and finding the hidden cost reduction opportunities and extra values in the relationships.

The means to secure these elements develop through joint improvement initiatives with an eye to sharing any further savings discovered. It becomes a sequential process resulting in the identification of specific joint actions that will provide the next level of improvements to the relationship. With the successes gained through SRM, the firm determines, from the many options available, how to automate as much of the remaining sourcing as economically feasible through electronic engines. The company will also be in a much stronger position to initiate CRM initiatives, as discussed in the next chapter.

10

MODELS FOR CUSTOMER RELATIONSHIP MANAGEMENT

As we continue our journey through Level 3 and higher of the supply chain evolution, we make the passage from supplier relationship management (SRM) to customer relationship management (CRM), a natural progression that combines the learning and experience gained from techniques described in the previous chapters with the ardent desire to keep growing the business. Now the firm begins paying serious attention to using supply chain techniques for building top-line revenue as well as reducing costs that affect the bottom line. Such an effort starts when a firm has the internal house in order by virtue of achieving many of the previously discussed initiatives. It expands as the firm moves into the networked arena with the help of equally skilled business partners. In many industries where the number of customers is small, firms will find CRM becomes a necessary effort to sustain the most important customer relationships, but it certainly is not a self-funding exercise. The links to supply chain become an imperative under these conditions, to include improvement benefits that help fund the effort and achieve the goal of better acquiring, satisfying, and retaining the most profitable customers.

To accomplish this goal, companies seek the means to merge advanced supply chain management (ASCM) and their customer management efforts into a CRM process that yields profits and growth. With access to a wealth of information relating to specific customers, buying habits, and market trends, the sales, marketing, and customer service personnel, along with some selected business allies, work to find opportunities for using knowledge to enhance relationships and increase revenues with the most desired customers. Gathering information on key customers, identifying the means of satisfying those with the most value, and increasing long-term loyalty through customized products and services meeting actual needs, become the business imperatives behind the CRM effort. Understanding that the focus on building a profitable customer relationship is reliant on the ability to deliver through an integrated supply chain, is a central concept behind the effort.

CRM EXECUTION HAS BEEN SPOTTY

The fundamental requirements supporting CRM are not exactly novel. Improving profitable revenues with targeted customers and retaining their loyalty have long been central tenets of business strategy. With access to helpful knowledge buried in burgeoning corporate databases, it becomes a modern art enhanced through technology. For that reason, CRM now appears on virtually every business supply chain radar screen as a technique to increase sales, retain existing customers, and acquire new customers. Our research indicates the subject currently receives more attention than any other specific topic related to supply chain management. Indeed, based on surveys of 100 business technology professionals, *Information Week Research* wrote, in its October 2001 report, that "98% say CRM is a strategic program at their company."

When it comes to integrating these systems with ASCM efforts, however, a different picture appears. The mind seems dedicated, but the heart appears to be stalled. Of the 100 companies *Information Week* polled, only 48% said alignment had been achieved. Most firms seemed more concerned with linking CRM to sales and marketing and strategic planning (an internal effort) than with achieving significant revenue growth through external efforts (Maselli, 2001, p. 88). At this stage of its development, the concept of applying CRM to create new business is well understood, but practical applications appear to be very limited, due, in large part, to a poor appreciation of what the real intentions are all about. CRM has been characterized by stovepipe thinking and silo activity constrained to sales and marketing efforts versus being an integrated enterprise initiative. The results have led to CRM becoming a source of many failures. From a related perspective, Darrell Rigby, Fred Reichheld and Phil Schefter, loyalty experts at Bain & Company, report that, "research suggests that one reason CRM backfires is that most executives simply don't understand what they are implementing" (Rigby, 2002, p. 102).

There seem to be some unusual factors relating to the subject. CRM was born of using strategy and process improvement to satisfy targeted customers and enhance sales, but technology has overshadowed the intent. As we researched the subject, we found most efforts were characterized more by an emphasis on applying software and reducing costs, particularly sales and service head count, rather than building revenues with key customers. In addition, cost cutting has become pervasive following the Internet adjustment, and many companies simply do not believe the claims associated with revenue growth through CRM. So far, the highest reported returns on the effort seem to come from call centers, where cost cutting and better resource allocation have led to savings and not to helping the customer. A second intention seems to be foisting a discipline on sales personnel that is often not appreciated, without explaining or demonstrating what is in it for them. Many CRM efforts languish as they become a control mechanism over the salesforce, sales personnel do not enter the necessary data, or the information is not used for the intended purpose.

In this chapter, we investigate the reasons behind this general lack of positive results from what should be a powerful supply chain tool, as we outline models and techniques for gaining greater benefits from an emphasis on the top-line of the profit and loss (P&L) statement. Assistance with this chapter came from Alex Black, Lynette Ferrara, and Patrick Molineux, with particular help coming from Paul Thompson, all partners at CSC Consulting.

MANY CRM EFFORTS LACK A DEFINING PURPOSE

As we analyzed the reasons for the spotty record and poor success rate behind a very desirable and certainly well-supported management initiative, we found, in addition to the issues cited, that much of the problem was associated with the absence of a defining purpose. There was no central imperative that would overcome the usual obstacles encountered in what also becomes a major business transformation. That problem starts with the definition of what we are considering. Gartner, Inc. offers its interpretation of CRM as "a customer-focused strategy aimed at anticipating, understanding and responding to the needs of an enterprise's current and prospective customers. The objective of a CRM strategy is to optimize profitability, revenue and customer satisfaction" (Gartner, 2001, p. 1).

Rigby and others present another definition: "CRM aligns business processes with customer strategies to build customer loyalty and increase profits over time" (Rigby, 2002, p. 102). We find these definitions are appropriate to the subject but lack the depth that would lead to defined purposes. For that reason, we add to these interpretations that CRM is the practical implementation of business strategy for identifying, acquiring, and retaining profitable customers, through a focus on:

- Applying portfolio management techniques to customer segmentation so knowledge can be used to increase share of business with selected customers
- Linking customer-related processes throughout an extended enterprise network so valued and trusted partners can help in the pursuit of profitable revenues
- Enabling fundamental productivity improvements for customers, key business partners, and employees to enhance the desired relationships
- Creating a customer/seller environment that is substantially more beneficial to both buyer and seller
- Providing techniques of greater value and benefit for those doing the selling and customer service
- Integrating critical information throughout all customer channels and back office functions from customers through suppliers, for the purpose of establishing the most effective system of response to actual customer needs. The integration of customer information is to achieve the goal of creating a single view of the customer across the selling organization, no matter what channel they choose for communications.

In short, CRM is something a business organization and its business allies do...not something they purchase. CRM is not an off-the-shelf software tool that will manage relationships in a flawless manner and deliver higher sales and profits. Technology and software will support the effort; they will not provide the means to assure satisfaction of key customers or build new revenues. Any CRM effort must be capable of adding value and delivering results against customer needs. This requirement reinforces the need for supply chain integration as a means of fulfillment on the demand side of the chain. CRM should also not be confused with the traditional emphasis on improving employee applications such as salesforce automation, marketing analysis, and call center or help desk applications. The correct CRM strategy becomes oriented around supporting the sales and service personnel, making their jobs easier and more effective, and then enabling them in acquiring, satisfying, growing, and sustaining the right customers — those with the greatest long-term benefit for themselves, the firm, and the firm's business partners. The central concept in this strategy is to grow the business with long-term annuities through features of customer intimacy.

Within that perspective, CRM is not for all companies. Many firms indicated to us that they intend to spend little money in this area because their central focus will be kept on cost reduction and operational excellence. Some of these firms are producing and selling commodities and the feeling is that CRM is an unnecessary expense. As much as we disagree with this philosophy, it is dominant in some industry and market segments, and it inhibits a proper customer orientation and implementation of CRM.

Therefore, as a firm decides to embark on what will be a potentially very expensive and lengthy journey into CRM, the leaders had better be sure there is a defining purpose and cultural orientation toward the customer that will ensure success. They should also understand that many elements of CRM could be effectively satisfied by focusing on customer strategies and processes without employing technology. When a firm decides to go forward, these leaders will find such concepts are not new. The idea that the more customer-centric your firm's culture is, the greater will be its success in the new business environment has been an item of faith for some time, especially with those companies that interface with key strategic customers. What is new and necessary is a strong central focus such that CRM becomes the vehicle for the deployment of strategies, processes, and technologies that help acquire, develop, and retain desired customers. That becomes the mantra behind CRM and the guiding purpose.

A generally accepted business tenet that helps this purpose is: firms that become adept at garnering greater customer loyalty through a true focus on customer needs and satisfaction grow much faster than others in the industry. These leaders tend to track customer satisfaction metrics as much as or more than traditional business values. Industry leaders such as Cisco, eBay, Hewlett-Packard, Land's End, and The Vanguard Group tie a significant portion of employee compensation, for example, to customer satisfaction in their pursuit of this tenet. Unfortunately, our research indicates that more companies profess a customer-centric orientation when they actually favor operational excellence or product/service innovation as core strengths. That's a conflict that needs resolving before expecting success with CRM. If you want to look for root causes of CRM failure, you don't need to go beyond the lack of adequate change management skills within the organization and an absence of an orientation toward the customer as the vital organ of the firm.

The important questions for today's managers become:

- On which customers do we focus the greatest attention?
- Do we know the value of our customers or the cost of the services we provide?
- How do we use our database and that of our allies to find the means to do a better job of customer satisfaction?
- What are the specific ingredients of a network CRM effort that will establish the level of customer loyalty we know will guarantee success?

Answers to these inquiries demand a customer-centric defining purpose for the effort, something that has generally been missing. At the core of the correct orientation should be a strategic intent to create profitable new revenues with targeted customers and consumer groups, important distributors, retailers, and intermediary agents influential in the buying decision. In that sense, a short list of perhaps 10 to 20% of potential customers would become targets.

This purpose creates the need for narrowly focused analytical tools, which become the primary ingredients in CRM. From the appropriate analytics will come the operational techniques that take advantage of the knowledge to generate profitable revenues. This movement does not mean the effort is intended to automate marketing, sales, and servicing functions. Rather, it means the firm and its closest allies work on finding the most effective way to use customer and partner information and apply models relating to customer behavior to create discernibly better marketing and sales efforts that end with superior results. Included in this purpose will be the tactful elimination of the least profitable and often most costly customers and a new system that has strong intrinsic value for the sales and service personnel involved.

CRM BEGINS WITH A COMPELLING BUSINESS CASE

In spite of the advocacy we are giving to this subject, and the intuitive validity of the concepts, there must be a clear definition of return on the effort or the requisite management support will be missing in action, and that return must be garnered in the face of ever-increasing costs and difficulty. Customers today expect and generally receive superior service, so that has become the table stakes in the modern business game. Distinguishing your firm and its allies from the competition takes something extra. At the same time, maintaining a high level of customer satisfaction has become more complex and difficult as there are so many different approaches being taken.

From the vantage point of the customers, there are critical links between supply chain and customer touch points, the incidences of contact and service that distinguish the supplier's value. If we can define these points of impact and describe the value of supply chain improvements to strategic customers, many of the supply chain benefits can create substantial cost savings to fund ancillary CRM improvements. Furthermore, customers have multiple points of communication with suppliers, multiple channels of delivery and service, and some expect linkage all the way back to primary sources. Suppliers must allocate both automated and human interfaces with the appropriate customers and situations so the right company gets the right service through the channel of choice.

Dealing with these modern challenges requires investment in changing both the organization and the technologies on which it depends. That creates the need to have a compelling business case to encourage and assure the required changes to normal business activities. Such a case can determine the priority of CRM spending, where to start based on value to be added, and potentially make additional roadmap enhancements pay for themselves through initial benefits achievement. An ROI-based road map, with bite-size release strategies that define the functionality to be attained and the residual business benefits, is absolutely necessary. Those benefits should include the supply chain enhancements that get an organization closer to satisfying the most important customers.

Before we outline the techniques and models to be used, it is appropriate to consider a number of contemporary measurements that will help establish and confirm the business case. A critical doctrine of CRM is that it is substantially more efficient to maintain current customers than to acquire new ones. A measurement such as customer turnover rates, or what has been termed as churn, is often used to justify the substantial expenditures required for a CRM implementation. Emerging from this idea are new measurements, such as customer lifetime value and customer ROI, that attempt to relate the long-term value and profitability of a customer to the cost of maintaining the relationship. As the business case is constructed, other traditional measures should also be used.

We recommend that pursuing CRM improvements should include these types and magnitudes of quantifiable benefits:

- Increased satisfaction ratings with key customer groups reaching highs of 95 to 98% or more with the most strategic group
- Increased revenues in the targeted categories of the customer segmentation from 3 to 10% per sales representative
- Increased efficiency and effectiveness of customer service and sales organizations in terms of customer ratings and solutions provided
- Reduced operating expenses and nonsales expenses documented through a 5 to 10% reduction in general, sales, and administrative (GS&A) costs
- Improved internal satisfaction ratings from sales and service personnel evaluating the value received from their part in the CRM effort
- Reduced customer churn

Because of the newness of the technology, the complexity of the implementation required, and the magnitude of change to be accepted by the organization, building a fact-based business case can be elusive.

The measures indicated might be viewed as incomplete and others may be required. The second area to address then is the relationship between CRM and the sales and marketing strategy. The CRM business case is seen as most compelling when it is viewed as an enabler of a holistic sales and marketing strategy, one in which opening new markets, using new channels, and creating an environment that makes CRM a critical factor are necessary to achieve overall business objectives. The ability, moreover, to deploy CRM must be seen in the context of the firm's central purpose and the means of distinguishing the firm in the competitive arena. When trying to make certain there is a strong business case, definable business metrics must be determined to calculate success and the ultimate business value being added. There are also a number of questions that must be answered positively:

- Sales efficiency — What is the value of more face time with the right customers? Can you expect increased sales from increased attention? How will the improvements be measured?
- Customer segmentation — Have you identified the unique value of special customers to the firm? Do you understand the value propositions being delivered to those customers? Are you supplying service based on those values? Have you asked key customers what they value most?
- Resource allocation — Have we based our resource investment on adding customer value? Have we accomplished an improvement to the unrealized value of customers or potential for growth?
- Compensation — Is the firm's compensation system aligned with the sales focus the firm aspires to achieve? Does your firm reward behavior that leads to better customer relationships and greater revenues?
- Organization design — Do our infrastructure and assigned responsibilities meet our objectives for satisfying customer requirements and fulfilling needs?
- Call center deployment — How many call centers and customer service representatives (CSRs) are necessary to adequately meet the needs of our customers? Do these CSRs add value or mainly respond to low-complexity questions that could be automated? Are the responses and time to service adequate for segmented customer needs?
- Consistency — Do customers get consistent, timely answers through various mediums of interaction? Are you improving the cycle times of value to your customers to industry best levels? Do you have a single view of the customer no matter what channel they may choose for communication?

With answers that support the customer-centric orientation, the firm moves to a second consideration of great importance. The business case must also clearly spell out the values for those doing the selling and servicing. It must be a dynamic document that shows what is in the effort for the sales representatives, agents, brokers, dealers, or other people making the calls and doing the selling. The added value for the front-line contact people doing sales service must also be considered. These are the people on whom success depends and, without a clear definition of what value they receive for their effort, there should be little wonder as to why most CRM efforts fail. When completed, this business case will provide the organizational alignment required for success and will be the key to unlocking the potential benefits derived from CRM across the firm. In essence, the business case should be a living document that continues to be refined through every phase of the CRM journey to track costs and resulting benefits based on predefined measures of success.

CRM CONTINUES WITH CAREFUL CUSTOMER SEGMENTATION

The CRM effort then begins with something that has become a business essential — the segmentation of customers in terms of value to the firm. Using the knowledge from the network databases and the skilled intuitions of those responsible for building revenues, existing and prospective customers are carefully analyzed and fitted into a decision matrix similar to that used for SRM. Customer profiles, histories, lifetime value analyses, calculated risk analysis, special demands, historic relationships, and other pertinent data are reviewed, often with the help of trusted advisors, to complete the matrix and use it as a guide for the CRM effort.

In the best of the efforts we have reviewed, some form of activity-based costing or balanced scorecard is also used to make sure the firm and its partners know the true costs of servicing those customers that reach the highest target level. Telecommunication industry studies, for example, show that as much as 80% of the profits can come from as little as 3% of the buildings in a company's territory. The key is to then expand the effort to analyze and understand behavior and predict which customers will respond appropriately to what becomes very special attention and service. That becomes the art of turning a mountain of available data into a usable knowledge base to better satisfy the chosen customers, generate new revenues with better profits, and develop happier sales and service personnel. In one enabling effort, SAS International is working to link their demand intelligence module, which does predictive modeling around demand, with their value chain analyzer module that does activity-based costing. The result would be that a firm could do what-if scenarios around demand changes, and understand the resulting cost implications through the supply chain fulfillment steps.

Figure 10.1 is a four-square matrix useful with a customer segmentation analysis. On the vertical axis, the ranking moves from low to high profit. This part of the segmentation requires a solid knowledge of what the actual cost to serve might be and the actual profits derived from serving the customer. On the horizontal axis, the variation is from low to high strategic value to the firm. An analysis similar to that portrayed in Figure 9.4 for suppliers can be used here to place customers along the strategic value dimension. The actual criteria used must be specific to the company's capabilities and needs and should reflect consensus across the major sectors of the firm.

Starting in the lower left corner of the matrix, with the low profit and low strategic value quadrant, dubbed Usual Suspects, we find the group every firm possesses and is reluctant to face. These suspects are generally a drain on company time and resources and offer virtually no possibility of reaching higher categories of significance. They tend to survive on the

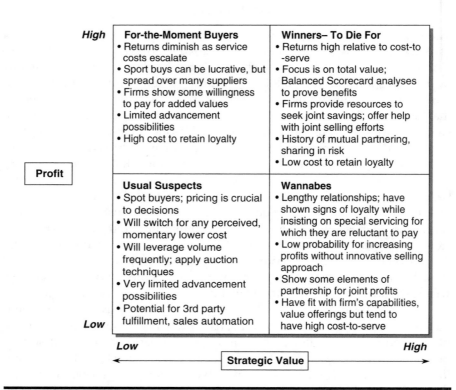

Figure 10.1   Customer Product/Service Segmentation

customer list because no one takes the time to question and purge the list. Decision rules for this category are relatively straightforward:

- Consider polite withdrawal and do not include these customers in any CRM effort
- Institute selective price increases for categories/SKUs for longer terms in areas of interest; maintain relationship only for categories with profit
- Strictly limit any new investments or special sales attention
- Establish minimum volumes and pricing; pass ownership to third-party organizations
- Automate processing with self-service features or abandon solicitation

Moving up to the area of high profits and low strategic value we find the For the Moment Buyers. Here there are profits worth pursuing, but with a very fickle constituency. CRM efforts should be avoided or very carefully applied in this segment, and the following decision rules should apply:

- Carefully cultivate a few potential winners that will react positively to demonstration of values rendered
- Match features and services with actual needs; emphasize self-service features
- Manage contracts limited to low cost and core competency categories and SKUs
- Orient sales effort around demonstration of full cost and values added
- Limit CRM involvement to only those with the highest long-term potential

As we move down to the lower right-hand quadrant, we encounter the Wannabes. These are customers that have strategic value but never seem to pay enough for products and services to garner a winner status. They are generally long-term customers that have a good match with the firm's capabilities but insist on shopping the industry or market to verify they are not overpaying for whatever they receive, and they always want the lion's share of special attention and service. The objectives in this sector become:

- Sort through to find a few candidates for higher status by virtue of limited special attention that returns above-average profits
- Try selective special introductions or promotions to test willingness to pay for added value

- Find hidden opportunities to match values with selective pricing
- Match limited investments with actual potential returns
- Establish cost controls on service costs
- Apply CRM very carefully to the highest potential firms

Finally, in the upper right, we see the highest profit and the greatest strategic value. These are the Winners, or the customers "to die for," and the core group to be included in any CRM effort. Now the objectives are oriented around retention and enlarging revenues with this group. The decision rules become:

- Allow highest access to connectivity features, use of extranet and advance information on developments, new features, and product promotions
- Invite into membership on advisory council; encourage joint development/investment projects
- Provide frequent communication on first offerings
- Delight, nurture, defend, sustain
- Avoid allowing cost to serve negate emphasis on overall value
- Begin and enlarge CRM effort with this group

For a particular firm or industry, this matrix and the decision rules can be modified in a customized manner. The point is there must be some solid mechanism for selecting the candidates for the CRM effort or it becomes a diluted exercise of trying to please all customers and will quickly run out of steam. Focusing on the area where the greatest opportunity exists is a simple mandate for success.

EFFECTIVE DATABASE ANALYSIS LEADS TO PERTINENT CRM KNOWLEDGE

Many companies have implemented operational CRM efforts, but have not realized the value of those investments due to an absence of integrated customer data. Because they lack a single view of the customer, these companies cannot move to analytical CRM, which is where much of the value lies.

Firms of any size in any industry can apply the type of matrix described in Figure 10.1 as an aid to establishing a single view approach to customer relationship management. CRM is not just for the largest and most powerful of companies. The technique requires knowledge typically found in existing databases and a concerted effort to use this knowledge as a tool for distinguishing the firm in the eyes of the most-valued customers. Figure

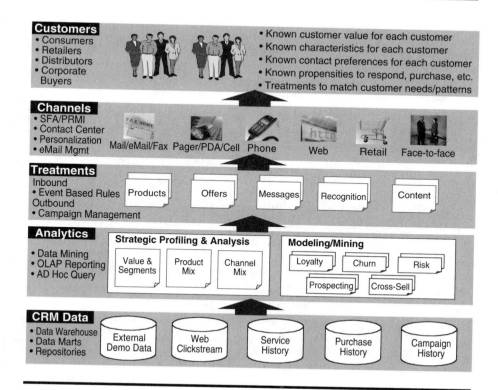

Figure 10.2   Data Acquisition and Analysis Are Critical to CRM

10.2 is a framework for conducting an effective data acquisition and integration analysis as a crucial ingredient in a successful CRM effort.

The process moves from bottom to top. It begins with assembly of the appropriate CRM data from the many sources available. It proceeds to cross-functional analysis that mines the data to establish profiling and modeling techniques useful in the segmentation and decision rules. The treatments sector matches the profiles and models with the products, offers, messages, content, and recognition that will be at the heart of the CRM methodology. Input from a few key customers can have great value in this area of the model. Channels to make certain key customers are getting their products and services the way they want them must be considered. The process culminates with the customers and value proposition that makes the most sense for those of most importance.

In a general sense, the more information you have, the more beneficial the analysis will be. In a larger sense, the care with which you analyze, consolidate, and use the data will lead to greatest results, and that is an element not restricted by company size. Discovering why good customers leave you, anticipating changes in buying patterns based on trend analysis, knowing how to take advantage of environmental factors, and being able to react properly to shifts in category preferences by age, gender, and ethnicity are part of the art behind CRM.

The whole effort yields the most benefit when several groups analyze the data together to make certain there are returns for all parts of the company. If the CRM strategy is to be a keystone in the firm's business, it must positively affect all constituents. While we advocate building CRM internally first, then expanding into a network effort, it is still advisable to involve a few selected allies on the supply and customer side to critique the process. To begin, the analysis should clearly show that the highest customer segment does have the greatest positive impact on the company's future. That's why we stress the need for activity-based costing and balanced scorecards. Increased revenues with firms that draw excess resources in relation to what they pay will eventually ruin a firm. Customers that constantly change schedules and require special attention unnecessarily are also drains on profits. We strongly suggest a general review of the data analysis so the CRM decision rules reflect the consensus of a cross section of all important company functions.

Next, the analysis should confirm that the most valued customers are receiving the most effective attention. That starts with asking some of these customers what value they would like to see added if the firm is going to make such a major investment in CRM. Our research shows the answers to that query are often unexpected. What products should be offered, for example, may vary from those perceived to have the most value. How the products are distributed, through which channels, which partners should be used, what the real delivery cycles should be, and so forth often come under scrutiny and new decision rules emerge. Finding out why some of these customers have defected is equally valuable as it quickly identifies problems needing attention.

Third, you should decide how technology could become an enabler for this coveted group of winners. With an understanding of the highest-value customers in hand, the firm targets direct marketing efforts that are matched with the identified needs. CRM starts to capture important product and service behavior information and feeds data back to the desired customers, which will induce them to increase buying activity, make joint developments, and participate in shared risk investments. Process transactions can be improved and automated where appropriate. Access to important supply chain information can be offered to those having a need for real-time exposure. In the most effective systems, this knowledge sharing extends from end to end in the supply chain network. The goal becomes oriented around building an interactive relationship with customers and growing overall satisfaction based on increased knowledge and understanding. Also, there is an underlying objective to predict when and why customers might be predisposed to leave, and to find the right incentives for retaining them. Bringing the solutions offered through advanced supply chain management closer to the customers can only serve to satisfy them better than competing networks and thereby increase their loyalty.

With an effective database analysis will come the right consolidation of information and knowledge so the firm can garner the desired improved relationships and revenues. When the use of the knowledge is discussed with the sales and service representatives to determine how it will be beneficial to them, the loop begins to close. Now the firm clearly explains why the extra work will bring value to those doing the work and how it will result in personal value. This combined knowledge launches the CRM effort through a methodology that takes advantage of the total company consensus.

CRM METHODOLOGY GUIDES PROCESS CONSTRUCTION AND IMPLEMENTATION

Figure 10.3 is a general version of a methodology used to guide a CRM implementation. It follows a staged progression across three phases:

- **Assess,** during which the firm evaluates its current situation in specific functional areas such as marketing, sales effectiveness, salesforce automation, or customer service. The intent of this

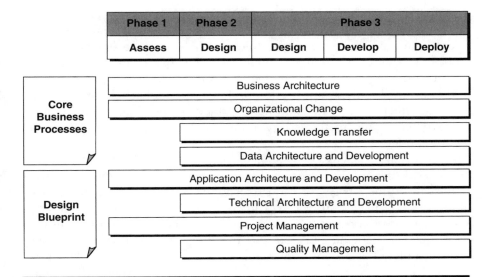

Figure 10.3   A CRM Methodology

activity is to define a functional strategy for improving CRM operations and results, internally and externally, while identifying options that can be pursued to provide further benefits. The assess phase concludes with the creation of an in-depth business case for implementing the CRM strategy.

■ **Design,** during which the firm refines the value proposition and purposes supporting the CRM effort. High-level business processes critical to execution are identified, an activity that is facilitated with input from the blueprint that emanates form the core business processes identified as being critical for CRM success. A second blueprint that defines core system components is also used to define the architecture needed to implement the solutions. Business and technical requirements are mapped to select the most appropriate enabling software for the specific situation. A release plan that outlines follow-on implementation activities is created at the conclusion of this phase.

■ **Implement,** which is organized across three sub-phases — create, develop, and deploy. From current best practices and applications and knowledge of techniques that work, business processes are established in detail and mapped to software package capabilities. Business scenarios are written for use during development to configure and customize software according to the firm's actual needs, particularly in relation to what key customers have indicated would be the most beneficial CRM features.

Initially, activities are grouped according to functional areas in which the firm sees skill sets working together to accomplish mutual objectives. Bands spanning the three methodological phases represent the activity blocks that aggregate similar activities. These activities include: business architecture, organizational change, knowledge transfer, data architecture and development, application architecture and development, technical architecture and development, project management, and quality management. This methodology is at the heart of the model to be recommended.

The steps and activities that take place in the implementation are illustrated in Figure 10.4. Here we see the various activity blocks arrayed against the three phases of CRM execution. Beginning with the activity of establishing the **Business Architecture** intended to support CRM, an assessment step appears to ensure that members across the firm understand the vision being pursued and that the segmentation analysis has been completed in a consistent manner. There should be a good understanding of the value of closing any gaps between current performance and intended results and using those values to substantiate the payback

Activity Block	Assess	Design	Implement		
			Create	Develop	Deploy
Business Architecture	• Confirm current state of business • Map current customer-facing processes • Understand the business vision • Segment and prioritize the customer base • Identify competitive environment and capabilities • Create future-state vision of business architecture • Perform gap analysis for business • Develop implementation road map • Develop business case	• Define business principles, constraints and assumptions • Identify business context and processes • Identify candidate system functions • Identify and profile user groups • Identify usability requirements and performance metrics	• Confirm business objectives and requirements • Design business processes • Identify and define business rules • Identify and define content and knowledge requirements • Create content development plan • Define report requirements • Map business requirements to application capabilities • Identify and define application configuration requirements • Identify and define customization requirements • Prepare business scenarios	• Develop content and knowledge base materials • Finalize process design • Finalize report design • Update business case	• Monitor business process effectiveness and recommend changes

Figure 10.4   Activities in the CRM Methodology (continued)

on the effort. The business case should be developed and an implementation road map accepted before proceeding.

In the design phase, the firm defines its business concepts and any constraints that could interfere with execution. From the segmentation analysis, the highest category-targeted customers become candidates for

| Activity Block | Assess | Design | Implement | | |
			Create	Develop	Deploy
			• Design user interaction • Define usability goals and performance metrics		
Organizational Change	• Understand current customer-facing organization and work distribution • Understand current performance metrics • Create future-state vision or organization and management • Develop implementation road map	• Identify potential organizational impact • Create management alignment strategy • Gain executive alignment (ongoing)	• Identify opportunity for organizational changes • Identify policy changes • Identify skills • Identify key roles • Identify locations • Create organizational roll out • Gain executive alignment (ongoing) • Create monitoring systems	• Develop policies, values, beliefs and culture necessary to support the new system • Develop organizational roll out • Develop performance measurement system	•
Knowledge Transfer	•	• Identify training and knowledge transfer requirements • Identify transition approach	• Create training plan • Create education and communication materials • Create final transition plan	• Develop training and communication materials • Develop training program • Develop transition program	• Develop training • Develop client transition plan
Data Architecture and Development	•	• Identify data and content categories	• Identify data sources and owners • Load test data	• Develop reports and analyses	• Finalize and test data model
Application	• Assess	• Confirm	• Create	• Run	• Finalize

Figure 10.4 (continued)   Activities in the CRM Methodology

action and the firm identifies how the system will respond to their needs. The CRM users are identified and profiled for needs and enhancement possibilities and metrics are established to track improvements. Once again, we strongly recommend interviews with at least a few of the

Activity Block	Assess	Design	Implement		
			Create	Develop	Deploy
Architecture and Development	current technology landscape • Review latest techno-capabilities and opportun-ities • Consider future-state vision of technology landscape • Perform gap analyses for technology and identify strategy for filling gaps • Begin implementa-tion roadmap	current system landscape • Define system principles, constraints and assumptions • Identify candidate functions and applications • Identify candidate software packages • Select software packages • Create conceptual application architecture	technical scripts • Identify and refine interfaces to other applications • Identify and design to-be-built component and interfaces	technical scripts • Execute business scenarios • Identify interfaces • Develop and test interface functional specifications • Develop and unit test integration objects • Develop reports and analyses • Execute interface projects • Configure applicaton • Identify gaps between business requirements and package configuration • Reconfigure application to solve gaps • Iterate gap identification resolution activities • Revise con-figuration workbook	application architecture
Technical Architecture and Development	•	• Confirm current tech-nology landscape • Define tech-nology plat-form, infra-structure and hardware requirements	• Specify and acquire technical infrastucture • Install appli-cation and technical infrastructure	• Install and configure production environment	• Finalize technical infrastructure • Deploy business solution in production environment

Figure 10.4 (continued)   Activities in the CRM Methodology

included candidates to determine what they would like to see in a more focused and intense effort at relationship building.

The implementation phase has many activities as the firm creates, develops, and deploys its CRM methodology. Now the business objectives and requirements for change are confirmed. Business rules consistent with

Activity Block	Assess	Design	Implement		Deploy
			Create	**Develop**	**Deploy**
		• Identify candidate technologies • Prove candidate products • Select technologies • Design conceptual technical architecture	• Install and configure network • Design and install development environment • Design production environment		
Quality Management (Testing, Performance Engineering and Configuration Management)	•	• Capture business volumes	• Identify testing requirements • Identify testing tools and environment • Identify performance engineering requirements • Identify and define service-level agreements • Identify configuration management requirements • Identify configuration management tool • Identify configuration management environment	• Install testing environment • Create test plans and scenarios • Define and develop user acceptance plan • Run unit and component tests • Run integration and user acceptance tests • Conduct stress test • Optimize performance • Maintain and support configuration management environment	• Maintain and support configuration management environment

Figure 10.4 (continued)   Activities in the CRM Methodology

the CRM orientation are established, as well as the content and knowledge requirements that will become new operating parameters for the company. An important step is to map the business requirements with the application capabilities to identify any possible gaps between intentions and poor performance before the customer discovers the resulting problems.

Activity Block	Assess	Design	Implement		
			Create	Develop	Deploy
			• Train users of testing and configuration management tools		
Project Management	• Confirm project objectives and scope • Prepare project plan	• Define project scope and releases • Mobilize team and define roles and respon-sibilities	• Create release plan • Perform ongoing project management actvities	• Prioritize gaps discovered during Situation Demonstra-tion Lab (SDL) • Create and finalize plans for gap resolution • Update business case	• Deliver project • Obtain sign-off • Gather lessons learned

Figure 10.4 (continued)   Activities in the CRM Methodology

Business scenarios are prepared and user interaction defined so the system can be tested with a pilot group of customers.

In the develop step, the content and knowledge base materials are defined as a key to gaining higher satisfaction and loyalty from the target group. Here the process design is finalized around features that will add value to the firm's offerings to the key customers and the reporting system established for tracking and documenting results. It is very helpful to also update the business case to support such an extensive effort as CRM. Finally, deployment takes place as a system is launched to monitor business process effectiveness and recommend any changes needed going forward.

In the **Organizational Change** activity, the assess step ensures that people across the firm understand how the current customer-facing activities are organized and function and what metrics are used to calibrate success or failure. An improved future state vision is considered and an implementation road map is started. The design step identifies the potential impact on the organization and its key customers, establishes executive acceptance of the premises and strategic intentions, and aligns support for the effort.

As this activity moves to implementation, the create phase is used to identify the organizational changes required and the opportunities to be addressed. The policy changes are detailed and the required new skills, roles, and locations for execution are identified. The organizational roll out is established and, with executive alignment, the monitoring system is created. The develop phase includes setting and understanding policies, values, beliefs, and cultural imperatives that will assure success with the new system. The rollout sequence is detailed and the performance measurement system established. The deploy phase covers executing the rollout and monitoring the results of the crucial organizational changes that must take place — and adjusting, if necessary, for actual results.

The **Knowledge Transfer** activity moves directly to the design step and identifies the training and knowledge transfer requirements. It also identifies the proper approach to transitioning the firm from its current environment into the new CRM environment. It progresses to implementation with the creation of a training plan, the supporting educational and communication materials, and the final transition plan. Then the training and communication materials are developed, the training program finalized, and details of the transition plan established. Deployment comes with the delivery of the training and execution of the transition plan, often moved through the firm one business unit at a time.

The **Data Architecture** activity moves in a similar direct manner, starting with the design and identification of the necessary data and content categories that will support the CRM effort. It proceeds to creating the data sources to be accessed, identifying those responsible for ownership of the data, and instituting a test to determine that the correct information can be effectively accessed. The proper reports and analytical procedures are developed and the data model is finalized and tested under operating conditions.

The **Application and Architecture Development** activity is more complicated. In the assess step, the current technology landscape is reviewed against the latest technology capabilities and opportunities being demonstrated within and without the industry. A future state vision of an improved technology landscape is considered, while a gap analysis is performed to determine the difference between what can be accomplished with the current technology and what is possible with an improved condition. An implementation road map is then started toward selection of the appropriate enabling technology tools.

In the design step, the company confirms its current system landscape, taking care to be critical of strengths and weaknesses. The system principles, assumptions, and constraints are defined and the firm moves to identify candidate functions and applications for improvement. Candidate software packages are considered and evaluated and selection made, often after demonstration of capabilities that match identified needs. Then the conceptual application software is created.

In the implement step, a team creates the technical scripts needed to direct execution. Interfaces required with other applications, internally and externally, are identified, as well as the to-be-built components. Under the development step, a team will run the technical scripts while executing various business scenarios and options. The necessary interfaces will be clarified, finalized, and tested. Customized components will be watched closely as reports and analyses are developed to prove the value of the effort. Interface projects will be piloted and applications configured to identify gaps between business requirements and the package configuration so problems can be resolved and the configuration workbook revised. When all parameters are satisfied, the application architecture is finalized and prepared for roll out.

The **Technical Architecture and Development** activity is meant to assure that the technology landscape is defined and matches well with the prescribed needs of the CRM effort. It moves through the matrix in a manner intended to make certain members across the organization view the final design and deployment as beneficial for the internal functions as well as the key customers.

The **Quality Management** activity, which includes testing, performance engineering, and configuration management, moves first to the design step where the team captures the intended business volumes with the targeted customers. That means an outline of the business activities to be impacted by the CRM effort is drawn. With this information, implementation begins. The firm identifies the testing requirements and environment and selects tools and performance requirements that assure success. Service level agreements must be identified as well as the configuration management tools that will be used. These tools are installed and users are trained to implement them.

As the effort moves to develop, the testing environment is installed, test plans and various potential scenarios are created, and the user acceptance plan is defined and developed. Unit and component tests are performed as well as integration and user acceptance tests. The idea is to do enough preliminary work to make certain the effort will result in optimum performance while maintaining and supporting the intended management environment. When ready, deployment begins with the expectation that all the necessary preliminary work has been completed to maintain and support the configuration management environment.

Finally, in the **Project Management** activity, an assess step is included to confirm the project objectives and scope. A special team is mobilized and assigned to define the roles and responsibilities required to kick off the CRM effort. In the design step, this team releases the project scope and begins the effort. The ongoing activities now include completing and updating the CRM project plan, developing and managing risk management throughout the effort, producing status reports, holding status and review meetings, producing delivery assurance reports, and holding deliverable meetings with key customers to obtain acceptance.

The implementation steps are fairly straightforward and include creation of a release plan and performance of ongoing project management activities. They also include prioritizing gaps discovered during a situation demonstration lab (SDL) conducted to simulate the changed conditions, creating and finalizing plans to resolve those gaps, and updating the business case when appropriate. The deployment phase includes delivering the CRM process across the firm, obtaining executive acceptance, and gathering lessons learned for enhancing the CRM effort as it goes forward.

THE REQUIRED LINKAGE TO ASCM CANNOT BE OVERLOOKED

With CRM in place and ready for activation, another typical mistake must be avoided — the lack of a supply chain system prepared to meet the improved demand from key, targeted customers and consumer groups. It is axiomatic that, if a CRM initiative is embraced and rolled out with appropriate support, a spike in demand will be one of the beneficial results. At the same time, if the proper linkage with those in the supply chain responsible for fulfillment is not equally prepared, much of that spike can be lost as orders are not completed. The merging of ASCM and CRM is not as readily accepted as it should be, to assure success with most efforts. Firms typically launch CRM and then rely on basically manual processing to satisfy handling the new revenues through telephone and facsimile communication to heroically expedite response.

When the supply chain is particularly long and extends through many partners, the results are predictable — failure with what would otherwise have been a very successful roll out. CRM demands a successful and dynamic relationship between those responsible for generating the new revenues and those responsible for fulfilling the generated expectations. Simply put, that means an alliance between efforts to optimize plant and labor efficiency (maximum quality and minimum cost) with sales and marketing effectiveness (flexibility and satisfaction). In some cases, a third party can play a very important role in that integration.

When Mountain View, California giant, Intuit Inc., decided to use CRM to enhance the sales of its products, including the Quicken and Quick Books products, it also engaged Modus Media International Inc. to reproduce the CDs, boxes, and manuals that make Quicken a reality. Modus Media has great experience helping firms such as Intuit stick to their core strengths while the firm handles the details of packaging and delivery. Ingram Micro Inc., a Santa Ana, California-based technology distributor, was also engaged to streamline the fulfillment process for Intuit's retail customers. The three organizations are working as one with the common goal of responding effectively to the sales growth.

Multiple participants will be a factor in any modern distribution system and, as CRM becomes a tool for generating greater revenues, it will be imperative that the linked partners react appropriately to swings in demand from the targeted customers and consumers. That can only be done with visible, real-time connectivity across the total extended enterprise. Information sharing, especially on what is needed, and exchange of knowledge, especially on what can be provided, become the new tools of success. Anything less will doom CRM to failure.

TECHNOLOGY USED AS AN ENABLER

With the methodology in place and the roll out under way, attention can turn to making sure the technology being used will be an effective enabler. That can require multiple areas of support. When Madison, Wisconsin-based Alliant Energy decided to apply CRM as a means of improving its relationships with its most important commercial customers, management decided to center its CRM strategy on face-to-face contact. According to Mike Nutt, manager of sales systems support, "Account managers and support personnel on the road have remote access to Alliant's Saratoga Systems CRM software with all relevant customer data and billing information" (Maselli, 2002, p. 55).

As the effort progressed, the firm discovered not all customer support was reaching its intended standards. The process of notifying a customer that a power interruption would occur, for example, was not happening in a timely manner. Since Alliant has tariff agreements with most of its largest customers, which include incentives for curtailing energy usage during peak periods of demand, service agents were required to alert customers about power interruptions. The volume of such calls and the difficulty of reaching the main person on the first attempt meant that more than an hour could pass before the right information was in the right hands. This lack of timely contact was considered a significant problem by Alliant and its customers.

To resolve the issue, Alliant implemented a real-time message alert and delivery system from EnvoyWorldWide Inc. in combination with its core CRM software. Through this system, the firm sends messages to key business customers' "wired and wireless devices about impending power-downs." The system is able to notify multiple people at the customer site by facsimile, pager, or PDA. "Now we can alert 20 people or more from each company at once," Nutt reports. "To ensure that businesses receive the notification, business contacts call a number that's hooked into the Envoy system. Alliant can monitor the responses online and in real time to ensure all customers acknowledge receipt of the notification" (Maselli, 2002, p. 55).

In this case example, the firm followed the correct path to success. It began with a small group of core customers and developed a business case that would assure greater satisfaction. It then proceeded to design an improved system and install the enabling software to facilitate the intended results. Customers and suppliers are both happier and the interaction is faster and more reliable.

KEYS TO CRM SUCCESS

Before concluding this chapter, we should take one last look at the factors most important to assuring success with what will be a major investment and significant change to the firm's culture. As any firm constructs and implements its CRM effort, there are key aspects that appear in all of the successful efforts we have researched, including these favorites:

- Focus on business needs before technology implementation. When a firm introduces CRM without a clear connection to its business needs, it falls into a trap. The salespeople do not populate the database with the required customer information and other functions struggle to get data into a usable form for their needs. To be successful, the company must take the time to present the compelling business case behind the CRM effort and clearly articulate to the sales and service people involved in execution how the improved methodology will help them in the execution of their work. With the business needs identified and the objectives tied to personal benefits, the technology or software can be installed in a way that will assist the people and make more money for everyone. Without these ingredients, most efforts fail.
- Design process steps and enabling systems to help the customer, not plug-in software that automates back-office procedures. Getting CRM right is all about how all parts of the business interact better with key customers. Included in the execution must be a fail-safe system to make it easy and effective for these customers to conduct business with the firm. That goal requires new and different approaches, unfamiliar to many in the organization. The best approach begins with a sustained focus on a strategy oriented around satisfying what the key customers want and need. This approach should then be extended to determining how to make life easier and more effective for the sales and service personnel. When properly in place and working, the back-office connectivity can be improved as well.
- Align CRM objectives with the business strategy. Above all else, don't try to ram the CRM effort through without taking the time to win support across the firm and making certain the objectives

and intended deliverables match the overall business strategy. Remember that CRM is not a product or a single business application; it must be an integral part of the firm's business strategy and behavior, oriented around a customer-centric culture. The firm must accept the fact that CRM encompasses the entire organization and many activities of its business partners. It involves integration across disparate functions and systems, from the front office to the back office and to network relationships across the supply chain network. This linkage must be of the highest caliber possible. That will not happen unless everyone sees the direct link between the CRM effort and the strategic imperatives the firm is trying to accomplish.

CONCLUSIONS

In today's business environment virtually every firm, with perhaps the exception of those most upstream in a supply chain providing feed stocks and commodity products, must accept that becoming more customer centric and making it easier for the most critical customers to do business with the firm is at the heart of sustaining loyalty and creating a competitive advantage. Achieving the goal of satisfying the most crucial customers better than any competing network demands the application of the best techniques and practices across an extended enterprise network. That begins with a customer relationship management effort that is central to the business and its strategic imperatives. There can be no alternative for success.

The analysis of most CRM efforts, unfortunately, indicates there has been more interest in using the technique for cost cutting and sales discipline than for building relationships and profitable revenues with the most desired customers. There are also strong indications that software was sold as a panacea before the organization was prepared for such a serious and influential change process. Most firms failed to recognize that the foundation under CRM is not technology, but an understanding of how a firm uniquely connects with its most important customers. To overcome these obstacles and get the proper returns on what will be an expensive and arduous journey, firms are better advised to build a compelling business case for CRM, placing the need for customer attention at the heart of the effort, and introducing a value proposition that explains how CRM is relevant to the firm and its customers. They are then advised to adopt a methodology that includes all parts of the organization and selected external partners.

The model described proceeds with a solid analysis of what could be in the effort for the customers, the firm, and those doing the implementation. With an understanding of the benefits, it proceeds through a carefully staged methodology that builds the enabling design and architecture. When that framework is complete, the enabling technology and software will assure that the desired goals are met and the proper connection is made to the supporting supply chain activities.

With the Internet and other cyber-based technologies, companies today have the means to better integrate customer relationship activities with supply chain support. As CRM becomes an activity of ever-increasing importance, and advanced supply chain management is recognized as the key tool of support, it is only logical that there should be a strong technical integration occurring between the two allied efforts. CRM will help companies improve relationships with their key customers and drive new revenues and profits. ASCM will assure there are no failures in the responses to the expected increase in business and that the special features offered to the most desirable customers are met. Integration across these disciplines must occur seamlessly and in a real-time environment.

As the effort progresses well with the top-segmented customers, most firms discover they can move CRM into *partner relationship management*, or a technique to be used across the firm's selling and servicing efforts. That means the successful CRM techniques can be used to move down the segmentation matrix from the most-valued winners to those customers requiring less attention and service with slightly fewer features being included at each segment.

11

MODELS FOR COLLABORATIVE DESIGN AND MANUFACTURING

Once a firm has developed advanced supply chain management (ASCM) relationships on both the upstream (with key suppliers) and downstream (with key distributors and customers) sides of its supply chain network, it is in a strong position to begin working collaboratively with key business partners on new design and manufacturing techniques. The internal house will be in order and experiments with external partners should be showing the value of advanced networking with trusted allies. Once again, the concepts involved are not new, but their use is gaining momentum. Companies in a wide range of industries are finding it advantageous to use collaboration and technology to speed the design, development, and possibility of success with new product and service introductions. Advanced firms are moving even further by enhancing the life cycle management of these products from design through manufacturing to consumption. Improved manufacturing techniques are also part of the potential from this part of ASCM.

There is one important caveat. Nearly every firm thinks it has the ultimate secret to bringing the best and most accepted products to market, so sharing their design and development process with any outsiders is not a natural part of business life. But the results, showing as much as 10 to 30% or more shortened cycle times and 2 to 5% new revenue, have made believers of some of the most obstinate critics. When lower costs are also documented, the concept tends to be more easily accepted. Advocates must be wary, however, of the intrinsic discomfort with which most firms approach the subject, and realize any pitfall could quickly throw the company back to an internal-only development process.

COLLABORATION MUST BECOME AN ACCEPTED PRINCIPLE

To begin a convincing argument, we should first accept that informal alliances have been on the business scene for some time as firms build close relationships with business partners they know can assist with supply chain activities, even product design. What is new, and becomes part of a more mature supply chain system, is the ability to link communications and cooperation across an end-to-end network and deliver innovative goods and services to targeted customers and consumers in record time and in a user-friendly manner. Through the application of information technology and cyber-based communication, firms around the world find they can collaborate on a full-time, real-time basis and transfer data, drawings, specifications, ideas, prototype information, and new designs among trusted allies in a network effort to gain the high ground in a market. Those in manufacturing also find that building the products becomes easier as synchronized flows and full network acceptance of specifications make the new products more compatible with manufacturing capabilities.

The automobile industry offers a good example, having shaken off its old image of bringing new models to the showrooms in four to six years, and is working on delivery to the buyer's home within days after a selection is made from a dealer or over the Web. The future for this industry holds the vision of delivering less-expensive cars and trucks that have been built to individual requirements in two weeks or less. Only through network collaboration and cross-enterprise application of technology and manufacturing skills will this objective become a reality.

In another example, the aerospace industry is taking advantage of advanced collaboration techniques. Lockheed Martin Aeronautics Co.'s ability to share complex project information across its extended supply chain was an important aspect of that firm's winning a significant contract ($19 billion) from the U.S. Department of Defense for 21 supersonic stealth fighter aircraft. Lockheed's platform lets "participants collectively work on product design and engineering tasks, as well as supply chain and life-cycle management issues," according to John Burdett, Lockheed Martin Aeronautics' IT infrastructure architect. "It is unlikely Lockheed would have won the contract without the modern collaboration system," he reports. "This is a new era in how we contract for business and how we execute on contracts" (Konicki, 2001, p. 30). These and other modern examples show collaboration has gone from simply working closely with a few business allies to forming network relationships that involve serious investments in capital, systems, and people, so a strong differentiated position can be gained in a targeted market segment.

The ability to adapt a business culture to this new environment is not without its difficulties. Some industries and firms have taken the lead, while others continue to resist outside assistance with any project of perceived value. That is unfortunate as a company's ability to foster collaboration across inter-enterprise networks will be what separates those that move ahead and those that fall behind. Supply chains simply function more efficiently when creating and producing products designed collaboratively, and making use of manufacturing systems that involve cross-enterprise cooperative interaction. In today's volatile business environment, there just isn't any room for unnecessary delays in getting what customers want in front of them.

The concepts are basic. Collaboration and technology establish the necessary foundation, which gets extended beyond point solutions between business partners and results in jointly developed and synchronized strategies that include optimized implementation across firms for the duration of a product's lifecycle. These factors also play a key role in reducing the number of potential obstacles that could arise during the life of the product. Synchronizing design, manufacturing, and supply chain fulfillment requirements in the earliest stages of the development process only prepares the network partners to efficiently produce and deliver what the customer needs throughout the course of a product's life.

In this chapter, we elaborate on how the use of collaboration and technology are providing the means to gain positions of industry dominance in this vital business area. Larry Huhn and Simon Buesnel, partners at CSC, provided special help with this chapter and we greatly appreciate their assistance.

A CONTEMPORARY FRAMEWORK GUIDES EXECUTION

To appreciate the linkage between collaboration, technology, and product design, we should start with a few simple observations. Collaborating and applying technology for product design and development with trusted supply chain partners is a powerful modern management tool aimed at improving costs and the time to market for successful new product introductions. The technique is advancing rapidly, especially in industries where external partners, such as contract manufacturers and subassembly suppliers, are an important factor in completing the work. Where multiple design engineering cooperation and specific outsourcing of key components are involved, the technique becomes a requirement for success. Online visibility and real-time information sharing become the elements used, leading to tracking progress across the full life cycle of the new product or service. Included in a typical effort will be a complete product design history — from initial concept to product use, disposal, or recycling — including quality assurance and use and repair information.

Advanced examples are now verifying the advantages of this type of collaboration. Solectron, a worldwide provider of electronics manufacturing services for a wide variety of manufacturers, uses Internet technologies to efficiently exchange product information and expedite changes to reach its markets faster than competitors. Adaptec, a manufacturer of data transfer and communication hardware and software, has dramatically reduced the design-to-delivery cycle time and saved millions in inventory costs by using cyber-based collaborative design processes with key suppliers in Hong Kong, Japan, and Taiwan. Ford has shown it can bring new models to market in less than 24 months by allowing key suppliers to design portions of the new model and even allowing these suppliers to participate on the assembly line.

The concepts to be considered go by many names and we have selected *collaborative design and manufacture* to cover the cooperation as early as possible in the creation of new products through more efficient manufacturing (enhanced through helpful suggestions from suppliers) and delivery to targeted customers. For purposes of definition, the more popular term, *product lifecycle management,* also includes the techniques, software, and network information systems used to manage the data and events associated with creating a new product, from concept through design and manufacturing and then through distribution and acceptance by the targeted consumer group. The capabilities of an effective system enable online interaction internally among important members of research and development and marketing and sales groups, and externally with valued business allies in the extended enterprise network.

Contemporary applications are constructed around a closed-loop process that begins with customer requirements and ends with successful introductions and renewals when appropriate. Most of the current systems came from an earlier effort at using computer-aided design (CAD) and computer-aided manufacturing (CAM) and product data management (PDM) systems, which were used to support business partners with online systems for creating and managing products and processes across an extended enterprise while maintaining living documentation of what was occurring as the product went to market.

Collaboration in this environment is based on the idea of interactive and joint development, and management of the most likely-to-succeed products and services for the most desired customer and consumer groups. Participation could extend to suppliers and their suppliers on the one hand and directly to the final customers on the other. Figure 11.1 illustrates, in general form, the path taken in effective product life cycle management.

The process begins with a joint analysis of what the market appears to be demanding, an effort that was previously the exclusive domain of the marketing department. In the collaborative scheme, key suppliers

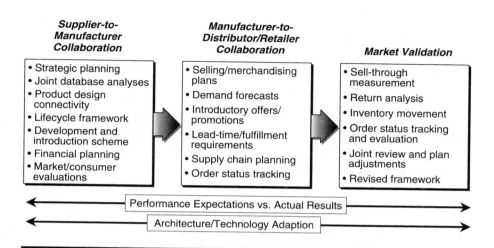

Figure 11.1 Product Life Cycle Management

are invited to participate in strategic planning around new developments and product introductions, as are internal representatives from operations. Together, the partners begin analyzing their capabilities and scouring their collective databases, sharing information pertinent to what the market needs and will accept and what they can provide better than any competitor. Generally, the partners find that bringing insights to this analysis from different perspectives helps select the right products and enhances the finished designs while better utilizing manufacturing capabilities.

Next, teams are established to begin co-designing new products or enhanced make-overs through a communications extranet established for that purpose. In the automobile example, suppliers and subassembly manufacturers have linked their design systems to that of the original equipment manufacturer (OEM) and are allowed to recommend new designs that match the OEM's manufacturing capability. In aerospace, it is now not unusual for a supplier to assume responsibility for the design of an entire major component of the finished aircraft. As the co-designing proceeds, a means to track the lifecycle of the products is accepted, usually through a merger of existing techniques. The teams then focus on the actual development, taking advantage of core competencies so the most effective partner assumes responsibility for the appropriate design steps.

An important step is to decide on an introduction scheme, which is created and approved and used to monitor progress. The first week in a new product's life can be absolutely critical to success or failure. A financial plan is also instituted to track results and measure return on the effort. Most importantly, market and consumer evaluation techniques are established so firms can jointly measure results and adjust plans for later involvement based on what the customers think of the final offering.

The designs are then moved into manufacturing where construction, assembly, or production takes place. Central to this part of the activity is making certain that manufacturing will move smoothly and at low costs so the new product is not put at a market disadvantage, and manufacturing costs do not escalate to the point at which there is a damper put on making time available for new product tests. Prototypes and test sequences are very important to ensure that the manufacturing needs, as well as expected market demands, are met.

Now the collaboration is extended downstream to helpful distributors or the retailer through which the products will be sold. Selling and merchandising plans are co-developed, reflecting the expertise each partner can bring to the preparatory work needed for successful introduction. Demand forecasts are analyzed to time the kickoff and develop the introductory offers and promotions, if appropriate. The lead times necessary to fulfill new orders are anticipated and decisions made on stocks, inventories, and delivery techniques. Supply chain planning comes into the scenario as a critical element to make certain the right stocks are at the right place and time. Order status tracking must be online, real-time to avoid the glitches that typically accompany new product introductions.

In an allied step, the team looks at market validation techniques. Here the intention is to track the news, good or bad, and learn from it so a higher success rate can be gained with each new introduction. Some form of sell-through measurement will be established to track actual sales, less any returns, so a reliable acceptance rate is determined. The return analysis is also used to determine what might be wrong with the product or where it can be enhanced. Inventory movement must be tracked so there are no problems with lead times and no build up of poor selling stocks. In modern systems, order status tracking is done over an extranet so key partners can view and evaluate exactly what is happening. An essential step is to have periodic reviews with the business partners so plans can be validated or amended as appropriate, based on actual market conditions. Finally, the framework for working on future projects is revised based on the findings.

Across the entire framework, the partners are matching performance expectations with actual results in a frank and open atmosphere so changes to the architecture and technology applications can be made during the introduction and throughout the life cycle of the product. With so much enabling software available today, it is important that consensus on what system will be deployed and how it will be maintained is reached early in the process. Then, as the life cycle proceeds, the partners must determine whether the software has met the intended conditions. The strategy that was established at the beginning of the effort should be kept dynamic and modified to reflect the actual service levels encountered, the costs to produce and deliver versus objectives, and unexpected developments from the life cycle analysis.

In an example of how this framework can be easily started, Cummins, Inc., a manufacturer of large diesel engines for trucks, began by sharing its customer order information with its key customers over a specially designed communication extranet. This process included providing the customers with visibility into future designs and new prototypes. A key customer, such as Peterbilt, could then recommend modifications based on their feedback from drivers and engineers. With this collaborative foundation established, Cummins found a means to maintain a loyal customer base, expand sales, and make a better determination of what it would take to satisfy key users of its equipment. Customers now provide the firm with insights on what features to add to its new offerings. When fully functional, the framework provides a means for buyer and seller, manufacturer and retailer to anticipate and realize higher-than-normal product success and profits. The typical result is greater market share.

COLLABORATIVE DESIGN CAN BE AN INDUSTRY ESSENTIAL

For some industries, the results are truly exceptional and necessary to sustain parity with the competition. In the apparel industry, time to market is critical in an atmosphere typified by adversarial relationships. Leaders have found collaboration becomes the key element to overcoming problems spawned by such conditions. Liz Claiborne took a first step by bringing key designers online and applying a very consistent set of technology tools. The designers were accustomed to hand sketching and had to be carefully moved to computer-aided design techniques. Hundreds of users also had to be brought online, often with painful results. The effort took five years but, in the end, reduced the design time by 50%.

While this is a good example of what can be done to cut design cycle time, other problems in the design area can be significant for manufacturers. Less technically developed suppliers of an important element in the manufacturing process, for example, might not collaborate because they have no CAD system. In this case, the manufacturer is faced with a disparate group of suppliers, some of whom can slow the overall process. Dillard's, the large retailer, found its information transfer problems to be very serious across a global network. At one time, the firm depended on massive faxing and overnight mailing of designs to private-label manufacturers and subcontractors willing to cooperate with the new designs.

The firm had a staff whose sole job was to send 300 to 500 faxes a day during peak periods. Twelve pages showing bills of material, sketches, cut and sew instructions, and other processing details would go out for more than 6,000 styles to be produced. Color pictures and print specifications had to go separately. It was a condition crying out for collaboration across a network that extended to China and India. A contemporary system now includes a collaborative product management system (such as Freeborder's CPM design) with virtual product folders to facilitate design, fabric development, product development, pattern-making quality, and delivery across the network.

CAREFULLY SELECTED ALLIES ENHANCE PERFORMANCE ACROSS THE SUPPLY CHAIN EVOLUTION

A crucial element in what is being considered is the cooperation of highly valued and trusted business partners, and that element introduces a very complicated selection process. The historical manufacturing supply chain has undergone extensive changes, moving from a simple linear process, as described in Figure 11.2, to the more complex arrangement involving the end-to-end work required for successful new product introductions. Today, there are a multitude of key partners involved in the design and what used to be a straight linear process can now span several firms working together. The need to have important information in the right hands at the right time makes the process considerably more complex. As a result, the entire product development effort is moving to a networked environment. As shown in the figure, that can involve transfer of information across many parts of several organizations without loss of clarity and accuracy.

In a manner similar to that described in the chapter on Supplier Relationship Management, the firm is advised to carefully cull through the list of willing participants in collaborative design and manufacturing and select those most likely to be able to enhance the process. Then the firm can build its own framework around pilot work with this core group. By carefully cataloging what works and what does not work, the framework will become a model for how to speed delivery of successful new products at better-than-normal operating costs. Now the company is in position to take the high ground in a market.

To describe what can take place in the collaborative design and development of products and services, and to calibrate your progress, refer to Figure 11.3. The supply chain evolution is used as a framework to detail the capabilities that are present as a firm moves through the five levels and makes ever greater use of external resources. In Level 1, product development groups are co-located, but since the focus is on internal-

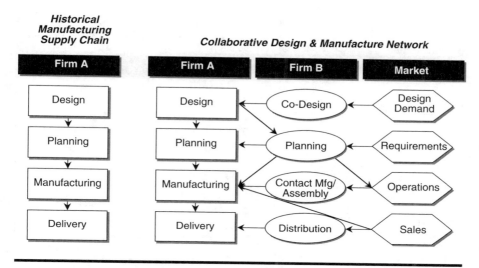

Figure 11.2   Emerging Networks Redefine Product Design

only activities, and the stovepipe mentality has not been subdued, they represent a loosely knit, independent organization. Products are developed without regard to high acceptance or commercialization rates and sourcing is not used as a processing enabler. Some common components and past learning is shared and a minimal amount of interactive data transfer occurs over the CAD-CAM systems. Local management is in total control of the process and dictating any changes to established procedures. In this environment, the cycle times and success rate are as good as the internal capabilities.

In Level 2, as the internal barriers to cooperation tumble down, projects are coordinated across domestic and global locations, using simple communications and the intranet set up for such purposes. Concurrent engineering methods are in place, as are metrics to measure improved conditions. The emphasis moves toward introducing shared or reusable components from similar sources to reduce costs. Typically, we see at least a 30% reduction of suppliers. In one example of processing in this level, a major car manufacturer insisted that product life cycle management be viewed as an enterprise system that had to be integrated with other corporate initiatives to optimize benefits from the development effort. When it was implemented, the firm found that more consistent and accurate product definitions yielded material savings of 10 to 15% and failure costs were reduced by 10 to 30%.

The third level begins the external partnering so vital to significant improvement in design and manufacturing. Now product development is done across several locations with the help of carefully selected suppliers

I Process Optimization	II Internal Excellence	III Network Formulation	IV Value Delivery System	V Value Delivery Network
Divisional	*Intra-Enterprise*	*Inter-Enterprise*	*External*	*Total Business System*
• Product development groups co-located, loosely organized and independent • Develop products without regard to commercialization and sourcing • Share common components internally for easily identified commodities • Minimal CAD/CAM information shared with suppliers • Local management of change control	• Projects coordinated across domestic/global locations using simple communication tools • Apply concurrent engineering methods (e.g., DF*) and begin to use key metrics, but not consistently • Emphasize use of shared, reusable components/sources • Reduce to 30% engineered component supplier	• Product development across several global locations using leading-edge communication tools (Web-based applications) • Involve key partners and suppliers early to co-design and rationalize capabilities, knowledge and costs • Develop shared data repositories to reduce version control errors • Metrics used consistently and rolled up for analysis	• Product development using leading-edge communication tools is structured to occur and be coordinated anywhere • Reduce time to commercialization and scale • Suppliers integrated into technology/product roadmaps • Collaborative design process involves 2nd- and 3rd-tier suppliers • Capture, share and review all design rationale with each business partner	• Dispersed teams function effectively to support design/manufacture anywhere in the network • Apply cross-enterprise scheduling tools for distributed projects • Product information from all partners captured and managed across lifecycle with consistent processes • Comprehend value-added services into product design/development across lifecycle

Figure 11.3   Design and Development of Products and Services

using an extranet, leading-edge tools, and Web-based applications. Key external partners are involved early in the process to codesign and rationalize joint capabilities as they apply to development. The linked partners in the network develop shared data repositories to significantly reduce the costs of changes and moving through various versions of design. Jointly developed metrics are in play and used consistently throughout the roll-out and follow-up analysis. Lockheed realized a 45% reduction in design review time while reducing error rates from 30% to less than 1% as they moved through this part of the evolution.

In Level 4, where the value delivery system appears, product development advances to the point where the partners are using highly sophisticated communication tools, often based around business process management (BPM) tools. The time from concept to commercial acceptance is reduced dramatically, often by at least 30%, but with some firms achieving 50% or more. Key suppliers are integrated into the technology and product development and introduction road maps are extended to second- and third-tier suppliers collaborating with the development effort.

Together, the partners capture, share, and review all aspects of the design rationale and modify it where necessary.

In one example, a manufacturer of medical devices, partnering at this level with key suppliers on design, implementation, and customization of solutions directed toward specific key customers resulted in dramatic improvements. Cycle times were reduced from 60 to 88 days to a range of 8 to 19 days, with an average of 15. There was significant quality improvement and new operational metrics have led to industry best standards.

Level 5 is rarefied and only a few organizations and their business partners have achieved this degree of full network connectivity and are working with a full business-system approach. In this most advanced area, dispersed teams, staffed by partners across the network, function effectively to support what has become a collaborative design and manufacturing effort. Cross-enterprise tools are used for scheduling and delivery. Product information across the life cycle of the new introductions is captured from each participant and managed with consistent processes. The value-added services that accompany the products are documented and made a part of future design and development efforts.

In the most advanced networks, the nucleus company can often create conditions far beyond most competitors. Coca-Cola and Frito-Lay have leading systems that include global aspects. Coke has plans to bring consumers into product development as early as possible in the processing. Ford is making extensive use of the Internet to input consumer information into its development process. At its Web site, www.hybridford.com, consumers "can comment on Ford's plans to develop a version of its Escape SUV with hybrid engine technology by 2003" (Whiting, 2001, p. 58).

MANAGING AND PROCESSING DESIGN INFORMATION SHOULD BE AN INHERENT FACTOR

When the design process is interactive and jointly managed across a network, an important feature appears, and that is the ability to manage the design information across the supply chain — from supplier to customer delivery and final disposition. This ability facilitates handling product changes or modifications, dealing with engineering change orders, coping with product obsolescence or the need for modifying design, and accessing a partner's enterprisewide resource planning (ERP) system to maintain a proper information flow regarding the product's acceptance or failure. Logistics data, delivery results, maintenance and repair requirements, and customer use can be analyzed to determine how to avoid and solve problems. In some contemporary systems, there is an ability to track details down to the crew name and date of manufacture.

With such a system, specific areas of opportunity can be addressed as follows:

- Better access to documents, specifications, and plans. With so much information still being handled through telephone, facsimile, and mail, there are many errors, missing data, and resubmission problems that do nothing but extend the cycle times and costs of bringing products to market. A Level 4 or above system will be fail-safe in quality and provide needed information to all network constituents with a high degree of accuracy.
- Full tracking across the product life. Current systems typically allow the author or original design group to maintain and contain access to information on what is happening with the product. Business partners that contributed to the introduction are kept in the dark regarding what is happening unless they petition for information. Contemporary systems provide visibility to those partners needing access to what is happening, so proper responses can be made throughout the life of the product.
- Determination of customer results and satisfaction. The true test of a new product introduction is that the customer or consumer likes what is received. Without full network connectivity, that information is wasted on a limited number of parties, and those who could help root out any complications are kept out of the loop so long that the product is history before beneficial changes can be made.
- Quality can be substantially improved. With real-time access to how the product is faring in the market, the partners can tailor changes to meet actual needs. In the process, quality features that enhance performance or overcome problems fed back by the customers can be introduced to the product and to the manufacturing system.
- Inventory management becomes a network responsibility. As the partners access information online, they find it becomes easier to match inventories in the visible pipeline to those which are needed to meet actual orders and planning.

CONCLUSIONS

Collaborative design and manufacturing is a new thing in the business environment. Firms around the world have found it simply makes good sense to share some of the design and development work with willing and able supply chain partners. The objectives may vary but consistent efforts yield surprising results in a variety of key categories.

Based on our research, we find product lifecycle management brings significant profit benefits to a firm and its allies. In general, we find the improvements can result in lower costs for development and manufacturing and dramatic increases in sales.

These benefits come from the following sources:

- Successful new product rollouts per year can increase by ten percent with an improved possibility of success due to better-targeted and better-executed product launches
- Concept test to product development ratio can increase from 60 to 66%
- Product development/introduction ratio can improve from 70 to 77%
- Introduction success rate can be increased from 20 to 25%.

While collaborative design and product development is not for every firm, it certainly should be considered as a key element in any complete advanced supply chain management system.

12

COLLABORATIVE PLANNING, FORECASTING, AND REPLENISHMENT MODELS

As companies learn and appreciate the value of not hoarding knowledge and instead realize that by sharing selective information with key business partners they can help each other, a number of new opportunities surfaces. For one thing, firms discover that they can strategize and plan in collaboration with suppliers, channel partners, and customers by openly sharing relevant consumer data and product availability, all focused on a single, reliable forecast shared across the network. The results are strengthened customer relations, more revenues for the partners, and considerably less expediting and excess inventory costs. The vehicle in this area is collaborative planning, forecasting, and replenishment (CPFR), a concept we consider to be at the top of the potential advanced supply chain management ASCM initiatives.

CPFR provides a good example of what can happen as firms evolve through their supply chain efforts and apply concepts including quick response (QR), just-in-time (JIT) delivery, efficient consumer response (ECR), and other demand management practices. When implemented, this can result in compatible objectives and win-win conditions between suppliers and buyers. Any contemporary business model will apply these replenishment concepts with ASCM practices to achieve superior satisfaction results with customers and consumers while adding profits for both the buyer and supplier. The result is a positive linking of specific customer requirements with cost-effective, flexible manufacturing systems using cyber information to track and move products across the network.

When considering this application, one overriding premise must be kept in mind. CPFR is not about improving a retailer's supply chain. Rather, at its heart, there must be a focus on better satisfying the customer, and an overall intention to create added value for customers, the selling or manufacturing company, and its distributors and suppliers. The concluding models for supply chain success will be oriented around what can be done with CPFR and what often does not occur because that premise is ignored.

A HISTORICAL PERSPECTIVE SETS THE STAGE

A bit of history will help establish the background for what we consider is the most important effort that can be derived from network partnering. Since this technique was born of interactions between manufacturers and retailers, it is best to understand what took place and why we believe there are applications across many other industries. To begin, while early supply chain efforts generally succeeded in making improvements to existing processing, many left gaps in achieving optimized inventory conditions, less than acceptable fill rates persisted, on-time deliveries were often mediocre, sales were missed at the point of demand, and the need for emergency expediting to meet actual demand was a common symptom.

As some firms began to concentrate on data sharing and process integration across their value chain networks, and looked for solutions to problems still needing resolution, the beginnings of a more collaborative approach started to emerge. Most likely, the seeds for what became CPFR were sown when Wal-Mart began working with Warner-Lambert — a result of the retailer finding inconsistent performance standards with in-stock averages on W-L brands. With the help of SAP, Manugistics, and Surgency (formerly known as Benchmarking Partners), the retail giant led an effort to create a process that would link actual customer demand with replenishment across its end-to-end supply chain.

A pilot was set up to focus on the stock of Warner-Lambert's Listerine brand sold in Wal-Mart stores. The purpose was to validate how a collaborative forecasting process could improve supply chain conditions. A framework for a controlled experiment was established and, in a computer lab, it was demonstrated that Web techniques would be beneficial in the exchange of information. After several tests, interesting results were achieved: Warner-Lambert's in-stock averages rose from 87% to 98%; lead times dropped from 21 to 11 days; and sales increased $8.5 million. As the pilot was limited to one W-L manufacturing site and three Wal-Mart distribution centers (DCs), the results were considered very significant. From the Wal-Mart perspective, there was also an internal benefit. The pilot identified an opportunity for organizational realignment that would improve communication between its procurement and operational functions. From another perspective, both firms came to understand that increasing the critical mass involved in the processing also helped the number of benefits; so they went in search of other participants.

The achievements sparked interest and the effort gained momentum. Whatever it was to be called, the processing started on its way to formality with work performed by the Voluntary Interindustry Commerce Standards Association (VICS). VICS, formed by retailers, textile suppliers, and apparel makers, was established in 1986 to develop bar code and EDI standards for the retailers. With the help of VICS, several other pilots were conducted, all with good results. In particular, a controlled test between Wegmans grocery chain and a Nabisco DC showed excellent returns.

Sharing data on 22 items, and using help from Manugistics, the Nabisco salesforce created a forecast for the items that was then compared with the grocer's store forecasts. When a variance occurred, the Manugistics' software sent an e-mail to both companies and responses were quickly instituted. Sales of the 22 Planters brand nut categories grew by 31%, while Wegmans' dollar units increased by 16%. All of this was accomplished with an 18% decrease in inventory. A similar test was later conducted between Nabisco and Schnuck's grocers in St. Louis with equally impressive results on the Planters and Milk-Bone brands. In particular, pet snack category sales grew 7% while Milk-Bone sales rose 8%.

VICS is now composed of large-scale consumer goods manufacturers and retailing firms, including such firms as Kimberly-Clark, P&G, Hewlett-Packard, Federated Department Stores, Circuit City, and JC Penney. Its CPFR committee is composed of retailers, manufacturers and "solution providers." This committee went on to establish a joint effort to improve manufacturing scheduling and responsiveness to demand fluctuations such as those occurring in most supply chains. A special group was formed to investigate the situation and recommend operational guidelines to reduce the impact of such fluctuations and improve costs and inventory management. In 1998, VICS published its *Voluntary Guidelines* to explain the business processes supporting technology and change management issues associated with effective implementation. VICS also registered a trademark for the term CPFR. The intention was for companies to adopt the guidelines and develop improved supply chain systems. CPFR has found its greatest acceptance with companies that experience significant demand variation, buy and sell products on a sporadic basis, and those driven less by price and more by market demand.

Newer methods of vendor-managed inventories (VMI) and jointly managed inventories (JMI) are offsprings of this effort. But in all cases, the focus is placed on meeting customer demand by improving the processes and methods used to plan production and manage inventories between the manufacturer and the retail stores or Web-based channels of distribution. The results expected are higher sales with lower stock outs, lower dependence on safety inventories, reduced working capital requirements, and higher customer satisfaction.

While studies of many CPFR efforts vary in their reporting, most indicate positive results with implementation. It is generally accepted, for example, that product stock-outs occurring at the retail level amount to about 7 to 8%, or about 5 to 7% of store sales. While a consumer may stay in the store and purchase other goods, it is also generally accepted that nearly 5% of the potential sales go to a competitor having the desired goods. This is a significant amount of lost revenue and drives retailers and manufacturers to find the means to eliminate stock-outs and have the desired goods available at the point and time of need.

Given this background, we believe CPFR has application beyond its root intentions for retailers and their manufacturers. In this chapter, we investigate the phenomenon known as CPFR and explain why, after more than half a decade, firms are still struggling to reap the benefits of this powerful tool. Special assistance with the chapter was received from Chuck Troyer, partner at CSC Consulting, and we express out sincere thanks to him for his help.

FOLLOWING GUIDELINES CAN LEAD TO IMPRESSIVE RESULTS

If a retail firm follows the VICS guidelines and succeeds in working with key suppliers to apply the concepts, we have noted that substantial opportunities can develop. There have been sufficient studies, pilots, actual implementations, and documented results to prove the validity of the inherent concepts. Among the leading possibilities are:

- Improving revenues through elimination of lost sales caused by a mismatch between demand and supply at the time a consumer is ready to make a purchase. Several studies have shown sales increases of 7% or more when suppliers and retailers work together to have product available at the time of demand, particularly for jointly developed promotional events.
- Reducing the need for inventories and safety stocks as the vagaries of supply chain uncertainty are reduced and online visibility to what is happening in the chain introduces the ability to move goods to the most urgent point of need. Sharing of actual retail point-of-sale (POS) information with manufacturers and suppliers lessens the uncertainty and enhances the forecast accuracy involved in joint

planning. Studies show a lowering of inventories when such collaboration takes place.

■ Improving return on investment (ROI) by increasing profits on the goods sold and investing fewer dollars in manufacturing goods that become obsolete. The whole issue of inventory has been revolving too much around pushing the ownership upstream in the supply chain. The more contemporary view includes working to make the need for excess stocks go away. As firms collaborate and keep the inventories more closely tied to actual consumption through joint analysis and adjustment, the result is a lesser need for stocks.

■ Improving return on technology investments as the results are shared and leveraged with other trading partners. By jointly evaluating the potential benefits of enabling software, firms and their partners can leverage investments and reduce the cost of purchase and installation. As they extend the results to other network partners, the savings can be leveraged even more.

Reaping these benefits and more will require selecting a few partners to begin a CPFR effort and using the guidelines VICS provides (not much sense in reinventing something that has received so much attention) for execution. A quick access to the CPFR Web site at www.cpfr.com will reveal a host of enabling information and we will draw from that as we go forward. You will note from a cursory observation of the Web site material that it has an application for virtually any industry and any network involved in buying, selling, and delivery to final customers.

VICS GUIDELINES PROVIDE ROAD MAP

To apply the guidelines, it is best to begin by considering how others have made progress and what type of road map will lead to similar success. The VICS material indicates there are three forecasting and replenishment processes being applied by retail supply chain networks. The most popular is called the aggregate approach, while the other two are vendor- and joint-managed inventory.

From the VICS material, these forecasting through replenishment systems are illustrated in Figure 12.1. Under the aggregate system, the manufacturer and retailer view the processing together following the steps of: assemble data, forecast sales, forecast orders, generate orders, and fulfill orders. The processing to occur in each of these steps is listed in the appropriate block of the matrix. In the aggregate approach, there is limited joint business plan development and the partners use only syndicated data plus historical sales information applied at a high level of detail

	Aggregate Forecasting	Vendor Managed Inventory (VMI)	Jointly Managed Inventory (JMI)
Joint Business Planning	Limited joint business plan development	Limited joint business plan development	Heavy emphasis on joint business planning and coordinated execution planning
Data Assembly	Syndicated data and historical sales	Point of sale (POS), warehouse withdrawal data; syndicated data	POS data by product, store, and week; syndicated data
Sales Forecasting	High-level sales forecast; category, week or month, market or region	Sales forecast generated by: product, customer distribution center (DC), by week; store-level VMI is by product, store, week	Sales forecast generated at the store level by product by week; identifies micro-marketing and micro-merchandising opportunities
Order Forecasting	Primarily focused on manufacturing support to its own DCs; frequently not done by retailers	Focused on retailer DC, driven by inventory and transportation cost targets; store-level VMI focused on store inventory; still focused on supply coming from supplier DC	Time-phased replenishment of stores, retail DCs and supplier DCs
Order Generation	Generated by retailer expecting 100% fulfillment from supplier	Generated by supplier based on the pull from store replenishment or consumer demand for store-level VMI	Could be generated by either party based on store-level sales that are time phased to supply capabilities
Order Fulfillment	Supplier provides what is available at its DC	Supplier fills orders from its DCs, giving priority to VMI customers	Supplier fills orders from its DCs or manufacturing, depending on the extent of integrated planning

Figure 12.1   Forecasting and Replenishment Processes (From Voluntary Inter-industry Commerce Standards Association, Lawrenceville, NJ)

for planning purposes. The primary focus is on manufacturing support for the retailer's DC from which the retailer expects 100% fulfillment.

The VMI approach developed as some firms found implementation problems with the aggregate technique, primarily oriented around information accuracy in the data assembly, the desire by one or more partners to preempt forecasts (to meet short-term targets), making unplanned shipments, and shortages determined late in the fulfillment process. An important technology enabler appeared here, as many firms used supply chain applications to manage inventories at retail locations, bringing demand and supply closer into synchronization at the retail receiving point. Most often this is at the DC, although some systems focus on the stores.

VMI involves a broader view of the inventory staging and deployment areas and what goes on in what becomes the visible pipeline showing flow of goods. This feature provides better inputs to the manufacturer for planning and inventory flow at a level much closer to the retailer's actual needs. This processing still includes limited joint business development activity, but now the partners are using POS information and warehouse withdrawals in addition to the syndicated data, giving the participants a much better feel for what is actually moving through the supply chain. The sales forecast is made by product each week for withdrawals from the retailer's DC and by product by week at the store level. The expectations are that the manufacturer (vendor) will manage the inventory needs by making shipments from its facilities. The focus, however, is on the retailer's DC, through which most of the goods still move, and the drive is to meet transportation and inventory targets. The manufacturer assumes responsibility for fulfillment getting priority in orders from the retailer by virtue of being a VMI vendor.

While VMI has some advantages over the aggregate method, it also has limitations. The overall level of collaboration is limited by the categories included in the process. The level of detail is still done at a generally high level, and the focus on warehouse or DC withdrawals is not as effective as working toward actual store sales. Most firms accept the progress made with VMI, but they continue to make product for stock and fail to leverage the customer-specific data that would indicate a need for changes to planning and inventory. It is also difficult to make special arrangements for VMI retailers and still provide the right level of service to other customers.

The JMI approach focuses on collaborative planning and implementation at a much lower level of detail. There is an increased focus on the actual consumption and on finding opportunities frequently hidden in the data analysis. JMI typically includes teams working on key accounts through frequent meetings. The improved understanding that results can be an important factor in building trust and increasing the amount of interaction between the partners. JMI includes a more intense planning effort with lots of coordination at each process step and greater use of core competencies to make sure the right partner takes responsibility for the right steps.

In the model, JMI starts with a heavy emphasis on joint planning and coordinated execution. POS data is more central to the processing, down to its use in trend analysis, micro-marketing, and micro-merchandising opportunities. There is a time-phased element to sales forecasting that helps planning and execution of fulfillment across the total supply chain.

As a reminder, in each of the methods, the focus must be kept on the end customer or consumer, and then the firms work back through the process linkage to find improvements that benefit all parties. Together, the allies end by managing the development of a single shared forecast of demand that drives planning and fulfillment across the network. The network partners, moreover, jointly commit to the shared forecast through sharing risk as work is performed and the constraints are removed. Since no single business process fits all supply chain partners, the allies must compensate for their differences in viewpoint, strategies, systems, investments, and analysis of market information as they go forward. That means they must work the data together to build a joint knowledge of what is needed at the retail store level, what is the most efficient means of matching demand in that area, and what investments should be made to customize the delivery system at a low level of detail for the best customers and consumers. Three options are provided and the recommendation is to pick one, get started, and modify the framework as results are documented. The obstacles and limitations can be dealt with as you go forward, and the necessary level of process customization needed can be determined by measuring customer satisfaction.

THE FINAL FRAMEWORK WILL EMERGE FROM JOINT EVALUATIONS

Using this premise to get started and adapt as you proceed, most firms will modify what they apply in any event, and the final model will reflect the customizing efforts of both parties. The enigma plaguing CPFR is that the process tends to get slowed more often than it gets supported to move forward. Although these systems have been available for some time and are generally in use across many industries, limitations to success prevail. Observers are left to ponder: with such purported virtues, it should have been simple. What went wrong? In the first place, there is such a lack of trust in the retail buying and selling processing that major obstacles and impediments quickly arise, even as businesses try to collaborate for the best of intentions. From another, both parties are fearful valuable information will be leaked to competitors if they enter into CPFR arrangements with a key supplier or retailer.

In other industries, similar results occur where the buyer-seller relationship also remains on the edge of confrontation or antagonism, and the would-be, could-be partners chase different objectives, rather than collaborating on how to make more money together. Retailers stay focused on meeting consumer demand in the store and on the shelf, which is based on their point-of-sale data, and they are loath to share what they consider very valuable data. Business customers in other industries focus on meeting their predetermined sales forecasts instead on of dynamic planning opportunities. The manufacturers and suppliers are more concerned with meeting productivity objectives, receiving bonuses for exceeding push-into-inventory plans, and reacting to sales forecasts at the point of shipment. Although collaboration offers an opportunity to merge the two perspectives, the real-world conditions generally override the logic and the focus goes to winning the inevitable negotiations. What could become a good mutual effort typically gets bogged down in local concerns and cultural pitfalls. There are many other instances from many industries showing the reality of these types of complications. Michael McClellan, president of Collaborative Synergies, for example, notes the prevailing aspects of the existing general planning and forecasting practices include these major inhibitors:

- Most companies generate multiple, independent demand forecasts for different purposes. This condition interferes with the recommended focus on a single pervasive sales forecast. Whose information should be used? What data is most relevant? These questions bog down the effort.
- Most forecasting is done at a high level of detail that focuses on a product category or family, a market or region, and a period of weeks or months. Accuracy and efficiency in supply chain fulfillment require a much lower level of detail, tracked online and kept in synchronization with actual customer withdrawals.
- Forecast accuracy is not measured frequently. Most firms simply give up on attaining high forecast accuracy. Instead, they rely more heavily on monitoring warehouse withdrawals, heroic expediting for specific problems, and making customer service responses than they do on building the kind of smooth flowing system that can result from collaboration on what is actually happening in the supply chain.
- Operational forecasts usually focus on interaction between two nodes on the value chain. These forecasts are not time-phased across the value chain. The contemporary thinking requires network partners to collaborate across the end-to-end processing and find ways to optimize at each point of hand-off between parties.
- Manufacturing usually pushes inventory to its distribution centers based on manufacturing economics and not on forecasted consumer demand. The push system is a relic of those industries still mired in the concept that efficiency derives from highly effective manufacturing processes and not from meeting the needs of actual demand (McClellan, 2003, p. 26).

These problems must be resolved as partners move forward together with a CPFR effort. The emphasis must be placed on putting aside the adversarial relationships oriented around getting the best price and terms, and focusing on best total costs in the network with the highest customer satisfaction ratings — not easy conditions for most companies and industries.

The required increase in reliance on technology introduces other problems as well. Real-time, accurate inventory information to support the business processing requires investment in systems and software by multiple constituents to the network. Business process-based event management requires quickly sharing data among all key supply chain partners in an atmosphere where each party thinks the information has such value that the data can be sold. Visibility across an extended enterprise needs access to material flow locations and applications. The need for flexibility to meet changing business conditions means there must be compromises made to the operating culture and normal sharing of knowledge. The solutions to all of these complications require a new business model oriented around collaboration that helps all constituents. Partners to CPFR processing must accept that no single application can manage all of the inherent steps necessary, and that each point of hand-off in the supply chain becomes a process gate that can be managed well or poorly.

In spite of these obstacles, success can be found in virtually any industry. The VICS-suggested approach was eventually oriented around a standard framework, dubbed the *generic process model,* presented in Figure 12.2. This model can be used by any business organization working in concert with key suppliers and customers. It prevails as the leading methodology for a CPFR effort and begins with an effort to integrate demand with supply.

In addition to this model, the CPFR Web site includes 23 pages of detailed explanation and supporting appendices to take a would-be practitioner through each of the nine steps involved in the model. Included are models to establish collaborative relationships, create joint business plans, create sales forecasts, identify exceptions for sales forecasts, resolve/collaborate on (sales) exception items, create order forecasts, identify exceptions for order forecasts, resolve/collaborate on (order) exception items, and generate orders. The VICS model has been around for some time and its inherent logic is still very powerful and will lead to improved conditions and results if enacted. We strongly recommend its use for any firm in any industry looking to embark on this high-level ASCM effort.

There is additional help as well. The VICS committee has provided a CPFR road map, which accompanies the generic model. The road map is divided into five steps:

Evaluate your current state
Define scope and objectives
Prepare for collaboration
Execute
Assess results and identify improvements

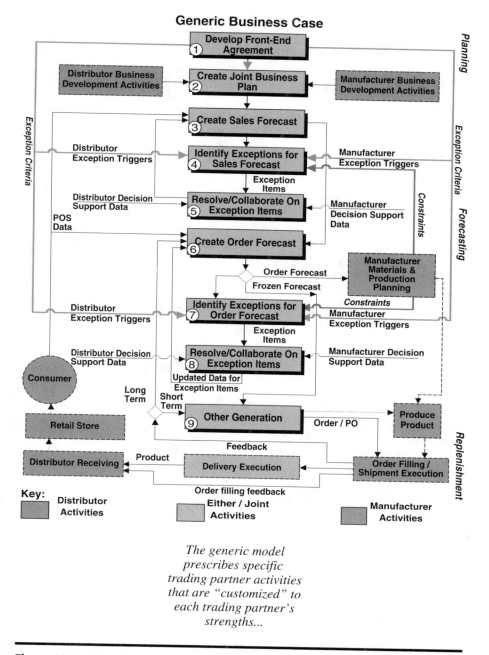

Figure 12.2   Generic Process Model (From Voluntary Interindustry Commerce Standards Association, Lawrenceville, NJ)

In the road map section of the Web site, another 26 pages of valuable information is provided to elaborate on each of these steps and guide the partners through the road map and on to successful implementation.

THE CHALLENGE IS BEATING THE OBSTACLES

Since each of the steps is detailed in the material available at the CPFR Web site, there is no need for elaboration here. The challenge for practitioners is to get started, stay the course, and make certain the final CPFR system:

- Integrates demand and supply knowledge across the network partners so correct responses that optimize returns on the effort can be made
- Facilitates end-to-end forecasting and demand planning through visibility of the actual interactions
- Matches actual performance with planned performance and makes adjustments as needed
- Signals all key partners about problems and quickly gets to solutions, eliminating the root causes

At the center of meeting these requirements will be the problem of coping with the lack of integrated systems across the network membership. In Figure 12.3, we see the three domains needed for synchronizing information across a linked supply chain network. The top layer includes the disparate planning systems the partners will bring to the early CPFR discussions. At each step, there will be somewhat rigid rules governing how planning is to progress and insistence from each culture that their system should prevail. In fact, the first problem will be to get the would-be partners to share information from their systems. In order to get started, pilots and test categories will have to be used.

One caveat is in order in this area of the effort. As the partners begin working out how to share across these planning systems, the trip from actual customer demand, as identified by point of sales (POS), to the need for materials and supplies could be rife with poor documentation, and the usual result is to load extra inventory to meet needs. The effort in this area should begin by collaborating on the single forecast that can reduce dependence on extra stocks to meet needs.

The second layer includes the operational cycles that trigger events and set the dates that must be met to stay on plan. Once again, there will be a lot of parochial thinking as the partners work on collaboration in this area. Having worked on their individual portions of the operational cycle for so long, partners can be expected to focus attention on the parts

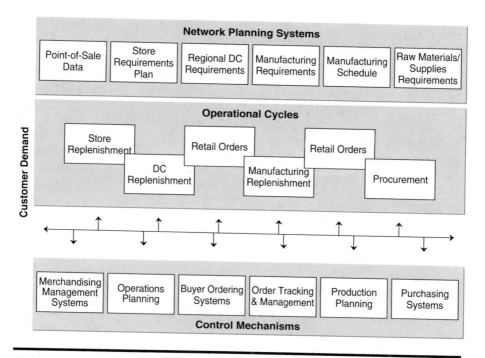

Figure 12.3 Synchronizing Information in a CPFR System

of the end-to-end processing closest to their parts of the supply chain. The CPFR model must prevail as data sharing focuses on the best overall cycle from demand back to original supplies.

The third layer includes the control mechanisms inherent in each constituent's operating system. Here we find the systems used to direct and govern actual processing. As much as the systems should be synchronized for optimized conditions, that rarely occurs. Each system has been built independently, and each has functioned for some time under local control. Most of the effort in this area is on linking the knowledge each system contains for the betterment of the total effort. Moreover, the data flows between these domains can be highly effective or highly ineffective, depending on the time and effort put into the designing and collaboration behind the desired improved system. Software advisers can be very valuable in this area as enablers of the intended improved processing.

Together, the partners must analyze the combining of these disparate systems and the implementation of the enabling technology and information sharing that brings the proper response to the actual business signal in a time-sensitive manner. Given the uncertainty that will always surround any demand analysis, flexibility becomes the watchword as the partners establish a system to monitor and evaluate what happens and take the proper action.

Under operating conditions, the process must manage the flow of information and goods in a way that minimizes the impact of uncertainty while providing an optimal flow of product to meet plans and actual demand. Whatever forecast error does exist is compensated for through the flexibility built into the response system and by matching deployment to highest priority need. Control limits can be set to bind the demand variation that will be met by the system and a special replenishment mechanism set up to handle unusual aberrations. Supply chain event management systems, for example, can be set so orders are monitored versus plan, and exceptions can trigger an alert to change a flow of goods in order to bring the system back within control limits at any point in the process.

CASE EXAMPLES SHOW THE WAY TO SUCCESS

The possibilities for applying CPFR concepts extend to many industries. Following are a few case examples that illustrate that point. Beginning with the area originally intended to reap the most benefit, let us first consider a case from the retail industry, one involving Sears, Roebuck and Company and Michelin Tires. The story begins when Sears was ready to run a special promotion for Michelin tires and the retailer received word that the manufacturer would be some 5,000 tires short of expected demand. Instead of dealing with the shortfall after the promotion was under way (the normal procedure), Sears applied techniques developed in a pilot test the two firms were running using the GlobalNetXchange CPFR tools. The shortage was detected, an analysis of the projections was confirmed, and the tire maker increased production to meet needs.

Essentially, a certain amount of tires were already in the pipeline when the tire maker began increasing shipments. Before the promotion, however, the retailer had sold more Michelin tires than forecasted. The CPFR tool allowed Michelin to compare what Sears had already sold, what it had on hand, and what it expected to need for the promotion. Then the firm was able to determine what was needed from the factories to make up the shortfall. To provide an idea of how much work it takes to get to this level, Jim Sullivan, director of demand-service planning for Michelin says, "The two companies worked together for more than two years to create and implement the system that made the promotion work" (Konicki, 2002, p. 42).

Sears and Michelin have developed the close, trusting relationship that eludes most other players in the retail arena. Using the GlobalNetXchange, a network with many other retail firms, including French giant Carrefeur, "Sears lets Michelin see sales of the tire maker's products and the inventory levels in stores and distribution centers. Michelin uses the data to help Sears develop a better replenishment plan. Sears has already saved millions by cutting its tire inventory by one-third" (Konicki, 2002, p. 42).

In another industry, we find that CPFR is not limited to consumer goods and large retailers. An essential element in the generation of electricity is buried in the hills of Wyoming and Montana, where there is an enormous supply of low-sulfur coal used by electric utilities because of strict environmental standards. Hundreds of millions of tons of this coal are delivered each year, especially to the Midwest, Southwest, and Eastern parts of the United States. Because of its weight and bulk, the carrier for this coal is a major national railroad, which uses 280-unit trains each week to make the deliveries, each train having 120 cars. During the handling of the coal, the railroad carrier often found it had 20 to 40 empty coal trains staged for the mine companies, which were loading coal at the various mines in their network. Sometimes the back up of trains waiting for releases from the utilities, which liked to add additional train sets for safety, could occupy more than 60 miles of sidings and track. The result and problem were increased train times and further congestion.

The problem was eventually addressed by a focus group set up by a transportation association representing many of the western coal operators. An early determination was that the mine producers and their utility customers had differing expectations about loading and delivering the coal. As a first step toward a better system, a monthly reporting system was put into place, based on e-mail, fax, and telephone communication among the involved parties. With this data, the railroad then attempted to reconcile the supply plans for coal with the demand plans from the utilities to assure the correct number of dedicated train sets was established. The flow of the coal supply was smoothed and many of the bottlenecks were eliminated for about 25% of the utilities involved.

Eventually, the railroad was able to launch an Internet-based collaborative forecasting tool that is expected to broaden participation, thus increasing scale, and provide additional benefits for the coal miners, utilities, and carriers. This forecasting tool allows the miners to accurately report the total tons of coal they produce while utilities can indicate their coal demand. Both parties and the railroad can track what is happening online. Any differences in supply and demand forecasts are quickly noticed and the railroad looks for solutions among the suppliers and users. This application allows forecasts of up to 13 months, although the immediate focus is on the next 30 to 90 days. On the sixth day of each month, the forecast is locked for the month, allowing the railroad to develop train-operating plans designed to assure an even flow of coal from mines to utilities. The operating plans essentially convert the coal usage forecasts into transportation requirements based on the location of the mines, utility destinations, expected transit time on the railroad and any connecting partners, and other variables. All network participants are able to view the single demand forecast so they can determine how to meet actual requirements.

THE ROAD BEYOND CPFR CAN LEAD TO MARKET DOMINANCE

Admittedly, CPFR is only one of a continuing series of transformation processes brought to a supply chain network. As the effort continues to take hold and a better understanding of the inherent concepts — particularly the need for customer focus and sharing of benefits — permeates the new models, a host of further applications can be envisioned. We elaborate on many of these future opportunities in the final chapter. For now, consider that CPFR can be extended to collaborative merchandise planning and optimization. This type of effort involves joint management of the processing related to item and category selection, product merchandising, and seasonal and promotional planning. In essence, partners come together and plan activities that better match product features and availability with consumer demand and a form of demand creation develops. This type of effort absolutely requires collaboration across the total merchandising process.

Consider further that the ultimate in forecast accuracy has not been achieved. Opportunities remain for leading firms to come together and combine their planning efforts, oriented around the actual needs of a market segment, while bringing the most current information and knowledge into play as decisions are made on what to produce and sell. Promotional planning can also progress, with the aid of many partners, from a hit-or-miss best-guess scenario to well-executed and successful events, which do not simply draw demand from a later time frame.

Using the full value of features of electronic commerce, the opportunities escalate. As business process management (BPM) technology continues its move into business practice, the means of collaborating across firms with different software, hardware, and operating systems is enhanced. As technology suppliers and users continue to work out the collaboration challenges through interoperability tests, the ability for CPFR to expand across more companies only increases. It starts with forming trusting relationships with a limited number of partners, and extends to using the full capabilities of joint knowledge for mutual benefit.

13

A LOOK AT FUTURE STATE
SUPPLY CHAIN MODELING —
THE NETWORK KEIRETSU

From their inception, supply chain efforts have been directed at improving the process steps occurring across an end-to-end supply-and-consumption network, beginning inside the four walls of a business and eventually expanding to include upstream and downstream partners. Fresh ideas, innovative concepts, bold techniques, best practices, customized applications, and a host of enabling technology and software have been infused into many efforts so firms and their allies could move as close to optimal conditions as possible. As these efforts continue and progress is made, the theories and underlying thinking will no doubt continue to change. Our look at the future includes some of that new thinking, but mostly it contains a few basic premises and two key factors — collaboration and technology.

The first premise is that there will be an inexorable move by industry leaders into creating and thriving in *networked enterprises* that dominate a market or industry. This movement will be directed more by the large, branded *nucleus* firms rather than by smaller entities, and it will come more slowly to some industries than others. Nevertheless, the value of using external resources to help a firm achieve optimized conditions is being proven on a daily basis and can no longer be ignored. The second premise is that network efforts will expand to include activities normally left outside the scope of supply chain. This expansion will include a collaborative focus on productivity, quality, and administrative issues that relate to achieving optimized supply chain conditions.

SUPPLY CHAIN WILL MERGE WITH TECHNOLOGY, QUALITY, AND PRODUCTIVITY

A clear example of the second phenomenon was demonstrated when Honeywell International asked Larry Bossidy, former CEO at Allied Signal, to serve as its CEO, following the failed attempt to make Honeywell a part of General Electric. After years of using Six Sigma processing to successfully drive quality and productivity improvement, Bossidy and the team he recruited determined that such a focus was not enough to achieve the aggressive goals being set for profitability at the Minneapolis-based firm. An early decision was made to focus on a reinvention of the firm and to "align and coordinate technology plans across its four business units and functional areas, including finance, human resources, legal, and supply chain" (Hartman, 2002, p. 24).

The plan, delivered by a corporate-level team, included targeted improvements to general and administrative costs (G&A) and direct and indirect costs of goods sold, as well as continued supply chain efforts. A $500 million savings target was set for accomplishment by 2005. We see this type of inclusion of other areas of focus coming under the supply chain umbrella in the future. Indeed, the hypothesis is: *There will be a merging of technology, productivity and quality efforts with an end-to-end focus on extended enterprise network supply chain optimization.* The overall objective will remain gaining market dominance through superior customer satisfaction, but a holistic approach will be taken to process improvement, with supply chain at the center of the strategy.

Procter & Gamble made a move in this direction as it used an effort termed *reliability engineering*, based partially on concepts discovered at the Los Alamos National Laboratory, to add nearly $1 billion dollars to its earnings. P&G has essentially applied defect-and-failure analysis, productivity analysis, manufacturing technology, and its drive for continuous supply chain improvement to forge a higher-level profit enhancement technique. The result has been significant savings across its organization. That type of blending of technology with productivity and quality improvements and end-to-end process improvement is the next frontier for firms looking to capitalize on their supply chain efforts. P&G found even further benefits from its efforts as it also developed operating arrangements with carefully selected key customers involving joint process management projects, thereby enhancing loyalty.

The steps applied at Honeywell were straightforward and in the direction being espoused. They included:

- Selecting a technology team to lead the efforts so the crucial ingredient would be included in implementation actions

- Taking inventory of existing and planned technology initiatives so the right blending of legacy and new systems would be enabling factors and not obstacles
- Analyzing and assessing budgetary allocations
- Developing an institutional planning process to include:
  - Using Scorecards to monitor and manage investments
  - Assigning a champion to drive success within each unit and function
  - Developing awareness of the value of digital strategies and ownership at the business unit level.

The Honeywell business units are hard at work developing leading practices and supporting systems in what amounts to a technology portfolio management technique. Based on published results, the firm is already showing good tracking with the targets established. More importantly, Honeywell is demonstrating the wave of the future — harmonizing the supply chain with other initiatives that cover all parts of the firm's operations. While this example is focused on internal excellence, we see a similar extension of that concept to collaborating firms in an extended enterprise. P&G has already offered its technique to other firms, including some of those in its supply chain network.

History provides support for the hypothesis. There is an inevitable force behind technology and continuous improvement. Both factors never cease to move forward, in spite of pitfalls and setbacks. The same can be said for supply chain. It has become an inevitable process that will go through many versions and transformations. The questions for those applying the inherent concepts include: How far will it go? Am I on the leading edge of the benefits? Have we missed important opportunities? How much more can we gain from our effort? What partners are we overlooking that could make serious contributions to progress? Where do we go to gain the next level of improvement?

The answers to these questions will come primarily from understanding that supply chain efforts require more than just integrating new tools and modifying old business models and infrastructures. The need is for a creative and guiding vision that includes the help of willing and trusted allies, along with enabling and advancing technology, to provide customers and consumers with satisfaction unmatched by any competing network. As progress is made with that vision, technology, quality, and productivity will become a part of the plans to increase profits and other metrics of importance for moving toward optimal conditions. In this chapter, we take a final look at supply chain modeling and where it is headed. As we do so, we show that the journey is toward a form of global keiretsu, where collaboration is at the heart of the effort, and there is an unbridled desire for optimized characteristics driving improvement of each and every process step.

NEW BUSINESS MODELS WILL PREVAIL

In a global business environment that has become very Darwinian in nature, the struggle is for survival. During these times, the more fit competitors prey on the less capable. All movement must be forward in areas of importance — costs, quality, productivity, asset utilization, customer satisfaction, time-to-market, and value-adding services. Any backsliding will be an instant opportunity for the competitor waiting in ambush to prey on an easy target. Solutions must be brought to the most demanding and important business customers and end consumers before another firm does so. And this is just the short list of requirements.

In essence, firms must review their current business models, strategies, and capabilities to honestly determine if their supply chains and network connections are sufficient for the new business jungle. University of Michigan business professor C. K. Prahalad puts it succinctly when he says, "Best practices are the table stakes. Next practices are where it is." Our analysis indicates most firms are less than half way through the evolution they need to make in order to sustain a dominant position in a market or industry, and most are still laboring under the delusion that they can optimize the results of their supply chain efforts while working in an internal vacuum. With the gap between the leaders and the followers widening, gaining the high ground in a natural selection atmosphere requires a fresh look at what is driving the business and how to make greater progress with supply chain efforts.

It also demands working ever more closely with trusted business allies in what we are terming a keiretsu environment, in which a leading company or nucleus firm works with a cadre of network partners, often sharing vital information and investments, to dominate a particular industry or market. With good transformation and attention paid to what is being demanded, the results can be truly astounding, as we have pointed out in the numerous case studies cited. Others have taken similar note of what can be attained, recognizing that "companies that have successfully mastered their supply chains have realized documented gains measuring up to 35% in market share" (Copacino 2001. p. 25).

Such market positions, moreover, are not limited to high-technology players such as Dell Computer and Intel or retail giants such as Wal-Mart. Consider the case of Scholastic, a leading publisher of children's books, which has parlayed its emphasis on supply chain into industry-high standards. Known mostly for its Harry Potter series of books, Scholastic is less known for its supply chain expertise that has produced cost savings and an enhanced ability to meet its customers' needs. Essentially, Scholastic's products have become customized, lower priced, and delivered more quickly than the competition. The transformation began with a better business model to guide the effort.

Scholastic started by carefully considering the delivery channels and customers that would best leverage its capabilities. The firm then invested heavily in a model developed around high-volume, customized fulfillment enabling it to dominate the direct-to-classroom book club business in the United States. Scholastic applies a combination of sharp supply chain capabilities with a focus on treating each teacher as an individual customer and each classroom as a targeted group of consumers, bringing multiple options and products to such customers and consumers in a coordinated and timely manner. The classroom book club that emerged in the model offers students a set of books, syllabus support materials, credits for free books, classroom technology support, and other media for their needs. With its supply chain house in order, Scholastic offers a set of products through a catalog, making sure of what it has available to ship, responding to variable order patterns and managing price relative to its offers and responses.

There are many strategies for many industries and market conditions, but central to those strategies under today's conditions must be a model driving the firm toward advanced supply chain management (ASCM) techniques and participation in a network enterprise. Minimizing costs will be a plank in that model, but so will a focus on building revenues and using collaboration and technology as the arches in the enabling structure. Completing the model will be the added focus on quality and productivity we see as keystones to success. So let us take a look at some of the features that could be a part of an improved keiretsu model involving participation in what becomes an extended enterprise dominating a competitive arena.

THE NUCLEUS FIRM WILL ORGANIZE THE KEIRETSU

Companies simply do not have all the resources required to respond in a real-time, effective manner to all of the pressures placed on their performance. Figure 13.1 is a pictorial description covering our general view of the future state of extended enterprise networks. These networks, and the nucleus firms in their center, need to learn how to dynamically balance often conflicting demands so a near state of optimization can occur. As the nucleus firms selectively partner with key business allies, they must discover how to create and deliver new value-adding propositions to the most important customers and consumers.

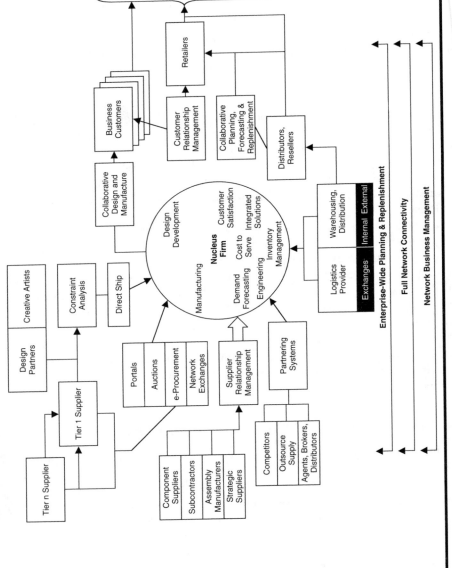

Figure 13.1 A Future State Extended Enterprise Network

The keiretsu-like processing that will emerge begins on the supply side as the nucleus firm sorts through all of its options and begins partnering with those firms most important to its core business model. Raw material suppliers might be sorted by tiers, but the closest suppliers will assume responsibility for delivering the right supplies to the nucleus firm at the right time. An extranet technology must become pervasive for sharing, viewing, and tracking critical information, even if that occurs through a number of communication mediums (telephone, fax, EDI, e-commerce, or other wireless, digital means). Constraint analysis will analyze the actual needs of the manufacturer's supply chain and the suppliers' capabilities for the direct flow of materials.

The actual goods will then be direct shipped to the point of need with any problems highlighted and action steps initiated where necessary. To augment this direct flow, we see a definite movement toward company-sponsored portals where key suppliers gain direct access to manufacturing schedules and make deliveries linked to codeveloped plans. The items of lesser importance will be handled by an e-procurement system while some of the supplies will be arranged by auctions, exchanges like FreeMarkets, and those industry exchanges that survive.

The subcontractors, assembly manufacturers, and strategic suppliers, so important to nucleus firms in automotive, aerospace, appliances, and other heavy goods industries, will be linked through a supplier relationship management (SRM) system. These systems will greatly simplify the processing within the keiretsu network, as these key suppliers play a direct role in achieving manufacturing and delivery goals. There will be another group of firms in the contemporary model. Firms needed as adjuncts to the manufacturing processes — such as agents and brokers bringing goods from around the world, suppliers to which part of the process has been outsourced, and even competitors making part of a product line by virtue of having a greater competence — will be contributing through a partnering system set up for that purpose.

To speed successful new products to market, the nucleus firm will include in its keiretsu design partners and creative artists — trusted allies who will be linked directly through the collaborative design and manufacturing system. These partners will be hard at work helping the nucleus firm stay one step ahead of the competition with innovative ideas and products flowing to meet actual needs as determined through sharing market knowledge and design capabilities.

Customer relationship management (CRM) systems will finally flourish and link the nucleus firm with its most important business customers, while collaborative planning, forecasting, and replenishment (CPFR) techniques will be at work with any retailers or business customers benefiting from this type of shared effort. Distributors and resellers will play a familiar role in this new model as they take products and services to specific markets or niches within the industry. Helping with the enabling will be logistics providers and those firms assuming responsibility for warehousing, distribution, and fulfillment.

THE KEIRETSU WILL FOLLOW A COMPOSITE SUPPLY CHAIN MODEL

With the nucleus firm guiding the construction of the keiretsu, a model illustrating the various elements of supply chain connectivity will be necessary to establish the required linkages from which the partners can help design the improved conditions. Basically, a process map must be drawn detailing the product, information, and financial flows occurring across the nucleus firms to its key partners. Figure 13.2 is a generalized model for that purpose, which can be modified by any nucleus firm based on actual conditions. For a complex manufacturing system, this model could grow in detail, but it should show the various systems at work within the nucleus firm and the other flows necessary for achieving optimized conditions. As external partners are included in the system, this model should be expanded to add their participation. Each step then becomes a target for analysis and improvement.

Technology plays a central role in this keiretsu-like supply chain. While there are many options available for technology support, Figure 13.3 illustrates a summary of how some of the activities will be enabled, first by electronic data interchange (EDI), the current mode of choice, and then by business process management (BPM), the emerging mode of choice. Higher-tier suppliers will bring their information forward to the first-tier suppliers via EDI showing schedules, inventory movement, logistics plans, and data pertinent to on-time delivery and high fill rates. The first-tier suppliers, and those attaining the strategic supplier designation, will interface directly into the nucleus firm extranet, making information visible on shipments, orders, and products. In a reverse flow, payments will be transacted electronically.

The nucleus firm applies enterprise applications to use the incoming data for planning and delivery purposes. Servers are set up to complete the knowledge chain linkage as data is sent forward to customers. Using BPM technology to increase the connectivity with key partners, the linkage moves to the most important business customers where shipments through the chosen distribution channels are arranged, inventory control takes place, systems are interfaced to share vital order and market data, and payments executed. Where the network extends to consumers, the linkage is directed at specific market segments to determine service needs and trends in buying patterns. Product selection is reviewed with the customers

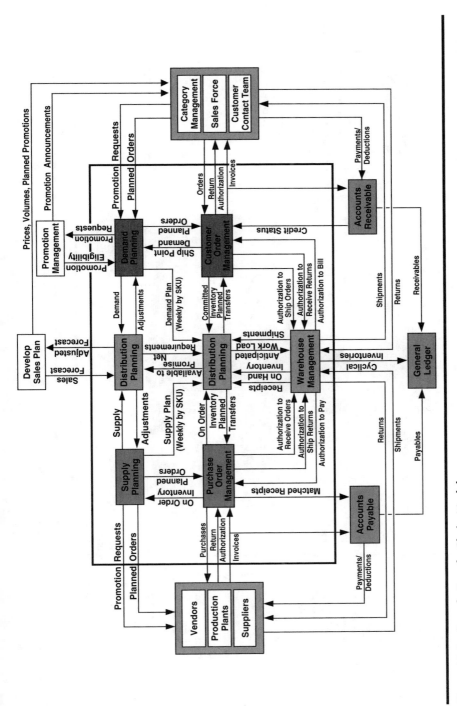

Figure 13.2   Sample Supply Chain Model

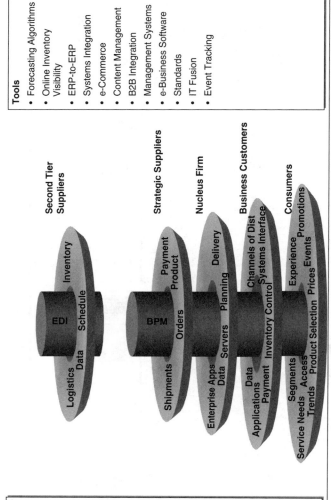

Strategies
- Access to Demand Signals
- Inventory Tied to Use
- Interactive Design
- Product Collaboration
- Planning Connectivity/ Control
- Automated Order Management
- Electronic Payment
- Strategic Sourcing
- Supplier Relationship Management
- Virtual Logistics
- Application/systems Integration
- Vendor Managed Inventories
- CPFR
- Decision Support
- Customer Relationship Management

Tools
- Forecasting Algorithms
- Online Inventory Visibility
- ERP-to-ERP
- Systems Integration
- e-Commerce
- Content Management
- B2B Integration
- Management Systems
- e-Business Software
- Standards
- IT Fusion
- Event Tracking

Technology Enablers
- eMarkets for Commodity Supply
- Smart Procurement for MRO and Supplies – Ariba, Aspect, Commerce One
- Middleware – Extricity, Syncra
- Shaved Scheduling – SAP, i2, Manugistics
- ERP Systems – SAP, Baan, JDE, PeopleSoft
- Retail Applications - Retek
- CRM Data - Siebel

Figure 13.3   Enabling the Networked Enterprise

so promotions can be jointly planned and implemented, events arranged and managed, and general experiences used to maximize the revenue lift. Pricing becomes a joint decision as the partners work the market for consumer satisfaction and mutual benefit.

Arrayed around the enabling model are the strategies that could be considered, the tools to be used by the network constituents, and some of the specific technology enablers. In essence, the contemporary model is a keiretsu that uses enterprise-wide planning and replenishment as the driver to gain the highest customer satisfaction. Full network connectivity becomes a reality as the players link together through the nucleus firms' extranet. In a collaborative manner, the partners spend some of the time they used to waste on reconciliation, error removal, emergency expediting, and other non-value-adding efforts on managing the business across the network. This is our view of the contemporary business model, and examples of how it is being constructed in full view are presented next.

FUTURE MODELS DEPEND ON A HOUSE IN ORDER

As we move to a futuristic documentation, one reminder is in order. Network participation requires having an internal house that is prepared for the kind of technical collaboration that will be expected from the keiretsu partners. That means the people inside the firm must be ready to participate on an equal footing with the technology being applied through the network connectivity. In other words, they must have immediate access to vital information pertaining to their part of the processing so they can help internal and external customers.

One example of such preparatory work occurred in the information-intensive public relations industry. Hill & Knowlton, Inc. created a half-million-dollar system, which it termed HK Net knowledge-management, to make information sharing more efficient inside its organization. Using a collaboration platform from Intraspect with instant messaging, this agency built an intranet that lowered costs and increased revenues. One of the applications included a searchable archive where employees can access important e-mail *strings*, bringing up-to-date information to new employees, representatives switching accounts, and new participants in client discussions. The system can also alert Hill & Knowlton personnel, who have requested notification, to a particular client or topic of interest that has been added to the database. "By embedding presence awareness — the ability to tell if a person is online and available — in those alerts, employees can use instant messaging to discuss an issue or invite other account team members into an online conference" (Kontzer, 2002, p. 38).

Another larger-scale example comes from the insurance industry. Lloyd's of London sits in the heart of London, England, where every work day hundreds of brokers from dozens of carriers carry large claims files under their arms as they go about looking for underwriters who have backed a specific policy or risk. Lloyds decided a better system would be beneficial and set out to electronically manage the claims "processed by the entire London insurance market." Xchanging is software owned jointly by Lloyd's and Xchanging plc, a business-processing outsourcer. This software was selected and used as a build-on to a claims-processing system already in use by a cluster of insurers to monitor claim transactions.

Linking that system with a new document repository from content management supplier iManage Inc. cut the cost of processing complex industrial claims, which can require thousands of people accessing the documentation, by about half. Related documentation of "some 80,000 processing claims reside in the repository. The repository not only lets brokers, underwriters, and adjusters digitally access the information they need, it also provides tools such as online chat, instant messaging, and video-over-internet protocol (IP) for real-time collaboration" (Kontzer, 2002, p. 36).

When it was time for real estate giant CB Richard Ellis to build its intranet, it decided to include a document library delivered to its employees by a content management system from Stellent, Inc. This library makes all the company's procedures and manuals available, reducing the costs for printing and distribution while increasing internal effectiveness. Employees gain instant access to the most up-to-date versions of documents and add to the content using a Web browser. The intranet system also allows the firm's "21 business units to search across the entire library or vertically within their individual business unit. The platform also includes a subscription feature that notifies employees when content is updated or new documents are made available" (InternetWeek.com, August 26, 2002).

Once this type of sharing is done throughout an organization, a number of possibilities develop. Employees across the firm are not only better able to recommend improvements and work on customer satisfaction, they become more interested in playing a role in the overall success of the supply chain effort. Ideas for applying technology no longer become the private domain of senior IT professionals. At ExxonMobil, for example, the idea for Speedpass came from a lower-level marketing manager versed in technology's potential. This manager was aware that most motorists wanted to get away from the gasoline service station in the shortest time and decided such an enabling technique would increase customer loyalty.

Speedpass is a small radio-frequency identification device the driver uses by holding it close to a receiver built into the gasoline pump. The driver transmits credit card information and customer ID to ExxonMobil's information network. The transaction is approved and the customer begins pumping gas. When finished, the transaction is automatically recorded and a receipt delivered. The result was a profit-making advantage in a very competitive marketplace.

From another perspective, there must be an understanding permeating the internal organization that any rivalry between the IT function and other business factions will be an impediment to success. You cannot expect a firm to do a good job of technically collaborating with key external partners if it does not possess the ability to cooperate inside its four walls. That cooperation starts with the necessary alliance between supply chain managers, business unit leaders, and the CIO and his or her staff. Too many companies fail to recognize that the cultural differences between their business managers and their IT professionals stand in the way of finding the optimized route to network processing.

The quality of and return on IT investments, for example, increase dramatically when the objectives and criteria for acceptance are oriented around how to increase the company's market value and customer satisfaction by each business unit. According to one story, "Credit-card issuer Capital One directly attributes its financial success to business and IT executives working together and applying technology properly to meet the company's strategic objectives. A Capital One executive cites the company's proprietary Information-Based Strategy (IBS) technology, which lets the company tailor products to the customer's needs, as the reason (for its success). The company also uses IBS to capitalize on new, promising markets, including auto financing and patient financing" (Logan, 2002, p. 32).

The most effective collaboration occurs when the IT leaders begin to think like their business unit colleagues and business executives understand the requirements, risks, and rewards of using advanced technologies. That knowledge comes from an interactive exchange of ideas, concepts, and strategies focused on mutually beneficial goals. With such an internal orientation, the firm is ready for significant external partnering.

NUCLEUS FIRMS MUST DEMONSTRATE CAPABILITIES TO BUILD THE KEIRETSU

As the firm then goes about building its network keiretsu, three capabilities will be present — the ability to establish and successfully implement process integration across the extended enterprise, automating the connectivity in areas of importance and practicality, and demonstrating how to collaborate with key business partners in a meaningful way. Technology links the constituents by leveraging existing internal intranets and information systems with the emerging public interface standards. That means the nucleus firm will lead the drive to automate processing in appropriate areas such as order management and planning, and then link enterprise-wide resource planning (ERP) systems and other means of exchanging knowledge in a real-time basis.

Figure 13.4 is a pictorial of the future technology linkage to which we are referring. Process execution and deployment facilities will be established with a limited, but critical, number of supply chain constituents. Their IT systems will be connected over an extranet designed for sharing important knowledge. A number of applications, which each firm believes add value, will be open for limited access, as will sections of the joint databases and directories set up to link the back-end applications. System convergence will be occurring through a number of languages and operating systems.

BPM technologies will be at the heart of the effort as process servers are set up to use the BPM language, developed by the BPMI.org group, and other languages to facilitate access to key information and its sharing across many companies. Business-to-business collaboration will be the central focus of this connectivity, applying a variety of protocols from among the many available today, to make the front-end connections needed by marketing and sales.

Global networks will become feasible as BPM emerges as the means to connect firms of any size with the nucleus firm. Now network enterprises will become the medium of competition, using knowledge as well

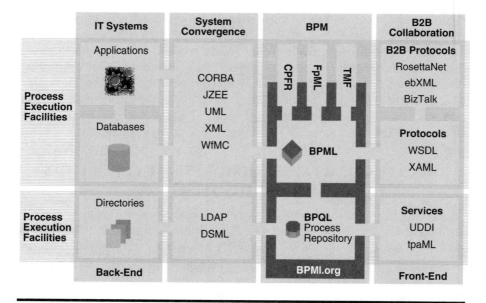

Figure 13.4   Technology Will Link the Value Chain

as cost and efficiency as the elements of differentiation. The focus of the supply chain effort will move from efficient processing to sensible innovations that add value across the network. The metrics of importance will be reduced total process costs, reduced cycle times, increased network sales, greater customer satisfaction, and retention of the most-valued customers. There will also be an inherent change in focus from machines and systems to people in the new business world as BPM enables any firm and its employees to participate in network improvement by virtue of having direct access to the collective knowledge of the network partners.

Your AutoChoice.com provides an example of this new technology-enabled network model. On this Web site, sponsored by Avis Europe plc, a consumer can browse for nearly new automobiles. Coordinating the effort are AVIS, Bank of Scotland, and the Royal Auto Club. AVIS, Navidec, Boston Consulting Group, CSC Research Services, and an independent marketing consultant providing creative collaboration. While browsing, the potential customer can trade in an existing vehicle, select a new car (with free delivery), select a finance option, and have seven days in which to return the car and get a refund, or twenty days to exchange the vehicle for another. The model that is applied can create and track flows across the multiple, inter-enterprise relationships. Ford is using similar techniques with its Supply Network, linking material suppliers to stamping operations and the assembly factory. All financial matters are handled through the extranet set up between Ford and its supply chain constituents.

As part of its effort to move to becoming a global e-business company, Germany's giant Siemens is undergoing a keiretsu-like transformation that will make its supply chain Internet-capable across internal business processes and with customers, suppliers, and other key business allies. Begun in May 2000, Siemen's enterprise-wide effort, with the company acting as a nucleus firm, was "designed to achieve a sustained increase in the company's value through the electronic networking of all business processes." Each of the firm's 14 operating groups is expected to assist by reorganizing its business to help the firm reach its objectives. A central assignment is to develop "cross-unit standards for the harmonized digitization of processes and for the software used within the company" (Goller, 2002, p. 58).

Following an investment that is expected to reach one billion euros, the company has already raised the percentage of online transactions by 50%. A company portal has been set up, called click@procure, for securing standard goods and material and providing all of the functions necessary for handling purchases on an electronic basis. Suppliers store their catalogs on the site, issue quotes, receive orders, send invoices, and obtain data on demand. Some 3,000 Siemens' buyers and another 30,000 employees have access to this platform. In a similar move, more than 20,000 employees use the company's ShareNet knowledge management system to exchange information and know-how, solve problems, and create bids for business.

In its battle with global giant Boeing, Toulouse, France-based Airbus, the European aircraft manufacturer, is using technology as a competitive tool. This firm has installed a large-scale supply chain automation initiative that will make it more competitive. This project has been dubbed Sup@irWorld and calls for spending $48.5 million to "automate procurement of direct and indirect materials, better manage its supply chain interactions, and closely track performance and data on suppliers" (Smith, 2002, p. 1).

As firms tend to start their external collaboration on the supply side, they find quite a bit of enabling software and applications. Ariba has introduced its Enterprise Sourcing 4.0 allowing buyers to create and manage multi-level groups of line items, develop bills of materials (B/M), and upload B/Ms directly into Microsoft Excel spreadsheets. The new software lets a buyer automatically create a request for proposal (RFP), assemble responses, and manage price lists in Excel. Enterprises can evaluate suppliers on a total-cost basis and rank and analyze supplier performance. Another Ariba offering, titled Category Management, lets companies model and map sourcing processes, create new projects, and search and retrieve all knowledge related to a given category of direct or indirect spend.

ERP SYSTEMS WILL BECOME A KEY ELEMENT IN CONNECTIVITY

One important step toward the modernization of the supply chain effort will be taking advantage of the potential offered by integrating the networked enterprises through linking ERP systems. Significant savings in inventory management, synchronized planning and fulfillment are among the possibilities when companies use ERP for its designed purpose — to optimize the entire supply chain. The real power of such systems comes from integrating data across the network and delivering on many of the promises that, so far, have not been kept. Indeed, the new frontier for supply chain is to finally reduce inventories to much lower levels. So far, most of the inventories in supply chain systems have simply been moved upstream to obliging suppliers. The time has come to rid systems of much of the extra inventory that really ends in the cost of the products sold.

Figure 13.5 indicates large savings are available to companies that have not faced the real elimination of inventory from their supply chains. Covering five industries and a relevant number of firms, Drayer and Wight have shown the one-time potential for inventory reduction. If each com-

	# of Companies in the Study	Fiscal 2000 Total Sales for Companies ($MM)	Inventory Reduction Potential	Annual Savings Potential (MM@10%)
Food, beverage, and tobacco	28	$351,602	$22,404	$2,240
Consumer products – Durables	17	$136,060	$11,632	$1,163
Nondurables	16	$126,944	$4,371	$437
Material and construction	14	$80,626	$3,573	$357
Paper and paper products	14	$72,789	$3,228	$323

Figure 13.5   Inventory and Cost Savings by Sector and Industry (From Drayer, R. and Wight, R., *Supply Chain Management Review*, May/June 2002, p. 46 With Permission)

pany could achieve the industry benchmark, reductions in inventory levels would be enormous. The annual savings column, using 10% carrying costs, indicates what could also be gained each year. In the Darwinian business world, these are costs that must be extricated from network performance. The secret is to share information that validates the total amount of material and products in the network, including days-on-hand at the primary and secondary suppliers, in transit between constituents, in storage throughout the network, and in distribution centers and stores. Any returned goods that are being re-worked or repaired should also be in the calculation.

The next step is to do something about the numbers and that means more than an end-of-period fiscal adjustment. Attaching a cash flow map to the numbers highlights the potential savings and a strong, centrally led impetus to reduce the levels to what is really needed to support consumption gets the job done. The best solutions derive when there is visibility across the network showing the forecasts, reliable data on amounts and locations of inventory, and the actual replenishment needs. Discussions with all key constituents, analyzing the information together, generally leads to a more robust model and lowering of stocks across the supply chain.

To gain this visibility and a better awareness of how to solve the problem, the IT departments must now step forward and achieve a return on their investments in ERP. To date, few business organizations have used these systems to effectively improve supply chain performance. The opportunity is now at hand. When connected, ERP systems will provide the data integration needed for network response. Planners will be able to access what they need to improve forecast accuracy and plan closer to actual needs, buyers will be able to lower the amount of stock ordered to match what manufacturing requires, stores will have what is needed at the point of demand. All of the extra costs that go into emergency expediting and special shipments can be dramatically reduced. Most importantly, many of the material shrinkages and lost product problems will surface and the firms can work on balancing material and products in a more optimized manner.

The ERP linkage can be shallow or deep, but getting started will propel the connected organizations in the right direction. Shaw's Supermarkets Inc. does not have a large-scale ERP system, but it does link its chain of 186 stores through a best-of-breed system using i2 supply chain and transportation planning software. The firm can decide when to use its own truck fleet for store deliveries and when to use part of a wholesaler's fleet. It can also determine which of its 11,000 items should be stocked at its distribution centers and which of the wholesalers' warehouses should be used. "If we add warehouse capacity," says Mike Griswold, Shaw's strategic process leader for supply chain, "we can rerun the model and, within minutes, we have a completed cost structure for the change" (Konicki, 2002, p. 22).

Ralph Drayer, founder and chairman of Supply Chain Insights LLC, provides a vision of what is possible when systems are properly integrated across a network. "Imagine a supply chain designed and operated by customer demand and customer requirements. Customer orders trigger master scheduling and raw material ordering. Raw materials arrive only when needed and finished goods are shipped immediately after being made. The whole supply chain runs using world-class information systems and with minimal inventory. This is the vision that has propelled Michael Dell's business from a college hobby to a $32 billion operation" (Drayer, 2002, p. 51), Drayer said.

In a move that can only help the effort to integrate ERP systems, Walldorf, Germany-based SAP AG, has announced a long-term strategy to help customers with supply chain management systems to "work together more intelligently and adapt to unexpected problems." The firm said it would "devote development resources to create a new generation of collaborative production and supply chain applications that would work together as one system" (Songini, 2002, p. 1). The new suite is expected to connect supply chain management and manufacturing operations, from raw materials procurement to the final shipment of goods to customers. The expected results include higher inventory turns, tighter manufacturing cycles, better quality, and a reduction in total cost of ownership.

Oracle plans a similar move with its introduction of E-Business Suite 11i.8. This release includes portal-based reporting and data analysis tools that measure supply chain performance. But continuing the chess game for dominance, SAP intends to focus on further technology advances helping supply chain professionals. The firm plans to include the capability to track radio-frequency devices that could replace bar codes in following goods through a supply network. Another plan includes developing adaptive software agents that use artificial intelligence to learn from past actions so the firm can then create business rules for how to proceed in the future.

OTHER APPLICATIONS BODE WELL FOR FUTURE SUPPLY CHAINS

These technological breakthroughs hold interesting promise for those designing their future supply chains. One application, about the size of a grain of sugar and the cost of a piece of candy, could have far-reaching effects — radio frequency identification (RFID) tags that incorporate tiny microchips. Each chipset contains a unique, 96-bit identifier code. When scanned with a radio-frequency reader, the code matches with a table over the Internet. The details of the age, characteristics, and location of each product can be read by those with access to the system. As these tags come down in cost to about a nickel, companies like P&G, UPS, Target, Unilever, and Wal-Mart are hard at work determining how best to take advantage of a system that would enable tracking of products throughout the entire supply chain cycle. RFID tags can be applied to individual boxes, cases, or pallet loads, and provide suppliers, manufacturers, distributors, and retailers with the ability to view data as products move from beginning materials to final consumption.

At the center of this development is the Auto-ID Center at Massachusetts Institute of Technology, which was founded three years ago and has seen membership grow rapidly to 67 companies interested in just how far this technical enhancement can take them. Sponsors such as Coca-Cola, the U.S. Department of Defense, Pfizer, and Johnson & Johnson are just some of the firms poised to take advantage of what could be an excellent tool in the supply chain arsenal. Depending on the results of one test, Home Depot, Inc. reports it could eventually put RFID tags on all of the 50,000 products it sells (Ewalt, 2002, p. 17). One expected feature will be the ability to track items after purchase so manufacturers would find it easier to recall defective goods. Another will be to follow any thefts.

Product movement and consumption information will help many firms divert shipments and trigger other control steps in their supply chains. A tag that could be applied by a spray gun is being investigated by the auto industry to monitor parts used on an assembly line for later service needs. Old Dominion Freight Line is using RFID tags on its trucking equipment to control inventory in its freight yard, track shipments, and monitor employee productivity. This firm claims a one-year payback for its effort.

As you watch this technical breakthrough, keep an eye on the adoption of *business intelligence extranets* by firms wanting to capitalize on all the money they invested in building their databases and interactive systems. These extranets are built basically for business-to-business users as they extract useful knowledge from databases to be applied to specific business issues. FedEx uses theirs to let partnering shipping companies, which provide Fed Ex service outside the United States, access reports about revenue, shipping volumes, transit-time analysis, and other performance data. Energy companies use such extranets to let commercial customers access power consumption data. Brokerages also get in the act with institutional investors analyzing portfolio performance. Although they are narrow in scope now, we see an enlargement of the concept to share knowledge buried in databases to increase loyalty and build new revenues.

Personalization is another phenomenon growing in importance for those in supply chain. On the one hand, this effort is expanding from static pages on the Web to e-mail, multi-media contacts, and voice messages. On the other, it is moving past simple marketing functions and into customer service and logistics. In both cases, the results include improved business processing and better sales revenues gained through online contact. Anderson Trucking in St. Cloud, Minnesota, offers its version of a personalized Web portal for its customers so they can view the status of loads and service availability. Independent drivers in the system can track payments and get alerts on when loads are available for pick up. Office products distributor Quill Corp., based in Lincolnshire, Illinois, uses personalized e-mail that applies customer data to encourage the customer to buy online. Quill has been careful to distinguish between those customers preferring to use the Internet, those wanting to order from catalogs, and those preferring a combination of channels.

An especially successful story comes from Dow Chemical. That firm's MyAccount@Dow e-business site has been growing in use and results for three years. It has increased from 200 pilot users to more than 8,000 registered users. Annualized sales over the site are more than $1 billion. The site provides customers a way to "collaborate with Dow in a private environment and enables some self-service capabilities, which are extended to save customers time and expense. Registered customers get access to transactional functions and customer-specific information whether they connect through an ERP system, My Account@Dow or other methods" (Koller, 2001, p. 1). Those firms in the hospitality business are trying hard to make similar achievements as that industry is moving rapidly toward using personalization techniques with targeted guests.

CONCLUSIONS

And what is in the biggest crystal ball? Consider Timothy J. Berners-Lee, the developer of the technology that led to the Internet, and his proposal of a Semantic Web — a smart network that will understand human language and make computers as easy to work with as other people. As envisioned by Berners-Lee, this network would understand the meaning of words and concepts and the logical relationship between them. If consummated, the effort could turn the world into one gigantic fount of knowledge. Every Internet-connected computer or cyber device would have access to all the information accumulated over tens of thousands of years. According to Berners-Lee, "The Semantic Web will help more people become more intuitive as well as more analytical. It will foster global collaborations among people with diverse cultural perspectives so we have a better chance of finding the right solutions to the really big issues" (Port, 2002, p. 98).

With these and other far-reaching efforts in the works, some including technologies derived from biology and the use of electrons, businesses could be forced to become as adaptable in their Darwinian environment as species across the Earth have for millennia. In a business context, what we see is a merging of these new technologies with the desire for business optimization while better satisfying customers and end consumers than any competitor. The new business models will be networked in nature, depending on a host of capabilities demonstrated by a number of member firms. The efforts will be, at the same time, interdependent with those individual capabilities and unique in the combined offerings to customers and consumers. Alliances will thrive in this new jungle as nucleus firms and their keiretsu constituents pull upon each other to gain an advantage, just as the early human tribes must have done. The future holds much promise as technology and collaboration become the tools of survival in the brave new business world. Supply chains can only benefit by leveraging these tools.

BIBLIOGRAPHY

Ampuja, J. and Pucci, R., "Inbound Freight: Often a Missed Opportunity," *Supply Chain Management Review*, March/April 2002, pp. 50–57.

Bowman, R.J., "European Grocery Supplier Shows How CPFR Really Works," SupplyChainBrain.com, January 7, 2003, pp. 1–6.

Colkin, E., "DuPont Jumps out of Dark Ages into E-Commerce," Information Week.com, December 10, 2001, pp. 1–2.

Copacino, W.C. and Byrnes, J., "How to Become a Supply Chain Master," *Supply Chain Management Review*, September/October, 2001, pp. 24–33.

Cottrill, K., "Savings and More," *Traffic World*, November 12, 2001, pp. 17–18.

Degraeve, Z. and Roodhooft, F., "A Smarter Way to Buy," *Harvard Business Review*, June 2001, pp 22–23.

Drayer, R., and Wight, R., "Getting the Most from Your ERP System," *Supply Chain Management Review*, May/June 2002, pp. 44–52.

Ewalt, D.M., "Pinpoint Control," *Information Week*, September 30, 2002, pp. 16–18.

Fontanella, J., "Exchanges: Logistics in the Fast Lane," *Supply Chain Management Review*, September/October 2000, pp. 23–25.

Forger, G., "The Problem with Collaboration," *Supply Chain Management Review*, November/December 2001, pp. 90–91.

Foust, B., Shin, D., and Shehab, J., "Current Offerings Vary in Support of Supplier-Relationship Management," www.informationweek.com, March 11, 2002, p 1–6.

Gartner Consulting — SRM, "Enterprises Drive Competitive Advantage through SRM," White paper prepared for PeopleSoft, San Jose, CA, April 16, 2001, pp. 1–14.

Gartner, Inc. — CRM, "CRM Solutions Outlook: A Look across Vertical Markets," June 20, 2001, Stamford, CT.

Gelderman, C.J., "Rethinking Kraljic: Towards a Purchasing Portfolio Model, Based on Mutual Buyer-Supplier Dependence," *Open Universiteit Nederland*, June 2000.

Gilliland, M., "Is Forecasting a Waste of Time?" *Supply Chain Management Review*, July/August 2002, pp. 16–23.

Goller, A. and Heinzel, H., "Seimens — the e-Company," *Supply Chain Management Review*, March/April 2002, p. 5865.

Gonsalves, A., "Customers in Demand," *Information Week*, November 19, 2001, pp. 45–51.

Hartman, A., "Why Tech Falls Short of Expectations," Optimize.com, July 2002, pp. 20–27.

Hickey, K., "Paving the Way," *Traffic World*, November 12, 2001, pp. 21–22.

InternetWeek.com, August 26, 2002.

Karpinski, R., "Part II: TaylorMade's End-to-End Supply Chain," *Information Week*, October 17, 2001, pp. 1–3.

Keenan, F., "Logistics Gets a Little Respect," *Business Week*, November 20, 2000, pp. EB 112–116.

Koller, M., "Dow Online Exchange Gaining in Popularity," www.internetweek.com, November 5, 2001, pp. 1-2.

Konicki, S., "E-Logistics Gets the Kinks Out of Supply Chains," *Information Week*, November 19, 2001, pp. 64–65.

Konicki, S., "E-Sourcing's Next Wave," *Information Week*, March 18, 2002, pp. 57–62.

Konicki, S., Shopping for Savings, *Information Week*, July 1, 2002, pp. 37–45.

Konicki, S., "Collaboration Is Cornerstone of $19B Defense Contract," *Information Week*, November 12, 2001, p. 30.

Konicki, S., "Chain Reaction," *Information Week*, June 10, 2002, pp. 20–22.

Kontzer, T., "Come Together," *Information Week*, October 7, 2002, pp. 34–42.

Kraljic, P., "Purchasing Must Become Supply Management," *Harvard Business Review*, vol. 61, September-October, 1983, pp. 109–117.

Lee, H., "Creating Value through Supply Chain Integration," *Supply Chain Management Review*, September/October, 2000, pp. 30–36.

Logan, J., "Can't We All Just Get Along?" Optimizemag.com, July 2002, pp. 30–37.

Martin, A., "Capacity Planning—The Antidote to Supply Chain Constraints," *Supply Chain Management Review*, November/December 2001, pp. 62–67.

Martin, L., "Charting Pfizer's Path to e-Procurement," *Supply Chain Management Review*, May/June 2002, pp. 20–26.

Maselli, J., "CRM Shines on in a Cloudy Economy," *Information Week*, November 19, 2001, p. 88.

Maselli, J., "CRM Goes Wireless," *Information Week*, May 27, 2002, p. 55.

McClellan, M., *Collaborative Manufacturing*, St. Lucie Press, Boca Raton, FL, 2003.

Moozakis, C., "Carpet Maker Automates Forecasts," www.internetweek.com, January 7, 2002, pp. 1–2.

Morphy, E., "Industry-Specific CRM Rules," www.crmdaily.com, January 7, 2003, pp. 1–4.

Neef, D., *e-Procurement: From Strategy to Implementation*, Prentice Hall PTR, New York, 2001

Neuborne, E., "Happy Returns," *Business Week*, October 8, 2001, pp. 12–13.

Port, O., "The Next Web," *Business Week*, March 4, 2002, pp. 96–102.

Reinartz, W. and Kumar, V., "The Mismanagement of Customer Loyalty," *Harvard Business Review*, July 2002, pp. 86–94.

Rigby, D., Reichheld, F., and Schefter, P., "Avoid the Four Perils of CRM," *Harvard Business Review*, February 2002, pp. 101–109.

Schultz, K., "SCM Turned inside out," www.informationweek.com, June 25, 2001, pp. 1–9.

Semilof, M., "Unilever Tackles E-Logistics," Internetweek.com October 30, 2001, pp. 1–3.

Smith, T., "Airbus Automates Sup@ir-Sized Supply Chain," www.Internetweek.com, August 22, 2002 pp. 1–2.

Songini, M., "SAP Touts New Generation of Supply Chain Apps," computerworld.com, October 30, 2002, pp. 1–3.

Trent, R.J., "Managing Inventory Investment Effectively," *Supply Chain Management Review*, March/April 2002, pp 28–35.

Walker, I., "Mapping the Supply Chain — A Route Map to Business Benefits," *CSC Research Journal*, September 2001, pp. 38–47.

Whiting, R., "Virtual Focus Group," *Information Week*, July 30, 2001, pp. 53–58.

Worthen, B., "Nestle's ERP Odyssey," *CIO Magazine*, May 15, 2002, pp. 62–70.

INDEX